A History of Western Philosophy: 8

Contemporary Philosophy

Thomas Baldwin is Professor and Head of the Philosophy Department at the University of York. His previous posts include lectureships at Makerere University, Uganda and Cambridge University. He is the author of *G. E. Moore* (1990) and is the editor of the *Cambridge History of Philosophy 1870–1945* (forthcoming).

A History of Western Philosophy

This series offers a comprehensive and up-to-date survey of the history of philosophical ideas from earliest times. Its aim is not only to set those ideas in their immediate cultural context, but also to focus on their value and relevance to twentieth-century thinking.

Classical Thought
Terence Irwin

Medieval Philosophy
David Luscombe

Renaissance Philosophy
Brian P. Copenhaver &
C. B. Schmitt

The Rationalists
John Cottingham

The Empiricists
R. S. Woolhouse

English-Language Philosophy 1750–1945
John Skorupski

Continental Philosophy since 1750
Robert C. Solomon

Contemporary Philosophy
Thomas Baldwin

For Ruth and Elizabeth

A History of Western Philosophy: 8

Contemporary Philosophy

Philosophy in English since 1945

Thomas Baldwin

University of York

OXFORD
UNIVERSITY PRESS

OXFORD
UNIVERSITY PRESS

Great Clarendon Street, Oxford OX2 6DP

Oxford University Press is a department of the University of Oxford.
It furthers the University's objective of excellence in research, scholarship,
and education by publishing worldwide in

Oxford New York

Athens Auckland Bangkok Bogotá Buenos Aires Cape Town
Chennai Dar es Salaam Delhi Florence Hong Kong Istanbul Karachi
Kolkata Kuala Lumpur Madrid Melbourne Mexico City Mumbai Nairobi
Paris São Paulo Shanghai Singapore Taipei Tokyo Toronto Warsaw

with associated companies in Berlin Ibadan

Oxford is a registered trade mark of Oxford University Press
in the UK and in certain other countries

Published in the United States
by Oxford University Press Inc., New York

British Library Cataloguing in Publication Data

Data available

Library of Congress Cataloging in Publication Data

Data available

ISBN 0–19–289258–4 (pbk)

1 3 5 7 9 10 8 6 4 2

Typeset in Stone Serif/Sans
by RefineCatch Limited, Bungay, Suffolk
Printed in Great Britain by
Cox & Wyman Ltd, Reading, Berkshire

Preface

I have tried to write this book in such a way that it will be found to be intelligible and helpful by general readers. It is emphatically not addressed to academic philosophers or graduate students of philosophy. Some background familiarity with philosophy is assumed, but no detailed knowledge of texts or terminology. Thus, for example, although there was no avoiding some discussion of logic if I was to do justice to the subject, no use at all is made of logical symbolism.

Because I have assumed no previous familiarity with this subject matter, I have concentrated initially on the work of the most important philosophers of the 1950s and 60s (Wittgenstein, Ryle, Austin, Quine, Sellars) and thereafter on the central debates in English-language philosophy from 1970 onwards. My hope has been that I could thereby have sufficient space to provide discussions that convey the interest, originality, and importance of this work. The most difficult part of writing this book has therefore been to decide what to leave out. The omissions I most regret are any discussion of recent debates concerning the metaphysics of identity, change, and causation, and any discussion of political philosophy (though in this latter case, readers should turn to Jonathan Wolff's excellent *Introduction to Political Philosophy* (Oxford University Press 1996)). I am also very conscious that I have omitted any discussion of such areas as the philosophy of mathematics, the philosophy of religion, and aesthetics, in all of which there have been many interesting developments and debates during the period.

One regrettable consequence of these omissions is that there is much interesting and valuable work by many contemporary philosophers which I do not discuss at all. So it is worth emphasizing here that this book is absolutely not intended to provide a survey of all the important philosophy of the period. I doubt if a book of that kind could now be written by one person and it would certainly be very different in intention from this. I have kept references to a minimum in the main text, but further details are provided at the end of the book.

Contents

1

Setting the Scene: 1945

At the end of the nineteenth century German was the dominant language of philosophy, and students from the rest of the world travelled to Vienna, Marburg, and Göttingen to study with the likes of Franz Brentano (1838–1917), Hermann Cohen (1842–1918), and Edmund Husserl (1859–1938). A century later, English has become the dominant language of philosophy, and graduate students in philosophy now travel to Britain and the United States to study at Oxford, Princeton, and Harvard. There are many reasons for this transformation, and it would be a mistake to point primarily to the Allied defeat of Germany in 1945. The policies of the Nazis did far more damage to the German philosophical tradition than resulted from the Allied victory, and the current cultural pre-eminence of the English language has more to do with the economic power of the United States than anything else. Nonetheless, the Allied victory in 1945 does symbolize the point at which the balance shifts within twentieth-century philosophy from a predominantly German culture to a predominantly English-language one, although throughout this century there has also been a vigorous and distinctive French tradition in philosophy, running from Henri Bergson (1859–1941) to Jacques Derrida (1930–).

Within the English-language tradition itself there is a significant break at 1945. Whereas the change of generations within a cultural tradition is normally only gradual, the impact of World War II ensured that a largely new team took over the leadership of the discipline from 1945 onwards. Thus, although those old pillars of the analytical and pragmatist traditions, Bertrand Russell (1872–1970) and John Dewey (1859–1952), were still active in 1945, it was the new positions being developed by John Austin (1911–60) at Oxford and Willard van Quine (1908–2000) at Harvard which captured the attention of post-war students of philosophy (I discuss Austin's work in Chapter 3 and Quine's in Chapter 4). There is, however, one all-important exception to this claim: Ludwig Wittgenstein (1889–1951), the Austrian philosopher whose academic career was based in Cambridge, England. Wittgenstein's first great work, his *Tractatus Logico-Philosophicus* (1921), had been enormously influential in Britain and Austria. After its publication Wittgenstein withdrew from the study of philosophy for some years, but he returned to the subject in 1929 and began the development of a new approach to philosophy while teaching at Cambridge during the 1930s. During this period, however, he published very little and the great work of this later period, his *Philosophical Investigations*, was published only in 1953, two years after his death. Although written in German it was published with an English translation which effectively inserted it into the post-war English-language philosophical tradition. I discuss this work, by common consent one of the most important of the twentieth century, in the next chapter.

The Analytical Project

If one looks back at philosophy during the first half of the twentieth century in a Whiggish frame of mind, it is the rise of 'analytical philosophy' during this period that will strike one as the most significant development of the period. Although this was, in fact, only one aspect of the philosophical debates of the period, and the very phrase 'analytical philosophy' was not used until 1945, there can be no doubt about the importance of the pre-war analytical project for post-war philosophy.

As far as philosophy in English is concerned, the story begins at the turn of the century with the young G. E. Moore's (1873–1958) revival of the old Cartesian method of analysis. Moore sought to provide an analysis of the meaning of disputed questions of philosophy which would clarify them in such a way that it would then be a relatively straightforward matter to determine their answer. Thus he thought that once the meaning of questions about what things are valuable have been clarified by differentiating them from questions of psychology, sociology, religion, and metaphysics, it is not difficult to recognize that the most valuable things that there are are the enjoyment of friendship and the appreciation of art. As this example indicates, however, the transition from the analysis of a disputed question to the provision of an answer to it is by no means as straightforward as Moore supposed.

The crucial development of Moore's method of analysis was that effected almost immediately by Bertrand Russell, when he took it that the analyses of language inherent in the new logical theory that he was constructing on the basis of the work of the German logician Gottlob Frege (1848–1925) and the Italian mathematician Guiseppe Peano (1858–1932) could be used to clarify, and in some cases resolve, disputed questions of philosophy. This was a historically decisive transformation of the English-language analytical project into one which gave pride of place to *logical* analysis, so that thereafter one of the distinctive features of those who practised 'philosophical analysis', as they called it, was that they assumed that this type of analysis took place in the context of the kind of logical theory Russell had developed. This was an assumption with important consequences for communication both amongst philosophers and between philosophers and the general public: those who did not understand the language of the new logic were simply unable to keep in touch with philosophical debates as they developed within the analytical tradition.

I have written this book in a way which assumes no previous familiarity with logical theory and does not attempt to teach it (no use is made of logical symbols). Nonetheless, because the way in which Russell's use of logical theory transformed the potential of the method of analysis is well illustrated by his 'theory of descriptions', and this theory was actively debated during the post-1945 period, it is worth looking briefly and informally at this theory.

Russell's theory of descriptions concerns the meaning of definite descriptions such as 'The Queen of England' as they occur in a sentence such as 'The Queen of England is wise'. Russell held that it is a mistake to regard such a description as a way of naming the thing it describes. For, Russell held, the meaning of a name is the thing it names, but the sentence in question would remain meaningful even if the description failed to describe anything. So, Russell held, the sentence is used to say that there is just one Queen of England and that she is wise, which is a complex statement which will be false, and not meaningless, if in fact there is no Queen of England. This claim may well seem unpersuasive. It certainly involves many disputable assumptions, and one of the symbolic acts of defiance whereby post-war philosophers sought to differentiate themselves from their pre-war predecessors was Sir Peter Strawson's (1919–) critical rejection in 1950 of Russell's theory (I say more about this in Chapter 3). But what needs to be explained here is why Russell's theory was widely regarded during the pre-war period as a paradigm of philosophy.

At one level, the explanation is that Russell's theory cleared away a range of issues that had bothered philosophers from the time of Plato onwards concerning the possibility of meaningful discourse about things which do not exist. For if descriptions are taken to be ways of naming the things which they describe, and the meaning of a name is taken to be the thing named, it is then difficult to understand how we can use descriptions when we deny the existence of something—as when we say 'The largest prime number does not exist.' This difficulty is swept away on Russell's theory, for the theory simply treats such denials of existence as the denial that there is any one thing of the kind in question.

This point had in fact been informally clear for a long time; what was more important was that Russell used the theory of descriptions in conjunction with logical techniques such as abstraction to argue that where there are sentences which appear to describe objects whose existence is for some reason problematic (for example, because we could not observe them if they did exist), there is in fact no need to believe in the existence of these objects since the descriptions are not names of these problematic objects. The objects are 'logical fictions', the illusory products of a misunderstanding of the 'logical form' of our language. Hence, it seemed to Russell and others, philosophically significant conclusions can be established by a purely logical analysis of the relevant discourse. This, then, is the explanation of the paradigmatic status accorded to Russell's theory of descriptions. It seemed to show that 'logic is the essence of philosophy', as Russell put it in 1913. In fact these applications of Russell's logical theory always incorporate further significant philosophical assumptions, so that his logic alone does not establish his philosophical conclusions. Nonetheless, it remained the case that Russell convinced a generation that philosophical argument is dependent upon logical analysis.

Among those influenced by Russell was his pupil, the Austrian philosopher Ludwig Wittgenstein, who proclaimed in his *Tractatus Logico-Philosophicus* that 'the object of philosophy is the logical clarification of thoughts'. Wittgenstein's remark continues, however, with the claim that 'the result of philosophy is not a number of "philosophical propositions"'; so it was certainly not his view that logical analysis establishes specific philosophical conclusions. Instead he thought that the analysis should make it clear that what looks at first like a substantial but deeply puzzling philosophical question is either a question which can in principle be answered within one of the natural sciences (so that its solution does not amount to acceptance of a 'philosophical proposition') or else is a question about which nothing at all can be said. In accordance with this approach Wittgenstein maintained that epistemology is just the 'philosophy of psychology', and thus required only a logical analysis of statements attributing knowledge and certainty. But, recognizing that this did not offer a response to sceptical doubts, he added that such doubts are senseless because they raise questions which cannot be answered; so here nothing can be said, and all we can do is to show in our lives what we take for certain.

Wittgenstein's *Tractatus Logico-Philosophicus* had a decisive impact upon the Austrian philosopher-scientists of the 'Vienna Circle' who met regularly for discussion under the leadership of Moritz Schlick (1882–1936) from 1922 until 1936 (Wittgenstein was himself briefly involved in their discussions when he returned to philosophy in 1929). Both Schlick and Rudolph Carnap (1891–1970), the most influential members of the group, came to philosophy from physics, and in particular from the debates initiated by Einstein's theory of relativity. Following Wittgenstein, they took the view that a proper understanding of these matters was to be obtained within science alone and that attempts by traditional philosophers to impose metaphysical principles upon scientists were illegitimate. On the contrary, they held, science provides the only genuine knowledge of the world there is since it restricts itself to what can be properly justified on the basis of observation. Indeed, since what is meant by a statement cannot include more than what would be known by someone who knew the statement to be true, there cannot be more to the meaning of a claim about the world than can, in principle, be determined through the forms of observation and reasoning which would enable one to know its truth, i.e. to verify it.

This last claim embodies the 'Verification Principle' that the meaning of a statement is given by its method of verification. This is often regarded as the core of the 'logical empiricist' position of the members of the Vienna Circle, but the impression of a single orthodoxy here is misleading because of radical disagreements concerning the nature of verification. Nonetheless, there was agreement both that all legitimate knowledge is either scientific or logico-mathematical, and that where traditional metaphysics involves claims that are wholly unverifiable, these claims are meaningless. Thus, as Carnap put it, since philosophy itself is neither a natural science nor a branch of mathematics, the proper activity 'left over for *philosophy* . . . is only a *method*: the method of logical analysis' ('The Elimination of Metaphysics', p. 77).

It is, then, in the anti-metaphysical context of Viennese logical empiricism that there occurs the transition from 'philosophical analysis', conceived of as *an* important method of philosophical inquiry which involves logical analysis, to 'analytical philosophy', which restricts genuine philosophy to logical analysis. This conception of philosophy was famously introduced to an English-speaking audience by A. J. Ayer (1910–89) in his book *Language, Truth and Logic* (1936). Ayer delighted in giving a particularly iconoclastic version of the position, using the verification principle to argue that religious statements as well as those of traditional metaphysics are meaningless, and that the only way to give any meaning to ethics is to interpret what appear to be ethical statements as expressions of emotions, such as disgust or delight. Not surprisingly Ayer's book attracted the ire of traditional philosophers, some of whom accused him of corrupting the youth, while the more acute among them argued that logical empiricism rests on an assumption that scientific inquiries are uniquely privileged as sources of knowledge which is just as 'metaphysical' as the non-scientific assumptions it stigmatized as meaningless.

Nonetheless, *Language, Truth and Logic*, with its characteristic logical empiricist thesis that philosophy is logical analysis or nothing, helped to set the scene for post-war philosophy in English. The influence of the Vienna Circle was further enhanced when, as a result of the Nazi seizure of power, first in Germany and then in Austria and central Europe, the leading members of the group, together with other philosophers sympathetic to a broadly scientific philosophy (such as Hans Reichenbach (1891–1953) from Berlin), emigrated to Britain and, especially, to the United States where philosophers had not previously been as receptive to the analytical project as they had been in Britain. This intellectual migration of the empiricist, and predominantly Austrian tradition of German-language philosophy was an event of great cultural importance because of the resulting impoverishment of German-language philosophy, and the corresponding enrichment of philosophy in English during the post-war period.

Common Sense, Naturalism, and Pragmatism

My aim so far in this quick survey of pre-war philosophy has been to chart the rise of the analytical project, which, in retrospect, looks to be the salient feature of the philosophy of the period. In order to prepare the ground for discussion of post-war philosophy it is desirable now to fill in some other aspects. One figure to whom we should briefly return is G. E. Moore: Moore accepted Russell's conception of the role of logic in the articulation of philosophical analysis, but although he was responsible for the publication of Ayer's *Language, Truth and Logic* he never accepted the logical empiricists' conception of philosophy, and in place of their emphasis on the natural sciences he emphasized the importance of 'common sense', our ordinary unscientific conception of the world. In this it was not Moore's purpose to insist dogmatically that common sense provides an unchallengeable touchstone of truth; instead, by reminding his audiences of what they were going to go on believing anyway, Moore's aim was to bring abstract philosophical theorizing which contradicts common sense down to earth. Though Moore himself never rejected the possibility of positive theorizing in philosophy, his deflationary approach to philosophical arguments prepared the ground for post-war doubts about the nature of philosophical theory. These doubts were reinforced by another aspect of Moore's technique: in the course of his discussions of our common sense beliefs Moore was often drawn into a detailed analysis of ordinary language—a discussion of certainty, for example, quickly turns into a discussion of our uses of the term 'certain'. For some of his readers these discussions of ordinary language were the most interesting parts of his work, and they took from them the moral that philosophical arguments should be based upon an investigation of ordinary language. Thus there is a direct link between Moore's work and the 'ordinary language' philosophy to be discussed in the next two chapters.

Russell himself was more sympathetic to the logical empiricist programme. But from 1920 he had embarked upon the project of combining his logico-analytical method with an account of thought and knowledge rooted in a fully scientific psychology. Russell's later writings in which he attempts to carry out this project had little direct influence on subsequent philosophy, though some of his ideas were picked up and developed by Frank Ramsey (1903–30), the most brilliant Cambridge philosopher of the post-World War I generation (I discuss some of Ramsey's work in Chapter 8). Nonetheless, in the light of the fact that contemporary philosophy sometimes appears to be dominated by the aspiration to combine an analytical philosophy of language with a 'naturalistic' philosophy of mind (a conception of the mind based upon the natural sciences) it is very striking that right back in 1920 Russell himself recognized the need for a combination of this kind.

Russell's later philosophy owed much to the influence of American philosophers, especially William James (1842–1910), and is indicative of the existence of an American tradition about which I have so far said nothing. From the point of view of post-war philosophy it is the work of James's great successor in the pragmatist tradition, John Dewey (1859–1952), which is most important. Dewey rejected what he termed the 'spectator theory of knowledge' of classical empiricists such as Hume (1711–76), which treats our situation as essentially that of a passive observer, and emphasized in its place the pragmatist thesis that our actions have a fundamental role in shaping our understanding of the world: the ways in which we think about things are 'instruments' to assist us in coping successfully with life's needs. Dewey combined this instrumentalist pragmatism with a commitment to naturalism, i.e. to an understanding of the world and human life which respects the discoveries of the natural sciences. But he added his own insistence that nature embraces all aspects of life, including values. Thus there is no fundamental fact/value distinction and a fully comprehensive, though still naturalistic, account of human life will take account of the role of values.

During the early post-war period Dewey's work was largely passed over. But recent discussions of naturalism in ethics and philosophy of mind return to issues he addressed and this has led to a new appreciation of his position. In addition his criticisms of the 'spectator theory of knowledge' have been used recently as the basis for an apocalyptic critique of contemporary philosophy which I discuss in Chapter 11.

Dewey was the most influential American philosopher of the pre-war period, and since there was nothing especially analytical about his work he is a useful reminder of the fact that most American philosophers of that time were not 'analytical philosophers'. They were not all pragmatists either: there was, for example, a group of philosophers under the leadership of Roy Wood Sellars (1880–1973) who developed what they called a 'critical realist' position, that combined a form of evolutionary naturalism with an epistemology that stressed the importance of sense-impressions as 'vehicles' of perception. But there was a small group of analytically minded philosophers in the United States at Harvard University. Pre-eminent among them was C. I. Lewis (1883–1964) who was responsible for the development of an important branch of logic, modal logic (to which I shall return in Chapter 6) and also for an important blend of American pragmatism and Kantian idealism.

Kant's (1724–1804) philosophy rests on the thesis that our understanding of the world draws on certain fundamental 'a priori' principles which are inherent in the ways in which we employ experience to understand the world. Kant argued that only one such set of principles is available to us, but, following the development of alternative systems of geometry, Lewis argued that there can be different systems of a priori principles, and that the choice between them rests on pragmatic criteria concerning the merits of the resulting conceptions of the world. The resulting position is similar to one developed simultaneously by the logical empiricist Carnap, and I discuss this in Chapter 4 in the context of Carnap's debate with Lewis's successor at Harvard, Willard van Quine. Lewis also re-interpreted Kant's account of the role of sense-experience in terms of a doctrine of 'The Given' according to which the 'sense-meaning' of judgements about the world makes reference to no more than the actual or possible occurrence of appropriate types of sense-experience. This influential doctrine provided a target for the son of Roy Wood Sellars—Wilfred Sellars (1912–89), whose work I also discuss in Chapter 4.

In this brief survey of pre-war philosophy I have concentrated on the writings and debates which set the scene for the main themes of post-war philosophy in English. For this reason I have said nothing about the major works of the phenomenological movement, including those by Edmund Husserl and Martin Heidegger (1889–1976). For the phenomenological movement had little influence within English-language philosophy until recently. The reasons for this are complex, but an important one was just impatience with each other's jargon: the phenomenologists did not take the trouble to acquaint themselves with the logical terminology characteristic of analytical philosophy, and most analytical philosophers found Husserl's talk of the phenomenological reductions and Heidegger's deliberately disconcerting neologisms tedious and impenetrable. There are in fact interesting comparisons to be made between positions advanced within the phenomenological movement and analytical philosophy, but these are largely external to the development of discussion within each tradition.

The Turn from Language and the Possibility of Philosophy

The importance attached by many English-speaking philosophers during the first half of the twentieth century to the logical analysis of language, and the related concern of some with the implications of ordinary language, constitute what is often called 'the linguistic turn' in philosophy. In the early post-1945 period attention to language increased, though with a shift of emphasis from logical analysis to informal investigations of ordinary language. I discuss several aspects of this concern with language in the first half of the book (Chapters 2–5). By 1970, however, the dominance of this concern with language was being challenged throughout the central areas of philosophy (metaphysics, epistemology, philosophy of mind and ethics), and I explore some of these challenges in the latter half of the book (Chapters 6–10).

The linguistic turn brought with it a conception of philosophy as a discipline specifically directed to articulating and establishing conceptual truths inherent in our uses of language. One objection to this conception arose from reflections on the use of language itself: as we shall see in Chapter 4, Quine argued that one cannot separate out the contribution of language to our knowledge of the world, and thus that there is no special category of conceptual truths, altogether independent of matters of fact. As a result many contemporary philosophers repudiate the conception of philosophy characteristic of the linguistic turn, and take the view that philosophy is best conceived as the reflective understanding of the implications of our knowledge of ourselves and the world, particularly knowledge gained through the natural sciences. As we shall see in Chapter 9, this thesis is especially prominent in contemporary philosophy of mind.

This emphasis on the natural sciences threatens the status of our ordinary understanding of thought and action in which we advance reasons which justify what we think and do, and among those most concerned to uphold the status of this ordinary understanding are those influenced by Wittgenstein's later writings, which I discuss in Chapter 2. In line with his earlier writings, Wittgenstein rejected the presumption that philosophy is a discipline directed to the establishment of truths at all; thus, despite his emphasis upon language, he and his followers also reject the conception of philosophy characteristic of the linguistic turn. Instead they affirm that the philosopher's task is primarily to clear away the misunderstandings that surround ordinary modes of thought so that we can both see that these modes of thought do not require the justifications which philosophers have tried to find for them and also appreciate that their legitimacy is not threatened by the natural sciences, to whose pretensions Wittgenstein became increasingly opposed.

Although this therapeutic conception of philosophy remains valuable, most contemporary philosophers do not accept its limitations. As Chapters 6–10 will indicate, there has been a tremendous growth in the variety of positions advanced within the central areas of philosophy. In some cases these positions are advanced as conceptual truths, established by the kinds of arguments familiar within analytical philosophy; in other cases they are advanced as implications of the natural sciences, though usually in conjunction with a further argument to show why the scientific details are philosophically important to the issue in question. But in most cases the positions are simply advanced as contributions to an improved way of thinking about ourselves and the world, and those who advance them draw on a variety of arguments which cannot be regarded as exemplifying a single, dominant, philosophical method. What makes their conclusions nonetheless philosophical is the questions they address, which range from metaphysical questions concerning identity and necessity, through epistemological questions about the justifications for belief, to ethical questions concerning value.

To some, mainly critics from other disciplines, this disorganized heterogeneity of considerations is unsettling and is taken as evidence that contemporary philosophy has descended into a babble of voices which vainly attempt to continue a tradition of critical argument whose central presuppositions are no longer tenable. In the final chapter I briefly address this concern as voiced by the contemporary philosopher Richard Rorty (1931–). My own opinion is quite the opposite of Rorty's: I hold that philosophical arguments do not need to be conducted within the confines of the old worn-out tradition that Rorty takes to be definitive of its possibility, and that it is altogether a sign of vigour that philosophy has for the moment escaped from domination by such methods.

During the twentieth century, the writing, teaching, and discussion of philosophy within the English-speaking world was predominantly conducted within universities. The numbers studying and teaching the subject were very small during the first half of the century but the teaching of philosophy underwent a large expansion during the general expansion of higher education that took place from the 1950s onwards. Hence there is now a much larger public for philosophy than used to be the case and it is an interesting question what its consequences will be for philosophical debate. The rapid growth in recent years of 'applied' philosophy, such as medical ethics and cognitive science, is, I think, one consequence; and it seems reasonable to expect an increasing diversity among the intellectual pursuits and interests that are addressed from a broadly philosophical perspective. Some traditionalists fear that this expansion will lead to a loss of serious discipline in the subject. But there is no reason to think that serious philosophy will flourish only among a very small church of committed disputants.

2

Investigating Wittgenstein

World War II was the common man's (and woman's) war, and when some of these common men and women returned after the war to study philosophy, many found themselves directed to the study of ordinary language, the language of common men and women. This kind of study was not entirely new: its importance had been implicit in some of G. E. Moore's pre-war writings. But Moore's interest in ordinary language was never developed in any detail, whereas a concern with ordinary language is central to the later writings of Ludwig Wittgenstein. Indeed despite the emphasis on logic in Wittgenstein's earlier *Tractatus Logico-Philosophicus* (henceforth just the *Tractatus*), Wittgenstein had protested vehemently when Russell, in his introduction to its English translation, had mentioned his own view about the need to replace ordinary language with a logically perfect language as if this were Wittgenstein's view. On the contrary, Wittgenstein pointed out, he had explicitly affirmed there that ordinary language is in perfectly good order just as it is, and that the purpose of logical analysis is only to make this order explicit.

Nonetheless, in the course of his subsequent reflections Wittgenstein came to see that in his earlier account of language he had mistakenly taken scientific language as a model for language in general. In the first half of his later masterpiece, his *Philosophical Investigations* (1953), therefore he develops an alternative approach, according to which, so far from our having to undertake complex logical analyses in order to clarify ordinary language and reveal the thoughts it expresses, respect for the fact that ordinary language is in good order as it is requires us to adjust our theoretical preconceptions concerning the way language works.

Philosophical Investigations

Wittgenstein's *Philosophical Investigations* (henceforth just the *Investigations*; but in giving references I abbreviate the title as *PI*) is Wittgenstein's own distillation of his work from 1933 or so until his death. During the 1930s Wittgenstein had been in Cambridge and in 1939 he became Professor of Philosophy there in succession to Moore. When World War II began, however, he left Cambridge in order to do something more useful than teach philosophy, and he worked in hospitals in London and Newcastle for most of the war. In 1945 he returned to Cambridge to resume his position, but finding the academic environment there uncongenial he resigned his professorship at the end of 1947, and lived mainly in Ireland before returning to Cambridge where he died in April 1951.

The *Investigations* is divided into two parts: part I, which is the greater part of the book, was completed in 1945; part II is derived from his writings during the period 1947–9. According to his editors it had originally been Wittgenstein's intention to incorporate this material into a modified version of part I, but his final illness made this impossible, and the book as we have it was published posthumously in 1953. It is a captivating but bewildering masterpiece whose content is inseparable from its form. As Wittgenstein himself says, it is essentially an album of sketches: part I consists of nearly 700 short sections, mostly just one paragraph in length. Although they are carefully ordered, they do not provide a systematic development of a position or point of view. Indeed, he makes it clear that he does not seek to advance philosophical 'theses' at all. For, just as he had held in the *Tractatus*, he maintains here that no important positive truths can be established by the practice of philosophy: instead philosophy leaves everything as it is, and the work of a philosopher consists largely of assembling reminders of our ordinary uses of language which enable his readers to see through the 'grammatical' illusions that give rise to questions that have been taken to be deep and challenging philosophical problems.

Much of the book is 'dialectical' in two senses: first, in the sense reminiscent of Kant, that Wittgenstein aims to expose the illusory basis of philosophical theories. An important question here is whether Wittgenstein can really accomplish this task without drawing on 'theses' that are more than mere reminders of what we have always already known; whether, to put the point in Kant's terms, there can be a critical dialectic that is not dependent upon a positive 'analytic'. The second sense in which the book is dialectical is that Wittgenstein often adopts the style of a dialogue, interrupting passages in which he appears to be putting forward his own position with objections from someone more sympathetic to traditional philosophy. These interjections reflect the fact that although Wittgenstein holds that the principal resource that we have with which to confront and undermine philosophical perplexity is accurate reflection on our ordinary uses of language, he also holds that these perplexities generally arise from misunderstandings to which we are perennially tempted by ordinary language itself. Hence if he is to dispel what he calls the 'bewitchment of our intelligence by means of language' (*PI* para. 109), it is not enough simply to show what is wrong with the theories of traditional philosophy; he has to bring to the surface, and then neutralize, the intuitive convictions which give rise to them in the first place. The purpose of these interjections, therefore, is to have the reader recognize the interlocutor as herself and be cured of her misunderstandings of the beliefs they express by following through Wittgenstein's critical dialectic.

These points make an attempt at a descriptive introduction to the *Investigations* perilous, but Wittgenstein himself indicates that his new thoughts will be seen in the right light when they are considered alongside the position he had advanced in his earlier *Tractatus*. Thus he still takes philosophy to be an activity whose goal is one of achieving clarity, the kind of clarity which 'means that the philosophical problems should *completely* disappear' (*PI* para. 133), and the approach he employs is still one of attempting to show that these problems arise from the illusion that certain possibilities are genuine, when in fact the sentences which describe them violate the rules of language. An important difference is, however, signalled by the fact that whereas in the *Tractatus* he had thought that these rules are prescribed by logic, in the *Investigations* they are said to be a matter of 'grammar'. Wittgenstein does not have in mind here the details of traditional grammar books;

but this new idiom is a way of emphasizing that the rules in question determine what makes sense, and Wittgenstein now wants to include among these the informal presuppositions of our uses of language which he thinks are at least as important as anything prescribed by formal logic. Furthermore, Wittgenstein now disavows the aim he had had in the *Tractatus* of providing a single characterization of language in terms of logic which takes the language of the natural sciences as its model. Instead he stresses the variety of ways in which language is used, each with its own 'grammar'; and this variety is important to him in his subsequent dialectic since he argues that some of the characteristic mistakes of philosophy arise from a failure to recognize the distinctive grammar of our different 'language-games', and in particular from taking the natural sciences as a universal model for language in which genuine knowledge is conveyed.

Language-games

The central concept in his development of this line of thought is that of a 'language-game'. He introduces this concept in order to capture the way in which the ordinary use of language is integrated into activities such as shopping, so that the only general truth about meaning is that the meaning of a word is its use in our language-games—a slogan which by itself explains nothing, but directs us to look and see the variety of ways language is in fact used instead of theorizing about meaning in abstraction. An important feature of the activities that constitute language-games is that they are themselves partly constituted through the use of language: for it is not as though, when out shopping, our use of language simply describes activities of selling and buying that could take place anyway. The relation between language and life is one of mutual dependence: our language with its meanings is integral to our life, but equally to imagine a language is to imagine, as he puts it, a 'form of life'.

The existence of these shared language-involving forms of life is in turn dependent on certain general facts about the world and ourselves: to take his example, buying things like cheeses by their weight would not be possible if a piece of cheese was constantly changing its weight. This case involves the existence of reasonably stable features of the world. Wittgenstein's more striking claim is that shared forms of life are also dependent on the existence of a substantial measure of agreement between people. If people could never agree about arithmetic, shopping would again be impossible: the shopkeeper and customer might agree in the abstract the price for a piece of cheese, but if they could never agree whether the price had been paid no sale could take place.

Wittgenstein's claims here are of the form: 'Necessarily, in general . . .' and are characteristic of the descriptive investigations into the limits of our language-games which he undertakes in the *Investigations*. These qualified claims contrast with the universal claims of the form 'Necessarily in all cases . . .' that are typical of the essentialist position that he now avoids. Equally, his new way of thinking about language, with its emphasis on the use of language in language-games, stands in sharp contrast to old views about language, such as the view that, for each speaker, the meaning of their words is determined in important respects by their own subjective experience.

A standard case here is that of colour words. Empiricist philosophers such as John Locke (1632–1704) held that when we describe an object's colour, we do so by matching its appearance with a subjective visual image (or 'idea') which shows us the meaning of the colour word we should use to describe the object. In order to show how this proposal is unsatisfactory Wittgenstein asks how it is determined whether the speaker is using the right word to describe their visual image. Since there is no point in supposing that the speaker might invoke further images to match that whose colour is in question, the empiricist's reply can only be that the question is misguided and that the speaker's visual image simply fixes the meaning of the word for him. The familiar objection to this is that it raises an insoluble question as to whether we share a common understanding of colour words. Wittgenstein's objection, however, goes deeper: since in describing the colours of things we seek to describe them as they are independently of our so describing them, an account of the way in which we describe them must allow for the possibility of our making a mistake. But if the meaning of colour terms is simply fixed for a speaker by his own current visual experiences, there is no possibility of the speaker mistaking this colour. So there must be more to the meaning of colour terms than the empiricist supposes.

Wittgenstein does not deny that we have visual imagery, or that it plays a role in memory. It is just the picture of this role as the presence before the mind of an authoritative inner sample that he rejects. In fact, as he remarks, ordinary physical colour samples often have a role in our language comparable to that which the empiricist assigns to visual imagery. But it is not his view that it is the physical samples we have to hand, or those we encountered when as a child we learnt our language which provide an authoritative grounding for the meaning of our colour words. For such samples are vulnerable to change and decay, but the meaning of our colour words is not thereby altered. Furthermore they cannot of themselves dictate how other objects are to be described. Wittgenstein famously begins the *Investigations* with an extended quotation from St Augustine's *Confessions* in which St Augustine maintains that a child learns a language by having objects pointed out to it at the same time as their names are uttered. Wittgenstein responds that unless a common understanding of the world, a shared form of life, is presupposed, such 'ostensive definitions' may fail to achieve what was wanted. For example, unless the child already understands what colours are and that sepia is a colour, when some things are exhibited to her as samples of 'sepia' she can take the word to signify whatever it is about the objects exhibited to her that strikes her as salient—perhaps, for example, their inedibility.

This case suggests that no objects, be they physical (such as colour samples), or mental (visual imagery), can by themselves constitute or determine the meanings of words, even though physical objects normally play a essential role in our language-games and the ability to use language requires memory, which often involves visual imagery. This conclusion is primarily negative, as befits Wittgenstein's general approach to philosophy; but it raises the question of how it is that the meaning of language is determined. Wittgenstein's argument requires that, for any word that is used with a definite meaning in a given situation, there is a right way of applying it in that situation, so that there is also the possibility of making a mistake by applying it wrongly; but his conclusion implies that there is no easy way to identify the right way. If even the association of a colour word with a sample of the right colour does not determine what the word means one may well wonder how it can be that words have definite meanings at all.

Rule-following

This issue brings us to the 'rule-following' debate which has occupied much of the recent discussion of Wittgenstein's later philosophy. The debate has this name because Wittgenstein treats the repeated use of a term, such as a colour word, as an instance of 'rule-following' comparable to the application of a mathematical technique such as long multiplication, where there is also a tension between the requirement that there be a 'right answer' and the fact that explanations of what is involved come to an end at a point where formulae, diagrams and the like can in principle be taken in more than one way. Wittgenstein (who had worked as a primary school teacher in Austria during the 1920s) makes the issue vivid by imagining the case of a child whose arithmetical instruction to date has only concerned numbers less than 1000 and who, when now told to continue the series of numbers generated by the rule 'add 2' past 1000, finds it perfectly natural to write a series that runs as follows:

994, 996, 998, 1000, 1004, 1008, . . .

We will say that the child has gone wrong after 1000; but how is this judgement to be justified? For his past practice is consistent with an interpretation of 'n add 2' as the following function (as we might put it, using ' + ' for addition as we understand it):

where $0 \leq n < 1000$, 'n add 2' denotes $n + 2$
elsewhere, 'n add 2' denotes $n + 4$.

Of course this is far-fetched, and Wittgenstein does not wish to suggest otherwise. His point is just that the possibility of these deviant interpretations has not been ruled out by the child's instruction.

Generalizing from this case, then, it seems that no training in the application of a rule ('add 2' 'things like this are sepia') can exclude deviant interpretations; and yet it remains the case that there is no possibility in general of saying something capable of truth unless there is also the possibility of being mistaken, which requires that our use of language be informed by rules which prescribe conditions under which what is said is incorrect. Wittgenstein resolves this 'paradox', as he calls it, by distinguishing action (including speech and thought) which proceeds in accordance with a rule from the attempt to act in accordance with an explicitly formulated rule. Since explicit rules can always be interpreted in more than one way, we must accept that insofar as we follow rules in using language, we basically do so 'blindly', i.e. without any explicit rule to guide us.

Rule-following so understood is an irreducible and fundamental feature of human life, absolutely essential to language and thought. In one of his writings from the 1940s Wittgenstein remarks 'Following according to a rule is FUNDAMENTAL to our language-game' (*Remarks on the Foundations of Mathematics*. VI para. 28). But the reference here to language-games raises the tricky issue of the relationship between rule-following and participation in language-games.

Although rule-following is essentially blind, there has to be some basis for drawing the distinction between actions which follow a rule and those which do not. Otherwise we are back in a situation in which 'anything goes' and there is no possibility of truth. The argument so far implies that this basis cannot be either something merely in the mind of the speaker, including an explicitly formulated instruction or formula, or just the speaker's physical surroundings; hence it must be external but not just physical, and Wittgenstein takes it that it is our participation in language-games. He holds that it is a natural fact about us that by and large, despite the fact that we judge blindly, we agree with each other; deviants are rare. Thanks to this large measure of agreement, our judgements take place in the context of shared language-games, and thus connect with a network of interlocking beliefs and intentions, such as the expectations of those engaged in buying and selling. These expectations and the activities they inform, therefore, provide a context which identifies and reinforces the rules inherent in our judgements. So although in speaking we apply our words blindly, our judgements are cases of rule-following because they occur within language-games.

Some critics and sociologically inclined commentators infer from this that Wittgenstein takes the view that to judge correctly is simply to judge in accordance with others. But Wittgenstein explicitly repudiates this view, and it seems to me that so far from undermining the possibility of objective truth in this way, his discussion is intended to show how truth is possible. The position he opposes is one according to which individual thinkers can, all by themselves, secure reference to objective features of the world. That, he argues, is an illusory picture since neither an individual's subjective experiences nor his physical surroundings provide a basis for the distinction between the correct and the incorrect application of language which is an essential precondition of objective truth. Instead, Wittgenstein suggests, this basis is to be found by considering the use of language in the context of language-games where there is a shared form of life. Since the existence of widespread agreement within a 'community' is a necessary condition for such a language, it is, as Kantians would say, a 'transcendental condition' of the possibility of truth. But it is the world itself which determines whether what is said is true or false and it is entirely possible that the community as a whole be mistaken—for example concerning some unobvious fact, such as the origin of the universe.

This account of objectivity can, I think, be compared with the account of freedom propounded by classical liberals such as J. S. Mill (1806–73). Such liberals reject the naïve view that individual freedom is just a matter of doing as one likes in the anarchist's proverbial 'state of nature'; for in fact the conditions of life in such a state preclude the exercise of freedom. Instead they hold that freedom can flourish only where there are political and legal institutions which enjoy widespread support and are dedicated to the protection of individual interests and the promotion of the public good. Similarly, Wittgenstein holds that individual thinkers cannot, just by themselves, achieve objective truth. This is instead possible only within the context of language-games which draw on general agreements about the world and contribute to shared forms of life. Thus the attainment of objective truth and the exercise of freedom are possible only in the context of communal institutions; but these institutions dictate neither what truth consists in nor how freedom is best exercised.

In fact there must be more than just a comparison here: the fact that Wittgenstein's argument draws on the existence of shared forms of life implies that his position has presuppositions concerning the political institutions necessary to support these forms of life. These presuppositions are not explored in Wittgenstein's writings. Nonetheless, his emphasis in the *Investigations* on the multiplicity and variety of language-games is suggestive. For it is reminiscent of pluralist conceptions of political authority which reject the traditional conception of the state as a single hierarchical structure of sovereign authority. That conception of authority resembles the monistic conception of language of the *Tractatus*, with its presumption that only when language is conceived as based on a system of simple names of objects is it possible for language to express objective truth. By contrast, just as liberal critics of the traditional conception of the state hold that freedom flourishes best where authority and power are divided among a variety of political institutions which protect different interests and avoid conflict, Wittgenstein holds in the *Investigations* that objective truth is not the privileged achievement of any one language-game, such as the natural sciences. Instead, different language-games have their own rules to capture different aspects of the world, and as long as outright contradiction (such as exists between creationist and evolutionary accounts of human life) is avoided, there need be no conflict between different types of truth.

At this point I turn to an obvious objection to the thesis that objective truth is possible only in the context of shared language-games. If one considers the situation of a person ('Robinson Crusoe') who has become isolated after growing up and learning language normally, it seems obvious that he can still use language to engage in objective thought about the world, and indeed that he can extend his vocabulary to accommodate new features of the situation—for example, by classifying previously unknown fruits and plants. This case is not a problem for Wittgenstein. For even without others to share his new judgements Robinson Crusoe can draw on his previous understanding of the world in the language he continues to use—much as we all do anyway. The question that is more challenging is whether a human being who has not grown up with other humans might not develop linguistic and conceptual abilities.

Wittgenstein does not explicitly consider this individualist hypothesis in the *Investigations* but a remark from some lectures notes for 1934–5 might be taken to apply to offer an affirmative answer to this question (though it is unclear from the context what is here presupposed concerning Robinson Crusoe's past history):

We can indeed imagine Robinson [Crusoe] using a language for himself but then he must *behave* in a certain way or we shouldn't say that he plays lang[uage] games with himself. (*Philosophical Occasions*, p. 237)

It is certainly not difficult to think of an absolutely isolated person having good uses for simple signs, and thus incorporating them into his behaviour—for example when he wishes to leave himself reminders for the future, such as marks to indicate what seeds he has sown where or which fruits are to be avoided. Admittedly, the sad tales of 'wolf' children—human infants brought up by animals such as wolves—suggest that the normal development of human cognitive and linguistic abilities requires a human environment during infancy and early childhood. But if one is prepared to engage in speculations which bend the ordinary pre-conditions for human development, it is not easy to rule out the individualist hypothesis, and there is much in contemporary psycho-linguistics to support it.

As the passage quoted above shows, this hypothesis does not challenge Wittgenstein's thesis that the meaning of language is dependent on its use in language-games. What it does challenge is the assumption which I attributed to Wittgenstein that such language-games are inescapably social, and this attribution can itself be questioned in the light of the passage quoted above, though this is not the place to pursue this question (I think that Wittgenstein's position is in fact more nuanced than the simple alternatives 'social or individual' allow). But a neat way to resolve this matter is to follow a suggestion of Otto Neurath (1882–1945), one of the most innovative members of the Vienna Circle, who proposed that hypothetical cases which involve only an isolated individual are best thought of as quasi-social, involving a simple language-game in which earlier and later selves take the part of other persons. Neurath puts the point in a remark which nicely complements that quoted from Wittgenstein: 'The Crusoe of yesterday and the Crusoe of today stand to one another in precisely the relation in which Crusoe stands to Friday' ('Protocol Sentences', p. 166).

The Private Language Argument

This discussion of the individualist hypothesis provides a bridge to the most famous, but also most disputed aspect of the *Investigations*—Wittgenstein's 'private language argument'. It used to be said that Wittgenstein's argument provides the definitive refutation of the conception of subjective experience to be found in the works of Descartes (1596–1650) which provides the starting point for all subsequent epistemology. As with all such sweeping stories, although there is something to it, there is also a good deal of exaggeration: and since Wittgenstein himself, characteristically, does not attempt to connect his discussion with the positions of earlier philosophers, I shall not pursue this matter though I shall label the position he opposes 'Cartesian'. For even as it is, Wittgenstein's discussion provides plenty of material for thought.

Wittgenstein's basic idea is that the critical arguments developed in the context of rule-following imply that it is a mistake to conceive of our sensations as states of consciousness whose identity is fixed for each of us by the way in which we experience them. The Cartesian picture he opposes is that which talk of introspection naturally suggests, according to which we identify our mental states by inspecting an inner mental arena that is inaccessible to others. His objection to this picture is that it rests on the illusion that we can identify specific types of mental state purely by means of 'inner' ostensive definitions of them to ourselves, by saying to ourselves, when we have them, such things as '*that's* what a twinge is'. In reality, until the use of such a term is incorporated into a language-game, the putative ostensive definition does not fix the identity of anything.

Wittgenstein suggests two ways in which our identifications of our own sensations can belong to language-games: in the case of pains, the obvious and familiar way is via expressions of distress, sympathy, and comfort in the context of attempts at relief and treatment of ailments, cuts, and other causes of pain. The other way he briefly mentions is that in which the occurrence of a distinctive sensation is noted because it connects with a physiological change, such as a change in blood-pressure (Wittgenstein actually developed a new device for measuring blood-pressure while working in hospitals during the war). Both these cases, however, involve language-games in which our judgements about our own sensations are connected with behaviour or physio-logical changes that can be recognized by others; so they imply that these are not ways of thinking about sensations whose use is regulated by concerns that are exclusively available to those who have the sensa-tions. Is there any alternative, more congenial to the introspective model of Cartesian philosophers, which lacks this feature?

Wittgenstein invites us to try to imagine such a case, a case in which a thinker employs a language for his sensations according to which these are conceived of as 'private' states of his own consciousness—i.e. a 'private language' such that

the individual words of this language are to refer to what can only be known to the person speaking; to his immediate private sensations. So another person cannot understand the language. (*PI* para. 243)

We know already that such a 'language' cannot rely only on ostensive definitions to establish the reference of words to kinds of sensations: the question then is whether we can envisage its being incorporated into a more complex form of activity such that it forms part of a language-game which does not undermine its supposed privacy. Given this last requirement, such a language-game could consist only of a broader, but still private, understanding by the Cartesian private linguist of his own mental states within which his putative private identification of a particular sensation might be critically assessed by reference to its connections with other mental states. The objection to this supposition is that the existence of this broader understanding assumes that which is in question here. For it implies that the private linguist already has a working, but still private, understanding of the structure of the rest of his mental life when it is precisely the possibility of this kind of understanding that is in question; Wittgenstein concentrates on the case of sensations only because we are intuitively most strongly drawn to the introspective model of their identification in this case.

So there cannot be a 'private language'. At one point Wittgenstein puts his objection by saying that, for the private linguist, there is no 'criterion of correctness', and thus that 'whatever is going to seem right to me is right. And that only means that here we can't talk about "right"' (*PI* para. 258). As before it is the need to provide a basis for the possibility of making a mistake that is crucial, and the complaint is that no such basis can be constructed from within the Cartesian private linguist's consciousness alone; the broader context of a language-game is required but is not available if privacy is to be maintained. It is often objected that Wittgenstein's argument is at this point excessively verificationist: he expects a private linguist who mistakes one of his sensations to be able to verify to himself that he has done so, whereas this is not a requirement that in general we impose on ourselves. But the objection fails to do justice to the constraints imposed by the private language hypothesis in the first place; for by excluding all public tests the only resource left to the private linguist is his consciousness. Hence it is indeed true that if this were to provide a 'criterion of correctness', the verificationist demand would also be met. But Wittgenstein's argument does not rest on the general legitimacy of this verificationist demand.

The Grammar of Mind

So far the conclusion is essentially negative. But it suggests a positive thesis, that if talk of sensations, experiences, and other mental states is to make sense at all, our conception of these states must include the fact that they connect with behaviour and physiology in ways which enable speakers to engage in shared language-games. Wittgenstein formulates this point by remarking that 'an "inner process" stands in need of outer criteria' (*PI* para. 580: but notice Wittgenstein's use of 'scare' quotes here; as we shall see, one theme of Wittgenstein's discussion is that all talk of mental states as 'processes' is dangerous). This remark raises the question of what the connection is supposed to be between the mind and behaviour, physiology and other 'outer' facts, i.e. just what this talk of 'outer criteria' amounts to.

Criteria are evidence, but not just any kind of evidence. Wittgenstein distinguishes criteria from mere 'symptoms'. The distinctive feature of the criteria for a concept is that they determine its 'grammar'; thus they are authoritative kinds of evidence, and understanding a concept involves a grasp of the relevant criteria. This may suggest that Wittgenstein is after all committed to a version of the verificationist thesis of the logical empiricists that the meaning of a sentence is exhausted by a specification of the evidence for and against it. But though Wittgenstein accepted this thesis during the early 1930s (indeed he was responsible for the famous slogan that the meaning of a proposition is its method of verification), he rejected the logical empiricists' emphasis on the priority of simple observational evidence and the reductionist implications which they drew from this. Hence his later slogan 'meaning is use', is intended to be wholly permissive concerning the admissible types of authoritative evidence: criteria are specific to language-games, and it is the philosopher's business to describe them, not to criticize them.

An account of the 'outer' criteria for someone's having a sensation such as pain is, therefore, to be found by looking at the relevant language-games, and thus at the kinds of evidence which are in fact central to the ways in which talk of pains is learnt, taught, and used. So if such investigations show that the criteria for pains, and mental states generally, are behavioural—and this is what Wittgenstein's remarks often suggest—it appears to follow that even if Wittgenstein is not a verificationist he is a behaviourist, that his view is that being in pain is just being in a state in which one is liable to groan, writhe, complain etc.

As any reader of the *Investigations* quickly recognizes however, Wittgenstein explicitly and emphatically rejected any such commitment. He agrees, for example, that there is all the difference in the world between pain-behaviour accompanied by pain and the behaviour by itself. But how is this consistent with his previous argument? Wittgenstein says that the key to understanding the situation here is 'to make a radical break with the idea that language always functions in one way' (*PI* para. 304). The mistake which both the Cartesian and the behaviourist make is to assume that the language in which we talk of sensations and other mental states is straightforwardly descriptive. For reasons that are intelligible, but misguided, the Cartesian construes this language as a way of describing private states of consciousness; the behaviourist rightly rejects this conception, but wrongly infers that the language is a description of behaviour. Wittgenstein maintains, however, that our talk of sensations and other mental states is essentially expressive, and not descriptive at all.

This thesis rests on the claim that there is a crucial difference between first- and third-person uses of psychological verbs (i.e. between 'I feel . . .' and 'she feels . . .', 'I believe . . .' and 'she believes . . .', 'I intend . . .' and 'she intends . . .' etc.). The third-person uses are, he acknowledges, descriptive; but the first-person uses are not—they are expressions of the relevant state and not descriptions of it; furthermore they are the basic uses. Wittgenstein's point here is most easily grasped in connection with intentions (I discuss sensations and beliefs later). The expression of an intention is an occasion for forming, or reaffirming, an intention; by saying 'I intend to serve supper at 6 o'clock' I make it true that this is my present intention; I do not simply describe my antecedent state of mind. Where someone describes something, we can generally ask them for the evidence which supports the description; but it would normally be inappropriate to ask someone what their evidence was for supposing that they have an intention they have just expressed; their expression of their intention is itself authoritative. For this reason, the first-person expressive use ('I intend . . .') is the fundamental one, since the speaker's authority implies that this use is the basic criterion for the appropriateness of third-person descriptive uses ('She intends . . .') by others, though other behaviour by the speaker is also needed to show that she understands properly the language she has used (it is this requirement which makes it so easy to interpret Wittgenstein as a behaviourist *malgré lui*).

According to Wittgenstein, the Cartesian recognizes that there is something peculiar about first-person psychological language, but misconstrues this peculiarity as epistemological privacy. The behaviourist rightly rejects the Cartesian's conception of the privacy of the mind, but ends up denying that there is anything special about our self-ascriptions of mental states. The result is a typical state of philosophical bewilderment in which as thinkers we do not know our way about (*PI* para. 123); but the way 'To shew the fly the way out of the fly-bottle' (*PI* para. 309) is to identify the fundamental mistake by seeing that:

The first step is the one that altogether escapes notice. We talk of processes and states and leave their nature undecided. Sometime perhaps we shall know more about them—we think. But that is just what commits us to a particular way of looking at the matter. (*PI* para. 308)

It is not easy to demarcate the extent of Wittgenstein's critique here. It is clear that in rejecting the descriptivist assumption he rejects the conception of the mind as a domain of real 'processes and states' which it is the business of a scientific psychology to investigate and tell us about (*PI* para. 571). Instead, he holds, once we look at our actual uses of psychological terms, and the language-games which surround them, we find that they are rooted in expressive roles. Hence properly conducted psychological investigations, of the kind he himself undertakes in his extensive later writings on the philosophy of psychology, have to start there.

So far the point is primarily methodological. The temptation is to press it further and interpret him as advancing an anti-realist conception of the mind. After all, he declares, in an idiom reminiscent of Russell's talk of 'logical fictions' (cf. Chapter 1, p. 4), that talk of mental states is just a 'grammatical fiction' (*PI* para. 307). Nonetheless, I think this temptation is to be resisted: it conflicts with his deep aversion to advancing philosophical theses, and it does not fit with the fact that he does hold that psychological inquiries informed by a correct grasp of the grammar of our language are entirely legitimate. Such inquiries should therefore show us how to obtain an objective conception of the mind, one that deals with the 'real' facts concerned, if this idiom is to be used. What matters to Wittgenstein, therefore, is not a metaphysical doctrine about the reality or not of mental states, but the characterization of a way of understanding, and finding out about, the mind which respects the deep grammatical differences between the languages of natural science and psychology.

First-Person/Third-Person Asymmetries

As I indicated, Wittgenstein bases these grammatical differences on the differences between first-person and third-person uses of psychological verbs. His claim is that the 'expressive' first-person uses are fundamental and not descriptive and I discussed how this claim applies to the expression of intention. But its application to the expression of feelings and beliefs requires more discussion.

The Cartesian interprets the special status of first-person expressions of feelings in terms of the doctrine of the special knowledge each of us has of our own sensations. Wittgenstein rejects this and suggests instead that our relationship to our own sensations is not cognitive at all but 'grammatical'. On the one hand, he claims, it does not really make sense to say of me that I know that I am in pain. For in my own situation, unlike that of others with respect to me, if I am in pain there is insufficient distance between myself and my sensation for me to have any serious doubt as to whether I am in pain; and on an issue concerning which there can be no real doubt, he holds, talk of knowledge makes no sense either. Hence, and this is then the 'grammatical' thesis, what is special about these first-person statements is just that we use them to express, rather than describe, the sensations we are having.

This 'grammatical' account seems, to me at least, too thin, and the claim that it simply does not make sense to say of me that I know that I am in pain has not attracted much support. A revised account can, however, be constructed on the basis of two other claims which Wittgenstein also makes, first that patterns of involuntary expressive behaviour (as when one exclaims 'Ow!') are one main ground for the ascription of pains to others, and secondly that as we learn to control these expressions of pain we learn to conceptualize them in the judgement 'I am in pain' and thereby make the kind of judgement concerning ourselves which, in a third-person form ('she is in pain'), the expressions of pain by others have already made familiar to us. On this account it need not be denied that people who are in pain normally know immediately that they are; but this knowledge is to be understood as a product of their learning how to articulate conceptually what was originally just an involuntary tendency to express pain which enabled others to judge that they are in pain. So there is still an important asymmetry between first-person and third-person judgements: whereas third-person judgements draw on observations of behaviour, including speech, (and, perhaps, neurophysiological changes), first-person judgements simply reflect our ability to express our sensations in conceptual terms.

The case of beliefs is rather different. In this case, the asymmetry between first-person and third-person statements is exemplified by a puzzle which Wittgenstein called 'Moore's paradox' because it had first been noted by Moore. It concerns the manifest absurdity of such remarks as 'It's raining, but I don't believe that it is.' The puzzle here is that what is said may well be true: it is often the case that it is raining at times when I do not believe that it is; and yet the remark is clearly absurd. But how can it be absurd for me to say something about myself which is, in fact, true? The asymmetry here arises from the fact that the absurdity is confined to first-person present-tense indicative statements: there is no absurdity in remarking of someone else 'It's raining, but she doesn't believe that it is,' or of oneself yesterday 'It was raining, but I did not believe that it was.' There is, therefore, something special about the circumstances of the first-person present indicative use of 'I believe' which sets it apart from the other uses of the verb, despite the fact that if someone says of me 'He does not believe that it is raining', what he says contradicts what I say of myself when I say 'I believe that it is raining.'

Moore's view had been that the absurdity here is to be explained by noting that when I say 'It's raining' I thereby *imply* that I believe what I have said, i.e. that it is raining. Hence if I go on to say '. . . but I don't believe that it is' the latter part of my statement contradicts what I have implied by the first part of it. Thus the puzzle that there is here a truth about me that I cannot sensibly state is solved by recognizing that once I attempt to state it I imply that I have a belief which, in the statement, I say that I do not have. This diagnosis rests on the claim that our language-game is such that speakers have to represent themselves as believing what they say (even when they are in fact lying), and it is the significance of this point that especially interests Wittgenstein. He in fact concentrates on a variant of Moore's original paradox, in which someone says 'I believe that it's raining, but it isn't.' In this case the absurdity is just as apparent, and Wittgenstein suggests that it shows us that when I say 'I believe that it's raining' what I say is tantamount to what I would have said had I just said 'it's raining', which directly contradicts what I then go on to say. Although the direction of this explanation is apparently the reverse of Moore's, the underlying point is much the same: that because we express our beliefs by simple indicative utterances, when we explicitly attribute beliefs to ourselves we commit ourselves as much to the truth of what we say we believe as to the fact that we believe it.

A point that Wittgenstein takes from this is that we cannot detach ourselves from our current beliefs: we can, as he says, 'mistrust our senses' when we wonder if things are as they appear to us to be; but we cannot similarly mistrust our beliefs. Hence we cannot regard our own beliefs merely as mental states which represent aspects of the world more or less accurately: by virtue of the fact that they are our own beliefs we are committed to their truth. We are ineluctably inside them. Moore's paradox thus shows us that a concept of belief which includes a first-person present-tense use is not just the concept of an explanatory mental representation; it is also a concept which characterizes, for each thinker, how things are.

It follows that if I have described the world without including a description of my beliefs I do not need to add a further description of my beliefs to complete my description of the world; they are included already. This way of putting the point is reminiscent of a notoriously enigmatic thesis of the *Tractatus*, that 'I am my world', and I think the relationship between Wittgenstein's early and late philosophy is well captured by the way in which he returns to these themes in his discussions of Moore's paradox, which are among his last writings. For in these writings the point is developed in the context of an account of our ordinary language-game of belief, and not as if it were some only improperly sayable insight of metaphysics. A remark he himself makes in the context of his discussion of sensations applies better here— 'A whole cloud of philosophy condensed into a drop of grammar' (*PI* II. xi. 222)

On Certainty

Wittgenstein wrote a series of notes on the topics of doubt, knowledge and certainty during the final period of his life (1949–51; the last entry is dated only two days before his death). They have been published as *On Certainty* (hereafter *OC*) and they are among his most brilliant writings. The context in which he began to compose them was a debate between Moore and the American philosopher Norman Malcolm (1911–90), who had studied with both Moore and Wittgenstein, concerning the propriety of Moore's claim to know for certain such extremely obvious, common sense, things as that the earth has existed for a long time and that he has two hands. Drawing on Wittgenstein's account of knowledge (exemplified in his denial that we know our own pains), Malcolm had argued that these common-sense matters are in fact too obvious for us to know them at all. But, Malcolm also argued, to reject Moore's position in this way is not to side with the sceptic who seeks to persuade us that it is doubtful whether we have two hands. Instead we should accept that Moore's common sense is too obvious for us to speak sensibly of either doubt or knowledge.

Wittgenstein sides with Malcolm in this debate. But what he brings to the debate is the broader context of the role of language-games in arguments of this kind. We have already seen that he takes it that the existence of a language-game requires the identification of criteria, authoritative types of evidence, for the application of the characteristic terms of the language-game and thus for the existence of the things referred to by these terms. But he does not take it that one can therefore just dismiss sceptical doubts concerning the existence of these things. Instead, in a further application of his insistence on the primacy of language-games for conceptual inquiries, Wittgenstein takes it that such doubts should be explored in the context of the language-game of claims to knowledge, i.e. the patterns of reasoning and practice in which we talk of 'knowledge' and 'belief', 'doubt' and 'certainty'. *On Certainty* is an exploration of this language-game.

Wittgenstein's central claim is that reflection on the use of these concepts reveals that, as with other language-games, important areas of background agreement are presupposed. In particular, the understanding of the general structure of the world implied by our common sense beliefs forms, he says, 'the essence of what we call an argument' (*OC* para. 105). It is not a 'more or less arbitrary and doubtful point of departure' (ibid.); instead it is 'the element in which arguments have their life' (ibid.). The kinds of things Moore claimed to know with such certainty belong to this general structure, and the certainty of our conviction concerning them is therefore to be understood in the light of this role, which Wittgenstein captures in a memorable metaphor:

That is to say, the *questions* that we raise and our *doubts* depend on the fact that some propositions are exempt from doubt, are as it were like hinges on which those turn. (*OC* para. 341)

Wittgenstein's position is a way of filling out Moore's faith in common sense. But Wittgenstein differs from Moore in distinguishing *certainty* from *knowledge*. The common-sense conception of the world is, he holds, a matter of certainty: taken as a whole it is something which 'stands fast for me' in the sense that I cannot make intelligible to myself how I could come to have any serious doubts about it; for even doubts have presuppositions—they require hinges which stay put. For this reason Wittgenstein holds (like Malcolm) that Moore was wrong to insist that these common-sense claims are things which he knows. For where we have no reason to doubt a claim of this kind we cannot provide any serious demonstration of its truth: and, Wittgenstein holds, where this is so, it is incorrect to speak of knowledge. Wittgenstein does allow that for each common-sense claim taken by itself one can envisage there being concrete grounds to doubt it, and thus that a claim to knowledge might be appropriate once these grounds for doubt have been dispelled; but situations of this kind are precisely not those which Moore had in mind when he confronted the sceptic with his claims to knowledge. So though Moore was right to think that there is a 'common-sense' response to scepticism, he mislocated it by expressing it in terms of knowledge. Instead, our common sense understanding of the world and ourselves is that of which we are certain, where this certainty is not a matter of rational or intuitive conviction, but enters into all that we do. As he had held in the *Tractatus*, we are to *show* our certainty in the way in which we lead our lives rather than seeking vainly for further grounds which we might *state*.

I am not myself persuaded that we do not have common-sense knowledge (surely we all know such things as that the earth has existed for a long time); but the disagreement here is largely verbal, and does not affect the substance of his discussion of doubt and its presuppositions. A question of greater importance concerns the implications of Wittgenstein's position once one takes into account the possibility that there have been, and still are, people with radically different common-sense convictions. This hypothesis cannot be excluded: for common sense is not a matter of a priori truth, and Wittgenstein himself takes the example of people with very different attitudes to religious belief as an example of this situation. As he acknowledges, it is an implication of his position that in such cases people will find it difficult, if not impossible, to convince those who differ from them. But this does not imply that he is committed to the relativist thesis that one should accept that there are alternative, incompatible, systems of belief of equal merit to one's own beliefs. This differs little from the scepticism to which he was certainly opposed and conflicts with the theme of his discussion of Moore's paradox, that we cannot detach ourselves from our own beliefs. Instead we must just accept that we have beliefs which others do not share but for which we can offer no reason which is likely to persuade them. He puts the resulting position nicely in the following passage in which he imagines Moore confronting some strange king:

Men have believed that they could make rain; why should not a king be brought up in the belief that the world began with him? And if this king and Moore were to meet and discuss, could Moore really prove his belief to be the right one? I do not say that Moore could not convert the king to his view, but it would be a conversion of a special kind; the king would be brought to look at the world in a different way. (*OC* para. 92)

Wittgenstein's Naturalism

This brief discussion of relativism brings me to a final question concerning Wittgenstein's later philosophy, namely whether he really manages to satisfy the aspiration that one should do philosophy without oneself advancing philosophical theses. The main issue here concerns Wittgenstein's account of the role of language-games and the related 'rule-following' discussion. Are there not some 'philosophical theses' here? Just as Kant's critical philosophy revolves around the thesis that a thinker must be able to make sense of his experiences as the experiences of someone with a single, persisting, consciousness (so that, as Kant put it, the thinker must allow that 'I think' can accompany all his experiences), does not Wittgenstein's critical philosophy revolve around the thesis that we only understand a problematic type of statement when we have located it within its proper language-game (so that, as we might put it, a speaker must allow that 'it is said that' can accompany all his statements)?

The analogy holds, I think; but the difference nonetheless is that whereas Kant attempts to ground his position by a very ambitious a priori argument (the so-called 'Transcendental Deduction'; I discuss 'transcendental arguments' of this type in Chapter 8, pp. 172–6), Wittgenstein's arguments, including the 'rule-following argument' and the 'private language argument' are essentially only negative arguments by *reductio ad absurdum*, and are accompanied by frequent reminders that it is a mistake to think that 'descriptions' of our language-games need to be followed up by 'explanations' (i.e. vindications) of them. In the end we can only remark '*this language-game is played*' (*PI* para. 654—emphasis in the original). Furthermore when Wittgenstein does sound a positive note, it is not to introduce some new a priori doctrine but to suggest that his position belongs to a broadly conceived form of anthropology or 'natural history' as he calls it:

What we are supplying are really remarks on the natural history of human beings; we are not contributing curiosities however, but observations which no one has ever doubted, but which have escaped remark only because they are always before our eyes. (*PI* para. 415; cf. *OC* para. 475)

Thus although Wittgenstein's critical method, with its emphasis on the limits of language, is often reminiscent of Kant, his underlying approach to philosophy is closer to Hume (1711–86), who also wanted to replace the bad metaphysics of traditional philosophy with an understanding of our ways of thinking of the world and ourselves that was rooted in a grasp of human nature. Whether the concepts of 'human nature' or 'natural history' can really bear the weight that Hume and Wittgenstein wished to place upon them is an important question to which I shall return in Chapter 9. For the moment it suffices to see that it is by representing his inquiries into the structure of our ordinary language-games as a form of natural history, rather than as the development of a systematic *philosophy* of language that Wittgenstein regards himself as avoiding any commitment to philosophical theses of his own.

3

The Oxford Movement

During the early post-war period, from 1947 until 1960 or so, the liveliest centre for philosophical debate in the English-speaking world was Oxford. It had long been the case that there were far more academic posts which involved teaching philosophy at Oxford University than at any other British university or, indeed, any other English-speaking university (with the possible exception of Toronto). During the first part of the twentieth century, however, most Oxford philosophers had been hostile to the new ideas emerging from Cambridge and Vienna which I described in Chapter 1, with the result that philosophical discussion there had tended to stagnate. After the war, however, there was a remarkable renaissance and the heady atmosphere of those times is nicely captured by Liam Hudson, now a distinguished psychologist, who studied philosophy there during the early 1950s:

It was said . . . that there were more than eighty men and women at that time in Oxford, earning their living as philosophers. It was their energy and sense of purpose that brought the processes of thinking alive to me. They created in a haphazard way an educational environment of a quality I have never seen rivalled; revealing to us a world in which ideas could be pursued for their own sake, and with formidable intellectual vigour. They offered us the chance— priceless, and accorded only rarely—to express in terms of our work our adolescent ideals of the scholarly life and the disinterested pursuit of wisdom. (*The Cult of the Fact*, p. 32)

At the 'pinnacle of this intellectual pyramid', as Hudson calls it, were the trio of Gilbert Ryle (1900–76), J. L. Austin (1911–60) and Sir Peter Strawson (1919–), and it is some of their writings which provide most of the material for this chapter.

Ordinary Language Philosophy

As Hudson's remarks indicate, there was a general sense of intellectual excitement at this time, generated by a belief that Oxford philosophers had not only caught up with the rest of the world, they had now themselves grasped the torch of intellectual progress. In a retrospective collection of radio talks from 1956, published under the title *The Revolution in Philosophy* (which tells one more about the felt need for 'revolutionary' change at Oxford than about the content of the lectures) a series of Oxford philosophers describe the recent history of the subject (i.e. the material covered here in Chapters 1 and 2) and then introduce the distinctive Oxford approach to philosophy, which they call 'conceptual analysis'.

Its hallmark was a detailed concern with ordinary language and its nuances. 'Back to ordinary language', Ryle wrote, is 'the slogan of those who have woken from the formaliser's dream' ('Ordinary Language', p. 317). Although Ryle and others certainly thought that it was important to familiarize oneself with the techniques of formal logic, they thought that it was a 'dream', an illusion, to suppose that the analytical techniques of formal logic would enable one to resolve philosophical problems. Instead, they thought, the conceptual resources of ordinary language provide a much richer source of insights. For it embodies, as Austin put it, 'the inherited experience and acumen of many generations of men', and though it is '*not* the last word' it is 'the *first* word' ('A Plea for Excuses', p. 185). This was even thought to be true within the domain of logic itself, where Strawson contrasted the arid elegance of formal logic with 'the logic of ordinary speech', which 'provides a field of intellectual study unsurpassed in richness, complexity, and the power to absorb' (*Introduction to Logical Theory*, p. 232).

Since a concern with ordinary language is also a feature of Wittgenstein's later philosophy, it is worth asking how far Oxford philosophy of this period resembles Wittgenstein's later philosophy. There are certainly important similarities with Ryle and Austin, both of whom shared Wittgenstein's hostility to traditional philosophical theorizing. Ryle expressed the point pithily: 'The gist of my position is this. There is no place for "isms" in philosophy' ('Taking Sides in Philosophy', p. 153). Again, both Ryle and Austin delight in 'assembling reminders' in order to drive home the critical points they wish to make. Austin is especially effective at this. In the following passage he is reminding his audience of our normal conception of evidence:

The situation in which I would properly be said to have *evidence* for the statement that some animal is a pig is that, for example, in which the beast itself is not actually on view, but I can see plenty of pig-like marks on the ground outside its retreat. If I find a few buckets of pig-food, that's a bit more evidence, and the noises and the smell may provide better evidence still. But if the animal then emerges and stands there plainly in view, there is no longer any question of collecting evidence; its coming into view doesn't provide me with more *evidence* that it's a pig, I can now just *see* that it is, the question is settled. (*Sense and Sensibilia*, p. 115).

Yet there are also important differences. There is an obvious stylistic difference: unlike Wittgenstein, Ryle and Austin use continuous prose to develop their arguments. Furthermore, though Ryle holds that philosophy does not discover new facts and proceeds largely by the negative method of finding contradictions, he certainly advances some positive philosophical theses in his writings. This matter is less clear in the case of Austin, who is usually more concerned to deconstruct traditional philosophical debates than to present a positive thesis, though in his last writings he attempts to present a systematic theory of speech-acts. Above all, however, there is a profound difference of temperament and character. When Wittgenstein writes that 'The real discovery is the one that makes me capable of stopping doing philosophy when I want to' (*PI* para. 133) he implies in the absence of such 'discoveries' he could not stop himself doing philosophy, and his massive unpublished writings bear this out. Ryle and Austin, by contrast, delight in witty allusions and jokes whose point lies outside anything specifically philosophical, and often give the impression of being motivated at least as much by a wish to correct the mistakes of other philosophers as by a concern to resolve the problems they are discussing. Moore famously remarked that what had stimulated his interest in philosophy was his sense of bewilderment and outrage at the remarks of other philosophers; and in this respect, as in many others, Ryle and Austin resemble Moore rather more than Wittgenstein.

Gilbert Ryle

Ryle was the oldest of this group of Oxford philosophers. His academic career began during the 1920s and during the pre-war period he was the main representative in Oxford of the new analytical style of philosophy: 'the sole and whole function of philosophy', he boldly declared in 1932, 'is philosophical analysis' ('Systematically Misleading Expressions', p. 61). His approach at this time was similar to Moore's, resting on informal analysis of ordinary language rather than formal logic. Nonetheless, he held that the purpose of this informal analysis was to reach conclusions that are essentially 'logical'; and his conception of philosophy always remained one of an activity primarily dedicated to clarifying 'the logic of our concepts'.

A surprising feature of his work during the 1930s was his interest in the writings of the German philosophers, Husserl, Heidegger and their Austrian predecessors, on whose work he used to lecture during the 1930s, much to the consternation of his Oxford colleagues. He wrote a long review of Heidegger's *Being and Time*, which was for a long time the only serious discussion in English of Heidegger's philosophy. It is surely a remarkable fact that Ryle, whose writing often affects the style of English no-nonsense 'common sense', should also have been for a long time the one point of contact between German phenomenology and English-speaking philosophy. It is also a good question how much Ryle took from this German tradition and incorporated into his book *The Concept of Mind*. Ryle's hostility to 'isms' entails that he has no time for the jargon of Heidegger's *Dasein* or Husserl's reductions. But there are significant similarities with some of the doctrines of *Being and Time*, and Ryle's survey of our mental life through a discussion rooted in our ordinary idioms is a way of realizing the founding slogan of the phenomenological movement—*zu den Sachen selbst* ('To the things themselves!').

In 1945 Ryle was elected to the Waynflete Professorship of Metaphysics at Oxford, and at the same time he succeeded Moore as editor of *Mind*, the most important British philosophical journal. These appointments confirmed his position in succession to Moore as the most respected British philosopher of the post-war period, and equally confirmed the shift from Cambridge to Oxford as the centre of British philosophical discussion. Ryle was also largely responsible for an institutional development at Oxford which helped to reinforce this position—the establishment of a taught postgraduate degree, the 'Bachelor of Philosophy' (B.Phil.), which was the first of its kind in Britain. This attracted to Oxford not only many of the best British philosophy students, but also many from North America and the rest of the world, and provided a regular audience for advanced debates and discussions in philosophy of a kind not previously found in the British academic system.

The Concept of Mind

Ryle's claim to fame now rests on his book *The Concept of Mind* (1949). This book is often now described, dismissively, as an exercise in 'analytical behaviourism', i.e. as a misguided attempt to analyse mental concepts as concepts which do no more than characterize the kinds of behaviour we are prone to perform; and it must indeed be acknowledged both that Ryle lays himself open to this charge and that he pleads guilty to it. Yet quite apart from the fact that this description conflicts with Ryle's repudiation of all 'isms' in philosophy, we shall see that it fails to do justice to the central claim of the book, which is that the fundamental elements of our mental life are abilities which are best understood in the context of our ordinary reason-giving explanations of action.

Ryle devotes the first, and most famous, chapter of the book to a polemical critique of what he calls 'Descartes' myth'—the myth of 'the ghost in the machine'. This is the view that although the human body is a marvellously well constructed 'machine' for life, it does not encompass such distinctively mental phenomena as thought, choice, and feeling. Hence, according to this view, these mental phenomena involve something else, the human 'mind', which is distinctively non-physical (i.e. 'ghostly'). Ryle makes the interesting suggestion that this conception of the mind is a transformed and enlarged version of the early Protestant conception of the conscience: where the Protestants used this conception to vindicate the possibility of religious faith detached from external rituals, Descartes and his successors used it to suggest a way in which mental life could be conceived quite generally without essential reference to anything external.

Although Ryle argues that the resulting position is deeply mistaken, he does concede that if one starts out by supposing that all proper explanations of events which involve physical changes (as human actions do) must be in some way ultimately mechanical or physical, then it is quite understandable, and even legitimate, that one should embrace the hypothesis of a 'para-mechanical' ghost in the machine in order to deal with our mental life. Indeed in the closing sentences of *The Concept of Mind* Ryle emphasizes that given a choice between the mechanistic materialism of Thomas Hobbes (1588–1679) and Descartes' mind-body dualism, the latter is to be preferred; for the Cartesian dualist has at least seen that materialist mechanism is inadequate as an account of mental phenomena. So Ryle's fundamental target is not the Cartesian hypothesis of the ghost in the machine: it is 'the bogy of mechanism', mistaken fear of which leads people to embrace the Cartesian hypothesis.

As against the mechanist's reductive concentration on physical explanations, Ryle maintains that it is just obvious that human affairs are susceptible to explanations of many different kinds. Thus despite the fondness of mechanists for treating all events as explicable in the way in which collisions of billiard balls are explicable, Ryle observes that the course of a game of billiards actually depends on much more than the physics of the billiard table: it involves the rules of billiards, the tactical strategies of the players, not to mention their further goals, beliefs and moods. So in explaining the course of a game of billiards there are all sorts of facts to which one will need to refer, most of which involve concepts that are utterly alien to the laws of physics.

This position obviously gives rise to the question as to how these different explanations fit together. Although, as we shall see, Ryle says a good deal more about our mental concepts, it cannot be said that he seriously addresses this question and thereby slays the bogy of mechanism. So I shall turn instead to Ryle's critique of the Cartesian hypothesis that men are 'ghost-ridden machines', which he does argue against in detail.

The Ghost in the Machine

In criticizing this hypothesis Ryle makes much of the idea that it incorporates a 'category mistake', the mistake of regarding mental states as inner acts or events which take place in addition to the observable acts and events of ordinary life. He compares this mistake to the kind of mistake that would arise if a student of politics who had studied British political institutions such as the Houses of Parliament, the Courts of Law, and the Monarchy, went on to search for some further institutional realization of the British Constitution and, not finding any recognizable institution of this kind, postulated the existence of a secret political institution which controls all the observable ones. Such a mistake would involve a misinterpretation of that systematically misleading description 'the British Constitution' as if it described a further political institution, instead of recognizing that it is the set of more or less informal rules which regulate the authority of the political institutions of the British state (Ryle's argument here is an application of Russell's theory of descriptions—cf. Chapter 1, pp. 3–4). Similarly, therefore, the Cartesian misinterprets our ordinary talk of 'the mind' as the name of a private space within which mental acts and happenings take place. Instead, we are just talking about someone's 'mental constitution', about their general capacities, inclinations, and abilities which are manifest in their straightforwardly observable activities.

The analogy here is not perfect, and Ryle is well aware that when we think about ourselves we attribute to ourselves experiences, intentions, and inclinations concerning which we like to think we ourselves know best, and that the Cartesian hypothesis is a very natural extrapolation of this self-understanding. So he needs to show how our ordinary understanding of ourselves and others is in fact undermined when it is extrapolated in this way.

One familiar point concerns the difficulty of combining the Cartesian thesis with any confidence in our ordinary understanding of each other; for on the Cartesian thesis, this understanding is conceived as the outcome of speculative inferences concerning mental states that are in principle unobservable. As such, our understanding of others can amount only to what Ryle calls a 'problematic divination of occult processes' (p. 54). But Ryle's preferred method of argument was always *reductio ad absurdum*, and his critical discussion of the Cartesian account of perception is a good example of this technique.

When I see a ripe tomato which looks red, spherical, squashy, etc. the fact that it looks these ways to me depends on my visual experiences. So it is uncontentious that perception involves sense experiences. What is distinctive about the Cartesian hypothesis is that these experiences are regarded as states of consciousness—mental phenomena of which we are aware in having them and which have just the properties which we are thus aware of them having. As a consequence, having a visual experience involves an awareness of the experience itself. This awareness is itself a form of perception, an 'inner' perception; hence, Ryle argues, since all perceptions involve experiences, this inner perception of our own visual experience must itself involve a further non-visual experience. But this now sets off a regress of experiences of which one has to be aware if one is to perceive anything—which is absurd.

This argument is not unchallengeable (e.g. perhaps the Cartesian does not have to accept that inner perceptions involve further experiences), but it is not worth pursuing the matter here, since the Cartesian position has already been critically discussed in the previous chapter. Ryle's own account of perception starts from the fact that when we are perceiving something or having sensations such as pains we are primarily attending to features of the world or of our bodies. We can, if we choose, attend to the experiences involved in perception and bodily sensations, but this attention is retrospective and as such inherently fallible. In the case of our intentions and decisions, there are not even any experiences for us to attend to. Instead our first-person statements ('I intend to . . .' etc.) are 'avowals' and not descriptions of our mental states. So the authority we attach to them comes, not from special knowledge of our experiences, but from the fact that in avowing them we make them true (there are obvious similarities here with Wittgenstein's position—Chapter 2 p. 29). In many other cases there is no such authority; for example, where questions of motivation are concerned agents often possess less knowledge than others who know them well.

Ryle summarizes these points in the Proustian thesis that, so far from our having 'privileged access' to ourselves, as Descartes maintained, the self is 'systematically elusive': in attempting to attend to ourselves as we are, we always find that by this very attempt we have put ourselves beyond the reach of our attention. This is not on the face of it convincing: although there are spontaneous feelings which are in this way elusive, there is typically no difficulty at all in attending to a toothache one has; if only, one may well wish, the pain would make itself elusive. There are also situations in which the self simply obtrudes itself: the embarrassment one feels when one is aware, say, that one's clothes are inappropriate for a public occasion at which one is present can make it almost impossible to think about anything else. So there is more to self-consciousness than Ryle's anti-Cartesian rhetoric allows. But by itself this is not a big point, and to assess Ryle's position properly it is necessary to turn to the positive conception of the mind presented in *The Concept of Mind*.

Abilities and Dispositions

Ryle maintains that having a mind is essentially a matter of possessing abilities, of knowing how to do things. One might think that knowing how to do something is based on knowledge of facts, e.g. that knowing how to play chess is based on knowledge of the rules of chess; but Ryle argues that knowledge of these rules requires understanding and intelligence which are general abilities not expressible as knowledge of more abstract rules; and, further, that knowing how to play chess includes the ability to apply the rules of chess to particular situations, which is not knowledge of further rules as to how rules are to be applied. Thus although he does not deny that knowing how to play chess includes knowledge of the rules, it is not reducible to knowledge of these facts; on the contrary, our knowledge of facts is itself based on our intellectual abilities. Hence the epistemological tradition which assumes the opposite starts from the wrong place in its search for good reasons for true beliefs. Ryle, noting this consequence, concludes that traditional epistemology is a largely misconceived discipline (this is one place where it seems to me quite possible that he was influenced by Heidegger, who had advanced a similar claim in *Being and Time*).

If understanding and intelligence are primarily instances of 'knowing how', rather than 'knowing that', then all aspects of our life in which we are engaged as thinkers involve the exercise of such abilities. Thus Ryle contrasts the Cartesian account of perception he has rejected with the view that perception is essentially the practice of skills in observation and recognition. Similarly, he holds, the imagination is not a quasi-experiential awareness of mental images; instead it is the ability to pretend to oneself that one is perceiving that which one seeks to imagine (this cannot be quite right: I can pretend to myself that I am observing a Himalayan Yeti when I cannot in fact imagine one at all since I have no idea what it would look like; instead the imagination is the ability to make apparent to oneself how the thing which one imagines would or does appear). The primary field for the exercise of abilities is, however, action itself, and Ryle's claim is that by interpreting our talk of thought and intelligence in terms of abilities actually or potentially exercised in action we can do justice to them without treating them as separate acts or states. Thus someone playing the piano attentively is not doubling up the physical activity of manipulating the keyboard with separate mental acts of attention; instead the pianist's playing is simply being described as a manifestation of her ability to respond sensitively to the demands of the music.

Ryle does not maintain that all mental states are abilities; he maintains, for example, that our emotions are inclinations and that our moods are liabilities to action. Insofar as he puts forward a general position it is that implied by a comparison he draws between mental states and the dispositions of physical objects such as the solubility of salt and the fragility of glass. The aim of the comparison is to persuade us to abandon the presumption that someone's being in some mental state consists in his possessing some property, concerning whose nature we might find out more by investigating his state of consciousness or his brain. For in talking of the fragility of a glass we are not, Ryle thinks, describing one of its physical properties. Instead we are just describing what would happen if the glass were dropped—we are saying how things would be if certain conditions were to obtain, not how they are now. Similarly, then, in attributing mental states to people we are simply saying how they would act if certain conditions were to obtain; we are not describing them as they are now.

I think Ryle makes a mistake here. The comparison with physical dispositions is a dangerous one for him to make, since in attributing a disposition such as fragility to a glass we normally accept that the glass has some structural properties which explain why the glass is fragile whereas, say, an apparently similar plastic tumbler is not. Hence Ryle's comparison suggests that the attribution of mental states to people carries a commitment to accepting that they have further properties which explain why they have the states in question whereas other people do not. Nothing so far follows about the nature of these further properties, but the alternatives appear to be that they are either immaterial or material. If they are immaterial, then we are back with a Cartesian conception of the mind; if they are material, then a materialist conception of the mind is inescapable (David Armstrong's influential materialist theory, which I discuss in Chapter 9, emerged from precisely this line of thought).

Ryle sees the danger here and to avoid it he denies that dispositions need to be grounded in properties of the things which have them. Instead his view is that in attributing a disposition to something we say nothing about its actual properties; we simply characterize the hypothetical implications of certain conditions which may never obtain. This does indeed avoid the danger of a commitment to either Cartesianism or materialism, but it lays him wide open to the charge of behaviourism, since if mental states are dispositions which are neither real properties themselves nor grounded in any other properties that one can take to constitute mental reality, the only conclusion to draw is the behaviourist one that there is no intrinsic reality to the mind.

Ryle's attitude to dispositions is part of the heritage of logical empiricism. It rests on the hypothesis that there is a distinction between an object's dispositions and its 'real' properties. In truth, however, there is no such distinction: all familiar physical properties such as mass, charge, etc. can be regarded as dispositions; an object with a mass of 50 grams, for example, is one which, if it were placed on an accurate scale, would exactly balance a standard 50 gram weight. In the general theory of relativity even the structure of space–time is regarded as a disposition. So there are no good grounds for denying the reality of dispositions; and once this is accepted and applied to mental dispositions Ryle's behaviourism disappears.

What, however, of the anxiety that the comparison between mental states and dispositions brings with it a commitment either to Cartesianism or to materialism? The way to respond to this is to see that in the physical case, we demand an explanation in terms of further physical properties only for some differences in physical dispositions. Thus although we take it that differences in fragility should be explicable, differences in mass and charge are not, since these are basic physical properties. Hence once the reality of mental dispositions is accepted one can in principle take it that there are basic mental dispositions which make possible explanations of further differences in mental dispositions without any need to invoke either non-dispositional Cartesian states of consciousness or physical properties in such explanations. In particular, the anxiety that there is an implicit commitment here to materialism depends on the assumption that differences in mental dispositions are to be grounded on differences in physical properties. But this reductionist assumption is not warranted by the reality of mental dispositions.

Having set out a position which, I think, Ryle should have adopted since it avoids behaviourism as well as the 'isms' he repudiated—Cartesianism, materialism; I should add that there is a separate question as to whether the position is in the end defensible: as we shall see in Chapter 9 there are further robust arguments for materialism which are not easily sidestepped. All I have tried to show here is that Ryle's anti-realist treatment of dispositions gets in the way of a proper appreciation of his concept of mind.

His position is based instead on a conception of the fundamental role of our abilities, in particular those which distinguish us as intelligent— i.e. the conceptual 'know-how' which, as he puts it, forms our 'second nature' ('The Concept of Mind', p. 41). There is, no doubt, a causal story to be told about the evolution of these abilities; but for Ryle such a story cannot determine their content—the distinctions we draw and the similarities we note. Concepts are our basic, irreducible, mental dispositions. We exercise these conceptual abilities in our deliberations as to what to do, and the role of these deliberations legitimates rational explanations of our actions which differ in kind from causal explanations which rely only on physical descriptions of ourselves and our environment. Hence although Ryle repudiates the metaphysical dualism of the 'ghost in the machine', he replaces it with an explanatory dualism according to which human affairs admit of two different types of explanation. When our mental abilities are functioning properly, our lives are to be understood in the terms of the familiar disciplines characteristic of the humanities and human sciences—such as history, literary criticism, economics, and anthropology. It is only when things go wrong—in cases, say, of perceptual disorder—that scientific psychology makes a contribution to our understanding. The resulting position is, it must be admitted, not straightforward; but, despite Ryle's suggestion to the contrary, it is far removed from anything helpfully, or indeed harmlessly, described as 'behaviourism'.

It will be obvious that there are many similarities between Ryle's position and that of Wittgenstein. Both are critical of the idea of psychology as a comprehensive science of the mind; for they agree that it is a mistake to regard the mind as a special domain of 'inner processes'—ghostly or just material—which might be the proper subject of a special science. Equally they are both regularly accused of behaviourism. In the case of Wittgenstein, the accusation is certainly misplaced; in the case of Ryle, as I have indicated, matters are more complicated because of his misguided treatment of dispositions (it is notable that although Wittgenstein treats understanding as a case of 'know-how' (*PI* para. 78) he rejects the suggestion that it should be regarded as a disposition for the reason that such talk brings with it questions about the inner construction of that which has the disposition, and these are questions he holds to be misguided in the case of understanding (*PI* para. 149)). But once Ryle's treatment of dispositions is corrected, it is again the similarities are salient: where Ryle's position is based on our basic mental abilities ('know-how'), Wittgenstein invokes our fundamental capacity for 'blind' rule-following, and both of them go on to argue that explanations of action which invoke these capacities are not reducible to causal explanations and belong instead to the disciplines (language-games) characteristic of the subject-matter involved, such as economics or history. (Ryle's position suggests another comparison, with Aristotle's ethical writings; yet there is a puzzle here—although Ryle was a distinguished scholar of ancient philosophy and proposed a challenging re-interpretation of Plato's works, he alludes very infrequently to Aristotle).

J. L. Austin

If, within post-war Oxford philosophy, Ryle was the establishment figure, J. L. Austin was initially the *enfant terrible*, and then, during his period (1952–1960) as White's Professor of Moral Philosophy, the most influential thinker of the whole group. He was only forty-nine when he died at the height of his powers, having published only a few papers (subsequently collected as his *Philosophical Papers*). During his lifetime his reputation rested in part upon his rapier-like wit which can still be enjoyed by reading his lectures on perception, which were post-humously published under the title which Austin (alluding to Jane Austen) used for them—*Sense and Sensibilia*. These lectures are unmatched as an example of the traditional arts of rhetoric in twentieth-century English prose.

Austin's influence rested primarily upon the ways in which he sought to sidestep traditional philosophical disputes by introducing fresh ways of thinking grounded in an unmatched sensitivity to the ordinary uses of language and to its abuses by philosophers. But Austin's appeals to ordinary language were not motivated by an unquestioning faith in its merits. He is insistent that the discoveries of sciences such as psychology have to be taken seriously when they supplement or even supplant ordinary language, and that ordinary language is not to be expected to apply in extraordinary situations. Instead Austin's invocations of language usually have two aspects—exasperation at philosophical positions which start out from simplistic misunderstandings of the relevant parts of language, and an optimistic aspiration that once the language has been better understood the old problems will, if not disappear entirely, at least be placed in a context which encourages fresh ways of thinking about them.

Sense and Sensibilia

The first of these aspects of Austin's method is especially prominent in *Sense and Sensibilia*. His topic here is the familiar old debate concerning the objects of perception—whether they are just the familiar furniture of the world ('moderate-sized specimens of dry goods', as Austin calls them) or are something more subjective—the appearances of such things. Austin thinks that this whole debate is misconceived, and is to be attributed to 'an obsession with a few particular words, the uses of which are over-simplified, not really understood or carefully studied or correctly described' (p. 3). His primary target is A. J. Ayer's thesis that perception of the physical world rests upon awareness of the appearances of things—'sense-data', as Ayer called them. As we have seen, Ryle had already criticized this thesis, but Austin takes the matter rather further by trying to undermine the two basic reasons advanced in favour of it, the 'argument from illusion' and the search for certainty.

The argument from illusion rests on the thesis that the familiar perceptual illusions (such as the way in which a straight stick looks bent when placed in a jar half-full of water) show us that we do not perceive things as they are (for the stick *is* straight but *looks* bent); and from this it is inferred that the primary objects of perception are the appearances of things (the appearance of the stick *as* bent) rather than the things themselves (the straight stick). This inference is notoriously questionable; and Austin rightly challenges the assumption that a straight stick should look straight in all circumstances. But because he wants to undermine the whole debate, rather than simply vindicate a 'realist' position opposed to that of Ayer, he concentrates on the way in which Ayer represents the point in question in terms of a contrast between 'appearances' and 'reality'. Austin jumps on the assumption that 'reality' is to be understood through a contrast with 'appearance' and argues that if we look to our actual uses of the term 'real' we find a plethora of different uses: 'real' coffee vs. instant coffee, 'real' flowers vs. artificial flowers, a 'real' Vermeer vs. a fake one, even 'real' numbers vs. imaginary numbers. The main thing that holds together this variety of cases, according to Austin, is that it is the negative terms here which 'wear the trousers'—i.e. which define, in a given context, the point of the real/ unreal distinction. Hence, Austin concludes, whatever one might want to say about the way in which straight sticks look bent in water, nothing general should be inferred about the reality or not of the objects of perception. For questions concerning 'reality' are inescapably contextual: is someone who is admiring some artificial flowers looking at something 'real' or not? Do I see the 'real colour' of someone's hair when looking at it under normal conditions if the hair is in fact dyed? There are no context-free answers to these questions.

Austin's strategy here is comparable to that currently described as 'deconstruction' (the term comes from the contemporary French philosopher Jacques Derrida; it is notable that Austin is the only post-war English-speaking philosopher for whom Derrida has expressed any great admiration). In Derrida's terminology, Austin seeks to 'deconstruct' the distinction between reality and appearance by showing how the application of the apparently positive term (reality) actually depends on the use of the negative term, which is itself inescapably contextual. Austin applies the same treatment to the traditional debate concerning the 'freedom of the will'. He argues that the term 'free' is to be understood by reference to the varied ways we have of being 'unfree' in our action, which are identified by the excuses we proffer for our behaviour. So there is no positive condition of the 'freedom' of the will to be defended against determinists and other critics; instead, when we talk of someone acting freely we are simply stating that some one, or many, contextually specified excuses do not apply.

I do not myself believe that this deconstructive dissolution of traditional philosophical debates is altogether successful: in both cases, even while acknowledging the significance of Austin's account of the uses of the terms 'real' and 'free' a clear-minded theorist can, I think, reinstate the issues which Austin sought to bury (though Austin's comments about the use of 'real' do have an important moral for philosophical debate: the only way to characterize 'realism' in some domain is by reference to the contextually appropriate form of 'unrealism', or 'anti-realism', for that domain). But the other aspect of Austin's critique of Ayer's position, concerning the search for certainty, is, I think, unanswerable. Ayer held that knowledge needs to be based upon an absolutely certain starting point, or foundation; and that whereas beliefs about material objects are never absolutely certain, beliefs concerning their appearances, or our sense-data, are. So, Ayer concluded, we should install sense-data as the primary objects of perception in order to provide ourselves with foundations for our knowledge of the world.

Austin argues the search for absolute certainty is both fruitless and unwanted. It is fruitless because however minimal the claim being made—e.g. 'it looks blue'—one can envisage circumstances in which one would want to withdraw one's claim; for example perhaps when looking at the sea one might judge, on further reflection, that the apparent shade of colour is, not blue, but only a blueish grey. More importantly, we do not want the kind of absolute certainty that excludes the possibility of being mistaken. For it is a condition of a belief's being *about* anything at all that the truth of the belief be independent of the fact that it is believed. Hence it must be possible for the thinker to be mistaken. Austin's argument at this point covers some of the same ground as Wittgenstein's argument discussed in the previous chapter. But Austin's application of the point to the traditional epistemological quest for absolute certainty ('one of the most venerable bugbears in the history of philosophy' p. 104) is not so explicit in Wittgenstein and clears away, once and for all, the conception of sense-data as indispensable foundations for knowledge.

Austin connects this rejection of the traditional epistemological quest for certainty with a denial that there is an abstract way of ranking sentences in terms of their evidential bearing on one another (such that, for example, 'it looks green' is always evidence for 'it is green', but not vice-versa). Instead the question of what is evidence for what is always context-dependent; there is no abstract totality of statements whose truth would verify the statement 'there's a pig in the shed'; for there is no limit in principle to the kinds of evidence that might, in some strange way, turn out to be relevant. Hence, Austin says, echoing Ryle's scepticism concerning traditional epistemology, if the Theory of Knowledge is supposed to provide an abstract recipe of the kinds of evidence that are appropriate to particular claims to knowledge, there can be no such theory.

This emphasis on the role of context leads directly into Austin's treatment of philosophical scepticism in his paper 'Other Minds' (1946). Austin takes it that the mistake we make when confronted with sceptical arguments is to suppose we should be able to provide an abstract recipe for removing doubt, when in fact we should begin by locating any doubt that is introduced in a specific context of inquiry. For once it is located in such a context, it will turn out that there is some specific ground for the doubt which should in principle, if not always in practice, be susceptible of resolution. Thus if a doubt is raised as to whether a distant bird is a goldfinch, the doubt only makes sense by being located in a context in which much is not called into doubt—e.g. the general physical environment; and given a suitable pair of binoculars, a reliable reference book, and a bird that co-operates by remaining visible, it should be possible to settle the matter. In such a context 'enough is enough'; we do not have to prove that it is not a stuffed goldfinch, nor that it is not a mysterious lookalike that is capable of quoting the novels of Virginia Woolf. Hence the persistence of sceptical doubts is proof only of the 'wile of the metaphysician' ('Other Minds', p. 87) who manages to persuade us that we should be able to prove 'this is a real goldfinch' without specifying what it would be for it to be unreal, so that we are, unsurprisingly, at a loss how to prove that it is real.

This line of thought is an important contribution to the discussion of philosophical scepticism, and I shall return to it in Chapter 8 (p. 185). A related aspect of Austin's position is the thesis that claims to knowledge are not straightforward descriptions of one's state of mind; instead, he suggests, in saying 'I know that S is P' I give others my authority for saying that S is P. Austin's idea was that making a claim to knowledge is like making a promise; it is something that one *does* by one's utterance. As subsequent discussion showed, this comparison is not perfect, since, unlike someone who makes a promise, someone who claims to know something can certainly be mistaken as to whether he knows what he claims to know; nonetheless the implication here that claims to knowledge have a normative element is correct. But what is more important is Austin's use of the case of making a promise as an example of a clear case in which the speaker's utterance is his way of performing the act in question. For this leads Austin to open up the whole subject of 'performatives', utterances in which we 'do things with words'.

Doing Things with Words

Austin's initial interest in these cases is that they reveal the 'descriptive fallacy' of supposing that the only use of language is to describe the world. Like Wittgenstein he was keen to emphasize the variety of the uses of language; and in a way that is also reminiscent of Wittgenstein's remarks about psychological verbs (though it also raises a question about those remarks, since Austin's verbs are not merely 'psychological') Austin stresses the asymmetry between first-person and third-person uses of verbs such as 'promise': we *make* a promise by saying 'I promise', but *report* a promise by saying 'he promised'. During the 1950s Austin developed these ideas further, and they form the topic of his William James lectures *How to do things with Words*, delivered at Harvard in 1955 and subsequently published posthumously.

Austin begins the lectures by introducing the phenomenon of performative utterances through examples such as a bridegroom's utterance of the words 'I do' at the appropriate point in the marriage service. He goes on to characterize the phenomenon as one in which utterances are made which, although grammatically indicative and thus apparently assessable as true or false, are not statements, true or false, at all. It is not, according to Austin, that the bridegroom *says* truly that he is taking his bride as his wedded wife—rather, occurring at the right place in a proper marriage ceremony, his utterance just is his way of marrying her. This case involves a conventional procedure, but Austin also classifies as performative an utterance such as 'I warn you that this ice is thin' where no conventional procedure is involved. In this case the presence of the appropriate performative verb ('I warn') suffices in normal circumstances for the performance of an act, namely warning.

Having generalized the notion of a performative utterance to include non-conventional cases, Austin observes that the acts in question can also be performed without the use of a performative verb: I may simply shout to a child 'the ice is thin' and thereby warn her that the ice is thin. This observation prompts him to change his approach to one in which he characterizes the kinds of act performed in making an utterance rather than identifying a special type of utterance, the performative. Austin distinguishes three main types of act, 'locutionary', 'illocutionary' and 'perlocutionary' acts. The locutionary act is what the speaker has said; this is fixed by general principles of meaning—in uttering 'the ice is thin' I *say* that the ice indicated by the context of my remark is thin. The illocutionary act is that which I do *in* saying that— e.g. I give a warning; and the perlocutionary act is what I do *by* saying what I do—e.g. I dissuade the child from walking on the ice.

The point of the illocutionary/perlocutionary distinction is that successfully carrying out an illocutionary act requires only that the audience should understand the speaker's intention in saying what he does, whereas carrying out a perlocutionary act requires the occurrence of a further consequence not guaranteed by the audience's understanding alone. This is why, in the case of illocutionary acts, the speaker can make his act explicit through the use of a performative verb which gives rise to a performative utterance; but in the case of a perlocutionary act there is no similar performative verb (e.g. 'I persuade you that . . .') because no such utterance could guarantee the occurrence of the further consequence which is essential for the perlocutionary act to have taken place.

Austin does not himself put his new, tentative theory to work in his philosophy, though he does suggest that it supports his deconstructive inclination 'to play Old Harry with the true/false fetish'. Instead he sees himself launching a new approach to the study of language, the study of the illocutionary 'forces' which accompany the locutionary acts that have been the topic of most linguistic investigation. Because of his untimely death Austin did not himself carry this any further, but his ideas have been the inspiration for much subsequent work.

Sir Peter Strawson

Considerations of context were central to Austin's theorizing, and they also play an important part in Strawson's early writings. In 'On Referring' (1950) Strawson challenged the icon of pre-war analytical philosophy—Russell's theory of descriptions (see Chapter 1, p. 4). Strawson observed that Russell insists that descriptions function in a very different way from names primarily because he takes it that the meaning of a name is the thing that it names. One consequence of this doctrine is that despite the fact that Russell's theory is supposed to show how one can talk sensibly about things which do not exist, Russell has to hold that where '*a*' is a name the sentence '*a* does not exist' is meaningless. But even Russell acknowledged that where such sentences use ordinary proper names, they are meaningful; hence he held that ordinary names are in fact 'disguised descriptions' and that the only real names are 'logically proper names' such as 'this'. This conclusion, Strawson argues, is absurd; in particular, the treatment of ordinary names as descriptions used only to make general claims is unacceptable.

In order to avoid these problems, Strawson proposed a unified account of the use of 'referring expressions' in which he included names, definite descriptions and demonstratives. One aspect of this was a distinction, strongly reminiscent of Frege's distinction between 'sense' (*Sinn*) and 'reference' (*Bedeutung*), between the meaning of a referring expression, which Strawson takes to be fixed by the general rules of language, and the thing, if any, actually referred to in the context of its use on a particular occasion. Using this distinction Strawson separated the question of the meaningfulness of a sentence which includes a referring expression from that of the existence or not of anything referred to on some occasion of its use. He therefore finds no difficulty in allowing for the use of referring expressions, including names, in meaningful denials of existence.

Strawson went on to maintain, however, that where a positive sentence which includes a referring expression has a vacuous use because nothing is referred to in that context by the referring expression, no statement, either true or false, is made on that occasion, even though the sentence remains meaningful. Strawson here takes it that it is statements which are primarily true or false, and his claim is radically at variance with Russell's theory of descriptions, which implies that where a sentences has a vacuous use, a speaker makes a false statement by uttering it. This disagreement gave rise to much controversy concerning which theory provides the best account of the vacuous use of sentences such as 'My next door neighbour is drunk' and 'I met my next door neighbour in town' in a situation where the speaker has no next door neighbour (most people agree with Russell concerning the second sentence, but opinion is divided concerning the first—and this very difference between the two cases indicates that the semantic phenomena involved are more complex than either Russell or Strawson allow).

In the course of subsequent debate, two versions of Strawson's position have emerged. According to the moderate version, because a sentence remains meaningful even when its use is vacuous, a speaker who uses it in such a situation does thereby make a statement, albeit one which is neither true nor false. As Strawson has acknowledged, however, the question as to whether to treat such statements as neither true nor false, rather than false (as Russell held), is primarily a matter to be settled in the light of the further development of logical theory in which considerations of overall simplicity can be weighed against intuitive plausibility. The radical version, which was especially developed by Strawson's pupil Gareth Evans (1946–80), sticks to the thesis that a speaker who utters a vacuous sentence makes no statement, and adds a further psychological explanation of this claim, that in uttering such a sentence a speaker expresses no thought.

This radical version of Strawson's position rests on the hypothesis that our ability to think and talk about particular objects depends upon the existence of the objects in question and I discuss this hypothesis in Chapter 9 (pp. 220–1). For the moment, however, I want to return briefly to Strawson's debate with Russell. Russell's treatment of ordinary proper names as disguised descriptions wrongly implied that sentences in which such names occur are used to make general claims that there is just one thing of some kind; Strawson's position, by contrast, upholds our normal conviction that we use such sentences to talk about particular objects (whatever exactly that involves). Strawson, however, extended this claim to sentences in which only descriptions are used; but for these cases Russell's theory, or something similar, seems preferable. As we shall see in Chapter 6, subsequent discussion has broadly confirmed this intuitive view that whereas Russell was right about descriptions Strawson was right about names.

In his early writings Strawson maintains that there is an important distinction between the contextual presuppositions of the use of a sentence to make a statement, true or false, and that which is logically implied by the statement itself. Strawson is therefore critical of logicians such as Russell who, he thinks, provide a distorted understanding of language by confining their attention to logical implications and neglecting the presuppositions which contribute much to our understanding of ordinary language. In retrospect, Strawson's discussion of this matter appears hasty: his own account implies that anything presupposed by the use of a sentence to make a statement is logically implied by the statement itself. Nonetheless, his discussion helped to bring into focus an issue raised in different ways by Wittgenstein, Ryle, and Austin concerning the relationship between the relatively formal accounts of the meaning of utterances characteristic of analytical philosophers such as Russell, and the informal explorations of the presuppositions and implications of their uses in specific contexts characteristic of 'ordinary language philosophers'. Stanley Cavell (1926–), the most distinguished American upholder of the ordinary language tradition, famously put the issue in terms of a putative contrast between 'what we (explicitly) say' (the 'semantic' content dealt with by the traditional analytical philosopher) and 'what we mean' by saying what we do (the 'pragmatic' implications explored by ordinary language philosophers); and he then argued that these latter implications are indeed normally an essential part of what we mean when we say something.

Conversational Implicature

There are many topics where the boundaries of this distinction remain contested, but a central contribution to its understanding was made by another Oxford philosopher, Paul Grice (1913–88). Grice seeks to draw a distinction between, on the one hand, the strict meaning of an utterance and, on the other hand, the further implications of its use which are contingent upon the context within which it is made. He identifies these latter implications as distinctively 'conversational' and presents a general account of 'conversational implicature' as a phenomenon not to be confused with that of strict, or literal, meaning. A straightforward example of the distinction is a case in which, when asked how well a student I am teaching is performing, I merely reply 'he turns up for classes'. Because my reply includes no evaluation of the student's performance, the conversational context is such that my remark implies that the student's performance is at best undistinguished, though this is not part of the strict meaning of the words I have uttered.

Conversational implicature of this kind, which draws not on the literal meaning of what is said but on reasonable expectations and their deliberate violation, is central to humour, irony, rudeness, and so on: we rely upon its recognition by others in ordinary conversation all the time. Life is too short and complex for us to wish to spell out all that is mundane, upsetting, or potentially offensive. In order to distinguish conversational implicature from logical implication Grice notes a characteristic feature of conversational implicature: the speaker can cancel an implication by adding without self-contradiction a further remark which excludes it—as when I say, concerning my student, 'He turns up for classes', and then continue 'and so far his performance has been fine'. For the fact that this is possible implies that the original implication was not part of the meaning of the initial remark and was therefore contingent on the conversational context—including what had not, so far, been said.

Grice thus showed that there is a way of thinking about the 'use' of language which respects the intuition that there are often important implications inherent in the use of language and yet holds that these implications need not belong to the literal meanings of the terms employed. Since it had been a familiar trope of ordinary language philosophy to try to subvert traditional philosophical disputes by arguing that those who engage in them fail to respect the use of the crucial terms employed, Grice's work, though grounded in a detailed investigation of the uses of ordinary language, showed that the appeal to use needs to be informed by careful consideration of the kind of implication involved. Austin's discussion of evidence for the presence of a pig, quoted at the start of this chapter, is a case in point:

But if the animal then emerges and stands there plainly in view, there is no longer any question of collecting evidence; its coming into view doesn't provide me with more *evidence* that it's a pig, I can now just *see* that it is, the question is settled.

To this a critic may well object that, even if when we talk about having evidence the context is normally such as to imply that the question is not yet settled, this implication is merely conversational. It can be cancelled, as when we talk of having 'decisive evidence'— such as that provided by catching sight of the pig.

Thus although Grice's work does not show that appeals to ordinary language and its use do not have a proper place in philosophical inquiry and debate, Grice does show that they are not quite the straightforward source of conceptual insight that some philosophers had hoped. To that extent, therefore, it marks the end of one of the distinctive 'schools' of post-war English-language philosophy. By the time (*c.*1960) that Grice was articulating this challenge, however, another, more radical challenge had been well under way for many years in North America, and it is to this that we must now turn.

4

The American Point of View

As I noted in the first chapter, the general style of American philosophy during the inter-war period was different from the analytical style then dominant in Britain and Central Europe. During the early post-war period, however, there was a marked turn towards a more analytical style. There were several reasons for this. In part it showed the influence of the distinguished refugees from Central Europe who had arrived during the late 1930s. All over the United States teachers and students of philosophy were exposed at first hand to ideas developed in Vienna, Berlin, and Warsaw through contact with Rudolph Carnap, Carl (Peter) Hempel (1905–1997), Ernest Nagel, Hans Reichenbach, Alfred Tarski, and others. Another influence was contact, direct and indirect, with Moore and Wittgenstein. Moore spent much of the war teaching in the United States and seems to have had a remarkable impact there. Wittgenstein also visited the United States in 1949; although this was a private visit to his friend Norman Malcolm, Malcolm's writings from this period brought Wittgenstein's later ideas to public attention well before the posthumous publication of Wittgenstein's later writings. But the most important development was the emergence of a distinctively American school of philosophy which differentiated itself from both Viennese logical empiricism and British ordinary language philosophy.

The central figure in this development is Willard Van Quine (1908–2000) whose career was based at Harvard. Quine's association with Harvard began in 1930 when he was drawn there by the prospect of studying logic with Russell's famous associate A. N. Whitehead, though to his disappointment he found that Whitehead had by then lost interest in logic. But after completing his Ph.D. he was awarded a travelling fellowship which he used to travel to Central Europe, where he attended meetings of the Vienna Circle and then moved on for 'the intellectually most rewarding months I have known' ('Autobiography of W. V. Quine', p. 12)—six weeks in Prague, where he discussed philosophy with Carnap, and six further weeks in Warsaw, where he met the great Polish philosopher-logicians Tarski, Lesniewski, and Lukasiewicz. In retrospect the crucial meeting was that with Carnap. Once back in Harvard Quine lectured on Carnap and it was largely thanks to Quine that Carnap himself moved to the USA in 1936.

Quine, however, has been no uncritical disciple of Carnap; on the contrary, Quine made a name for himself precisely by rejecting one of the central points of Carnap's philosophy—the 'analytic/synthetic' distinction. The disagreement was hinted at in Quine's early writings, but only became explicit in Quine's famous 1950 paper 'Two Dogmas of Empiricism'. Quine not only separates himself here from Carnap and the tradition of the Vienna Circle; he also sets himself apart from the British tradition of philosophical analysis discussed in the previous chapter. In a review of Strawson's *Introduction to Logical Theory* written at this time Quine picks out for critical comment the fact that Strawson employs a conception of logical implication grounded in the idea of analytic truth, and in criticizing this and the associated conception of conceptual analysis Quine recognises that he is rejecting one of the central ideas of philosophical analysis as practised within the tradition of ordinary language philosophy.

In what follows I shall concentrate on Quine's discussion of this topic; but it should be borne in mind that throughout his career Quine has made substantial contributions to logical theory and in particular to the study of the logical foundations of mathematics. So, very much in the manner of Russell, Quine writes about philosophy as a practising logician.

The Analytic/Synthetic Distinction

The 'analytic/synthetic distinction' applies to 'truths', which Quine takes to be sentences that are unambiguously true (the disambiguation of a sentence such as 'I am hot' required to handle its use by different speakers at different times is broadly equivalent to Strawson's conception of the statement a speaker makes by uttering such a sentence). Typically the truth of a true sentence depends both on the meaning of the words used and on the state of the world: the truth of the sentence 'Washington DC is the capital of the USA' depends both on the meaning of the words used and on the location of the federal government of the USA. True sentences of this kind are said to be 'synthetic truths'. 'Analytic truths', by contrast, are supposed to be true sentences whose truth depends only on the meanings of the words used.

There are, supposedly, two main types of analytic truth. The first is exemplified by 'all bachelors are unmarried men': in this case it is because the word 'bachelor' means the same as the words 'unmarried man' that the truth of the sentence depends only on the meanings of the words used. But in fact this point about the meaning of the word 'bachelor' implies only that the meaning of the sentence 'all bachelors are unmarried men' is the same as that of 'all unmarried men are unmarried men'. Hence the first is an analytic truth only if the second is one too. This second sentence is an elementary truth of logic, but the fact, if it is one, that its truth depends only on the meanings of the words used is not a consequence of an explicit definition. Instead the meaning of the logical vocabulary in sentences of the form 'all A's are A's' must be such as to guarantee the truth of instances such as 'all unmarried men are unmarried men'. And this in turn rests on the thesis that the principles of logic constitute 'implicit definitions' of the logical vocabulary that occurs within them.

The existence of analytic truths in general therefore depends on the analyticity of logical truths, which Quine rejects along with the extension of the notion of analyticity to embrace non-logical analytic truths via the hypothesis of synonymous expressions. In both cases, Quine argues, supporters of analyticity are mistaken in supposing that there is a well-defined notion of meaning sufficient to guarantee all by itself the truth of sentences. So where upholders of the analytic/synthetic distinction hold that there are these two different kinds of truth, Quine is insistent that all truths are of one and the same kind, dependent both on language and on the state of the world.

By itself this may well seem a rather limited thesis, primarily concerning the meaning of logical vocabulary. But it is indicative of the central position of logic and the philosophy of language within analytical philosophy that Quine's thesis necessitates a reconsideration of the very idea of analytical philosophy. Indeed a first thought here will be that if there are no *analytic* truths, then there is no possibility of logical *analysis* and nothing worth describing as *analytical* philosophy. This, however, is incorrect: it depends on the assumption that the truths of logic are analytic, which Quine rejects. As a logician himself, Quine does not deny the importance of logic to philosophy in virtue of its central role in articulating our practices of reasoning; and he also recognizes that logic induces what he calls a 'regimentation' of ordinary language which, by assigning a logical role to different elements of language, constitutes a logical analysis of it. Thus Quine denies neither the possibility of logical analysis nor the philosophical significance of such analyses; indeed his writings are full of logical analyses. What Quine does deny is that such logical analyses are analytic truths, true merely in virtue of meaning; instead he holds that they differ only in generality from chemical analyses, which no one would think of as analytic truths.

It is easy to lose a sense of historical perspective on this issue, and it is therefore worth recalling that throughout the first decade of the twentieth century when Russell was at his most creative he also held that truths of logic are synthetic, not analytic. The shift to a conception of logical truth as analytic came about primarily because of its presentation by Wittgenstein in the *Tractatus* (though Wittgenstein had himself been influenced by Frege's earlier adoption of this view). Russell was among those persuaded by Wittgenstein of the analyticity of logic, and during the 1920s this thesis became a standard element of the position of those whom we now classify as analytical philosophers, such as the Viennese logical empiricists. Among those was of course Carnap, and his position is worth special attention because of the special relationship between Quine and Carnap.

As I explained in Chapter 1 (p. 6) Carnap held that philosophy is just logical analysis. He also held that logic is analytic. For, drawing on Wittgenstein's discussion of logic in the *Tractatus*, he held that the truths of logic are a by-product of the meaning of the language we use for the purposes of reasoning and calculation. This was important to him because of the way in which it explains the fact that it strikes us that the truths of logic are necessary and that our knowledge of them is 'a priori' (i.e. does not require justification on the basis of observation). Empiricists have always found these features of logic difficult to accommodate since they hold that our understanding of the world is to be justified on the basis of observation alone. If, however, logic is analytic then someone who understands a logical truth is in a position to recognize its truth without needing to obtain further information about the state of the world; so an empiricist like Carnap who holds that logic is analytic can allow that a priori knowledge of their truth is possible. Likewise, since their analyticity implies that they are true however the world might turn out to be, it also implies their necessity.

The correspondence between these three distinctions—(i) the *semantic* analytic/synthetic distinction; (ii) the *metaphysical* necessary/contingent distinction; and (iii) the *epistemological* a priori/empirical distinction—with the semantic distinction providing a basis for the others, is a central feature of Carnap's logical empiricism, and manifests clearly a conception of analytical philosophy according to which priority is to be assigned to semantic (linguistic) considerations in resolving metaphysical and epistemological issues. One possible line of criticism here is that these distinctions do not match up as neatly as is here supposed. Kant famously argued that there are synthetic a priori truths, and, as we shall see in Chapter 6, from the 1970s onwards there have been powerful arguments in favour of the existence of necessary empirical truths and of contingent a priori truths. But these points should be bracketed here, for Quine at least agrees with Carnap that the distinctions do match up much as he supposes. His disagreement is just that he holds that there are no analytic truths; so he also holds that there are no a priori truths and no necessary truths, at least of the kind envisaged in traditional metaphysics (cf. Chapter 6, pp. 121–2). Thus he rejects Carnap's conception of analytical philosophy as providing a new 'linguistic' way of fulfilling the traditional philosophical tasks of articulating the a priori structure of knowledge and the necessary structure of being. Instead, he subscribes to a thorough-going empiricist naturalism while remaining committed to the merits of logical analysis; his position is one of analytical empiricism without analytic truths.

Quine is by no means the first philosopher to have criticized the conception of analytic truth. At the start of the twentieth century, for example, the British idealist philosopher F. H. Bradley (1846–1924) rejected it in the light of his thorough-going 'monism' according to which all truths are in the end connected as elements within the one ultimate Absolute reality. For this is incompatible with the thesis that there are some truths which stand apart from others as true merely in virtue of their meaning. But although there are similarities between Bradley's idealist monism and Quine's 'holism' (which I explain below), there is no doubt that in the twentieth century it is Quine's empiricist critique of analyticity that was the most important.

Quine's Criticisms of Analyticity

As one would expect, Quine has one line of argument against the narrow analyticity of logical truths, what he calls 'the linguistic theory of logical truth', and a different one against the broader conception which draws on synonymies, though both begin from the demand that there be some empirical substance to the notion of meaning which the supporter of analyticity invokes.

In considering the case of logical truths Quine begins by accepting two points which supporters of their analyticity bring forward: first, that those who disagree over the acceptability of some alleged logical truth (such as the law of excluded middle that all sentences of the form 'A or not A' are true) disagree over the meaning of the logical vocabulary involved (usually the word 'not' in this case); secondly, the fact that if we find an anthropologist maintaining that some 'primitive' people have a 'pre-logical' mentality which tolerates explicit contradictions, we will conclude that the anthropologist has mistranslated the native language.

These points appear to imply that the logical truths in question are true merely in virtue of the meaning of these words. Quine, however, urges that this last step does not follow. There is, he thinks, a simpler and better explanation of the phenomena—namely that the truths in question are just so obvious that we are bound to regard disagreement or deviance as overwhelmingly good evidence for some misunderstanding, just as we would also conclude there must be some misunderstanding of the language if a person with normal eyesight and a good view of the sky on a clear sunny day rejected the sentence 'the sky is blue today', which no one would suppose to be an analytic truth. Thus, for Quine, the thesis of the analyticity of logical truths is a gratuitous, and empirically unwarranted addition to the connection between the obviousness of logic and the fact that disagreement concerning obvious truths is proof of misunderstanding.

This claim is not persuasive: the persistence of disagreements from the time of the ancient Greeks to the present day concerning the law of excluded middle undermines any suggestion that its truth is obvious. Nonetheless, these disagreements still appear to be based on disagreements about the meaning of logical terminology. This point is not, however, fatal to Quine's position. For it turns out that his critical discussion of the broader conception of analyticity which depends on the existence of synonymous expressions leads into a more substantial objection to the thesis that logic is analytic.

The starting point of this discussion is the demand that there be some empirical content to the hypotheses concerning synonymy which the defender of analyticity advances. One immediate suggestion here will be that words have the same meaning when they apply to the same things. Quine rightly observes, however, that this suggestion would be disastrous for the analyticity theorist. Thus, to take an example from medieval discussions, human beings are the only featherless animals which walk on two feet ('featherless bipeds'); but no analyticity theorist would want to conclude that 'all and only humans are featherless bipeds' is an analytic truth, dependent only on the meanings of the words 'human being' and 'featherless biped'. So although words with the same meaning must apply to the same things, some further refinement is required if one is to separate the analytic from the synthetic, and if this refinement is to show the legitimacy of the notion of analyticity it must not draw on considerations of necessity and suchlike whose legitimacy is supposed to be vindicated by reference to analyticity.

Quine takes it that, for empiricists at least, this further refinement will be that terms are synonymous where their use is such that whatever counts as observational evidence for or against one is similarly evidence for or against the other. This produces the right negative result in the case of 'human being' and 'featherless biped', since the kinds of evidence that would confirm that something is a human being clearly exceed those that would confirm its being a featherless animal that walks on two feet. The question that he raises, however, is whether any putative analytic truths are such that their constituent terms pass this test, which I shall call the test of 'empirical synonymy'; and his claim is that nothing does pass this test.

His argument for this thesis starts from a thesis advanced by the French historian and philosopher of science Pierre Duhem (1861–1916). Duhem argued that the role of observation and experiment in science is misunderstood by those who think that observations and experiments can be by themselves decisive in refuting scientific hypotheses. For these hypotheses only imply predictions concerning the outcome of experiments and observations given further 'auxiliary' hypotheses. For example, current hypotheses concerning the amount of dark matter in the universe only imply predictions concerning the observable behaviour of galaxies given the current theory of gravitation and assumptions about the amount of matter which is not dark; furthermore, our observations of the behaviour of galaxies themselves draw on many auxiliary hypotheses about the significance of the observable distribution of stars within galaxies, not to mention those literally built into the scientific equipment employed.

Within the philosophy of science Duhem's thesis is widely accepted and taken to imply a 'holistic' doctrine, to the effect that scientific theories, including the associated auxiliary hypotheses involved in testing them, face the 'tribunal of experience' as wholes. For where a prediction fails, Duhem's thesis implies that scientists always confront a variety of alternative explanations of this failure—all the way from rejection of their theoretical postulates to the diagnosis of a fault in their experimental equipment. Some philosophers hold, however, that even if Duhem's thesis applies to prediction and explanation within the theoretical natural sciences, it does not apply generally, since in normal life we distinguish between more and less authoritative types of evidence, between 'criteria' and 'symptoms', to use Wittgenstein's terms (cf. Chapter 3, p. 28). I shall discuss this line of thought in the next chapter, but for now I shall follow Quine in accepting that Duhem's thesis does apply generally to reasoning which involves empirical evidence.

One important implication of Duhem's thesis is that it is not possible to provide a verificationist analysis of the meaning of a 'theoretical' sentence, a sentence which does not straightforwardly describe something observable, in terms of sentences which describe the kinds of observation which would verify or refute the sentence in question, since any such analysis would imply that there are suitable observations which can by themselves refute the truth of the sentence. Yet there is no reason to hold that the idea of analytic truth itself brings with it a commitment to the possibility of such analyses. Someone who holds that one can analyse the meaning of 'bachelor' as 'unmarried man' need not hold that it is a simple matter of observation whether someone is unmarried. So, on the face of it, acceptance of Duhem's thesis need not commit one to rejection of the analytic/synthetic distinction.

In 'Two Dogmas of Empiricism' Quine begins by distinguishing the two 'dogmas' he has in mind, the analytic/synthetic distinction and the idea of a verificationist analysis of meaning. Having argued that the idea of verificationist analysis is untenable in the light of Duhem's thesis, however, he goes on to maintain that this also refutes the analytic/synthetic distinction since 'The two dogmas are, indeed, at root identical' (p. 41). This is a puzzling claim. The combination of an analytic/synthetic distinction with explicit acceptance of Duhem's thesis, was, as Quine must have known perfectly well, the position of Carnap in *The Logical Syntax of Language* (1934; Quine helped with its English translation in 1937 and I suspect that it was from Carnap that he learnt of Duhem). So why did Quine think that this combination was untenable? Quine's reasoning at this point is, unfortunately, obscure. But the explanation of Quine's claim, I think, is that he latched onto Carnap's acknowledgement in this book that the truth of even what are supposed to be analytic truths may turn out to require revision in the light of experience. I shall return to some of the details of

Carnap's complex treatment of this matter, but on the face of it, this admission is tantamount to an abandonment of the traditional conception of analyticity. For if experience might suggest to us that not all bachelors are unmarried men, then the truth that all bachelors are unmarried men does not simply depend on the meaning of the words involved but depends also on how the world is discovered to be.

Carnap's acknowledgment is, in effect, an extension of Duhem's thesis. For Duhem, a scientist who finds the observational predictions of his theoretical postulates unfulfilled has a variety of ways of revising his beliefs to accommodate the apparently recalcitrant observations, all the way from changing his mind about what was actually observed to revising his theoretical postulates. What Quine takes from Carnap is an admission that previously unquestioned analytic rules, which govern both the structure of the fundamental concepts and the underlying logic and mathematics, are also available for revision. The resulting position, that nothing, *including* putative conceptual truths, logic, and mathematics, is immune from revision in the light of experience, is now widely known as the Quine–Duhem thesis; and it is from the perspective of this revised thesis that the two dogmas show themselves as 'at root identical'.

It is, then, this extension of Duhem's thesis which lies at the heart of Quine's objection to the conception of analytic truth, to the idea that there is a domain of truths that are insulated from empirical inquiries because their truth has already been established by their meaning. This thesis clearly poses a challenge to the supposed analyticity of logic and mathematics as well as to the broader analyticity of truths which rest on synonymies and conceptual connections. But is it true, first, that mathematics and logic are revisable in the light of experience? One can point to the development of non-Euclidean geometries during the nineteenth century, and then to the use of one of them, Riemann's, in physical theory during the twentieth century. But the defender of analyticity can observe that even though Euclidean geometry was long held to be a priori, no one has ever thought that it was analytic. Quine also brings up the suggestion that some standard principles of logic should be abandoned in order to resolve puzzles within quantum theory. Yet this case is also not persuasive: although the resulting 'quantum logic' is of considerable algebraic interest, it commands no support among physicists. Contemporary debates concerning quantum theory certainly do include some weird hypotheses, but they do not involve any challenge to logic or mathematics. In truth, where there are serious disputes concerning logical principles these disputes do not arise from empirical inquiries. They arise either from disagreements about the right way to give an account of meaning of logical terminology (as we shall see in the next chapter); or from disagreements about the relative weight to be attached to considerations of overall simplicity as opposed to sensitivity to intuitive judgements (as applies in the Russell–Strawson debate about descriptions discussed in the previous chapter).

The case for supposing that logic and (pure) mathematics are revisable in the light of empirical inquiry remains, therefore, at best unproved. There are, however, better reasons for supposing that putative synonymies and conceptual connections should be regarded as revisable in the light of experience. Quine's colleague at Harvard, Hilary Putnam (1926–), offered the example of the changes in our understanding of mass and other fundamental physical properties consequent upon the shift from Newtonian physics to the Theory of Relativity. There are indeed many cases where the etymology of words reveals long-abandoned beliefs—the planets were once the wandering stars, atoms were once the indivisible elements of matter, oxygen was supposed to be the distinctive feature of acids, responsible for their sharp taste; and so on.

The existence of these cases is undeniable; their significance remains disputable. According to Quine and Putnam they show that experience can motivate us to modify our beliefs in unpredictable ways, and that we have, therefore, good reason not to seek to identify some core implications of a term as definitive, or analytic. Putnam nicely captured the resulting account of meaning by describing it in terms of the existence of 'cluster concepts'—concepts whose identity rests on their role in a network ('cluster') of connections which collectively give the terms involved their meaning, but which are such that any element of the network can be revised in the light of empirical inquiry. For Putnam the fact that all significant concepts are in this way 'cluster concepts' is the important truth of Quine's critique of analyticity.

The intuitive response to Quine and Putnam is that these are cases of a change of meaning motivated by empirical discoveries which show that the concepts previously employed do not fit the phenomena. So it is not that what were supposed to be analytic truths are found in the light of experience to have been synthetic falsehoods all along; instead, even though the old words are retained, their old meanings, with their analytic truths, are abandoned as inapplicable and replaced by new ones. The most influential development of this position is, not surprisingly, that by Carnap, in his 1950 paper 'Empiricism, Semantics and Ontology'. Carnap suggests here that questions about analyticity should be set in the context of debates about the merits of 'linguistic frameworks' or 'languages', by which Carnap means ways of describing some subject-matter, such as physics or astrology (and not languages such as English and German). Each such language, he holds, includes analytic rules which provide a calculus for reasoning and a conceptual framework for describing its subject-matter. Such descriptions provide answers to 'internal' questions by applying the analytic rules of the language to the results of observation or calculation, though Carnap again endorses Duhem's thesis: the analytic rules do not dictate how internal questions are to be answered in the light of experience. Distinct from these internal questions, however, are 'external' questions concerning the merits and defects of a language, and it is in the context of these latter questions that analytic rules themselves become answerable to experience. Where experience shows that the language works poorly, in that it neglects distinctions, similarities, or possibilities which we have discovered we need to allow for, there is good reason to revise the analytic rules and thus the meaning of the language.

Quine's response to Carnap was that just as there are no purely analytic truths, there are no purely external questions; Carnap's external/internal distinction is just another form of the old analytic/synthetic distinction. Although this response manifests Quine's disagreement with Carnap, it does not provide any independent reason for rejecting Carnap's position. It is no surprise, therefore, to find that their subsequent debates on this subject were entirely inconclusive. In practice, most American philosophers have taken Quine's side, whereas most British philosophers have continued the tradition of conceptual analysis. As I see it, the issue here is one of substantiating, with Carnap, our intuitive sense that there is a distinction between an 'external' change in the meaning of a term and an 'internal' change of belief concerning the things to which the term applies, instead of accepting Quine's sceptical insistence that there is no substance to this distinction. I shall return to this at the end of this chapter.

Empiricism Naturalized

Quine's commitment to empiricism was a key premiss of his criticisms of analyticity. Another element of these criticisms was his Duhem-inspired holism, and this leads him to an important reinterpretation of empiricism. For he comes to see that there cannot be a sharp distinction between an account of the reasons we have for our beliefs and the understanding of our cognitive abilities with which the natural sciences provide us. Just as philosophical claims about meaning require empirical substantiation, so do philosophical claims about the justification of belief, and this leads him to reinterpret empiricism as a form of 'naturalism'. This is another feature of his philosophy that has been of enormous influence, especially in North America, where, thanks to Dewey, the term 'naturalism' has long had a positive resonance.

For Quine, to be a naturalist in philosophy is to repudiate the aspiration of those philosophers who have held that it is a proper task of philosophy to provide what in the Aristotelian tradition is called a 'first philosophy'—namely a demonstration of the validity of scientific methods of inquiry which does not draw on truths established within the natural sciences themselves. Quine holds instead that philosophical inquiries, including those into the legitimacy of scientific methods, always take place within an understanding of ourselves and the world provided by the sciences. This may seem to promise only a circular procedure of justification; but Quine argues that there is no better alternative and that the circularity is not vicious.

His argument for the first point is simply that the traditional epistemology of those who aspire for a first philosophy has, in fact, simply led to a sceptical denial that we possess any knowledge: 'the Humean predicament is the human predicament' ('Epistemology Naturalized': 72) as Quine once put it, drawing on the old interpretation of Hume as a sceptic (though, ironically, most scholars would now emphasize Hume's own 'naturalism' through which he mitigates his sceptical conclusions by an appeal to our natural, involuntary, propensity to unreflective belief in those matters upon which ordinary life depends). By itself this unargued claim may not be persuasive; but, as I have indicated, Quine's position does fit with the systematic holism to which he is antecedently committed.

The reason Quine gives for supposing that this position does not undermine any worthwhile epistemology is that although our beliefs form a network, there is sufficient redundancy among the connections between them to enable us to examine critically one group of beliefs without compromising all the rest. Quine likes to employ Neurath's picture of our situation: we are like sailors at sea who cannot take their ship into a dry dock but can replace leaking planks one at a time, and in this way keep the boat afloat. The dry dock option is the aspiration of those 'cosmic exiles' who seek for a first philosophy. This is unrealizable, but, because our beliefs interconnect in a variety of ways, it is possible for us to undertake a piecemeal critical appraisal of them while still retaining reasons for supposing that our understanding of the world and ourselves is broadly correct.

In his paper 'Epistemology Naturalized' (1969), however, Quine seemed to suggest that the result of naturalizing epistemology amounts to its replacement by cognitive psychology. Since this would involve the substitution of causal questions concerning the origin of our beliefs for normative ones concerning their justification, it would lead to the annihilation, rather than the naturalization, of epistemology. In more recent writings (such as *The Pursuit of Truth*, 1990), however, Quine has made it clear that this was not his intention: instead, the normative project of justification and criticism is indeed to continue, but placed within the context of an understanding of ourselves and the world provided by the natural sciences. As we shall now see, Quine nonetheless draws on this naturalization of epistemology to argue for conclusions that are not just subversive of a philosophical tradition, as was characteristic of his critique of analyticity, but threatening to some of our most deep-rooted beliefs about ourselves.

The Indeterminacy of Translation

Quine's rejection of analyticity rested upon empiricist scepticism concerning the notion of meaning employed, especially that of sameness of meaning within a language, i.e. synonymy. In *Word and Object* (1960) he turned his attention to the question of sameness of meaning across different languages, i.e. translation. But whereas in the first case he argued that the existence of synonyms cannot be substantiated at all once one considers the ways in which our beliefs are revisable in the light of experience, in the second case he allows that translation is often possible, but then argues that where it is possible it can always be achieved in a variety of ways which are, on a sentence by sentence basis, incompatible, even though they are nonetheless equally good overall. Thus in this case the sceptical challenge arises from the fact that too many meanings (translations) are available, whereas before the problem was that none are (because there are no synonyms). This appears paradoxical at first; but different standards for sameness of meaning are in play. In effect Quine is now arguing that, starting from an empirically legitimate, but coarse and holistic, conception of the translation of a language, one cannot refine a precise conception of the meaning of a sentence of the kind which we would need to vindicate judgements of synonymy.

Quine puts his naturalized empiricism to work in presenting this argument through a typically philosophical thought-experiment, in which he imagines a linguist who finds a previously unknown community, and then undertakes with unlimited resources the project of 'radical translation', the project of translating utterances by members of this alien community into her home tongue. Quine's naturalized empiricism implies that her translation should be based on a scientific understanding of the processes underlying alien linguistic behaviour, including an understanding of the stimuli which prompt utterances. When Quine first developed his thought-experiment he thought that this was unproblematic in principle: all the linguist needed to do was to identify that aspect of the perceptible environment (e.g. the visible presence of a rabbit) to which the alien's utterance was a response and mark that down as the 'stimulus meaning' of the utterance. In more recent writings Quine has argued that this is too simple and that it is necessary to adjust his position somewhat. I shall explain this adjustment later, and suggest why it is not altogether congenial to his naturalized empiricism; for the moment we can stay with the earlier conception of stimulus meaning.

For Quine, discernment of these stimulus meanings constitutes the empirical basis for the linguist's translation of the alien language. But whereas the translation of 'observation sentences' which describe what is being observed (once tentatively identified by the linguist as such) follows directly from an identification of their stimulus meaning, the translation of other sentences inevitably involves assumptions about the preferences and beliefs of alien speakers in ways which makes it inappropriate for the linguist to take the stimulus meaning of their utterance as a sufficient basis by itself for their translation. For example, if the linguist comes to think that the aliens sometimes talk about the past, translation of these sentences cannot simply amount to identifying the heterogeneous collection of stimuli which prompt their utterance. Instead translation will require the linguist to impute to alien speakers beliefs about the connections between present evidence and past events. Thus the linguist's situation is one to which Duhem's thesis about the role of 'auxiliary hypotheses' is directly applicable: when a question from the linguist based upon a tentative translation of a sentence which is not an observation sentence does not prompt the expected response from an alien, the linguist always faces a choice between revising her translation or modifying her beliefs about the alien's underlying beliefs and preferences.

For this reason, Quine argues, translation is inherently 'underdetermined' by the linguist's procedures; there will be more than one scheme of translation that fits the evidence, the observed stimulus meanings. The only constraint is that each translation-scheme, with its own package of imputed beliefs, preferences and other attitudes, should account overall for the pattern of observed stimulus meanings and associated behaviour. By making compensating adjustments within a system of translation and imputed beliefs and preferences, different schemes can be constructed which fit the observed stimulus meanings equally well however much data is collected.

It is essential to grasp that the resulting variety of possible translations is not supposed to be just the familiar phenomenon of alternative, and only partly adequate, attempts to accommodate linguistically idiosyncratic idioms such as one finds in attempts to translate poetry; nor is it just an implication of the vagueness inherent in much of our language; nor, again, is it a reflection of the difficulty of translation where one language draws distinctions that another does not. Quine misleads his readers by representing the aliens as 'natives' who live in the 'jungle'; instead the aliens should be assumed to live in an environment that is, objectively, precisely similar to ours. For even in the most apparently straightforward case, Quine holds that there will be different but equally good schemes of translation which involve substantively different translations of individual utterances—'utterly disparate translations . . . each of which would be excluded by the other system of translation. Two such translations might even be patently contrary in truth' (*Word and Object*, pp. 73–4).

This argument—the 'argument from above'—draws on holistic connections between the translation of utterances and the imputation of beliefs and preferences. Quine has in fact placed most weight on another argument—'the argument from below'—which concerns the relationship between translation of whole sentences and translation of the words they contain: the claim is that translation of sentences does not uniquely determine translation of the words they contain. Quine's uses his famous example of the utterance 'Gavagai' to suggest this point. He assumes that this can be regarded as a one-word observation sentence whose minimal translation into English, on the basis of its stimulus meaning, is 'Lo, rabbit!', and then invites us to consider whether a fuller translation should be: 'Look: there are some rabbits here' (which would imply that the use of 'Gavagai' involves our ordinary conception of rabbits); or 'Look: there is some rabbit here' (which would imply that 'Gavagai' is used as a mass term comparable to 'beef'); or even 'Look: it is rabbiting here' (which would imply that 'Gavagai' occurs as verb comparable to 'raining' and indicates that the presence of rabbits is thought of as an event comparable to a shower of rain). Quine maintains that each of these translations is tenable as long as it is accompanied by suitable similar translations of related parts of the language; hence, he concludes, in this respect also translation is radically underdetermined.

For two reasons, this example is not persuasive. Firstly, there are obvious syntactic differences between nouns such as 'rabbit', mass terms such as 'beef', and verbs such as 'to rain'; in particular, as Gareth Evans showed, they enter into patterns of inference in different ways. So Quine's linguist with unlimited resources should be able to identify from the observed patterns of speech and inference involving 'Gavagai' which translation is to be preferred. Secondly, if, for some reason, this procedure does not resolve the matter, the significance of the example is only that in this respect the use of ordinary language does not determine a precise conception of the metaphysics of substance. This is not a radical objection to the possibility of translation, but only a reminder that in some respects metaphysics goes beyond common sense.

There are other ways to fill out the argument from below, though they too are difficult to develop in persuasive detail. Nonetheless, the conclusion of the argument from below is supported by that of the argument from above. For the precise translation of a speaker's words brings with it the imputation of beliefs and other attitudes; hence if the ascription of beliefs and attitudes is underdetermined, the translation of his words should be likewise underdetermined.

However that may be, the conclusion, in my view primarily supported by the argument from above, is that translation is in principle underdetermined. Quine infers from this that translation is essentially indeterminate—i.e. he converts the epistemological pluralism of his undertermination thesis into a metaphysical scepticism to the effect that there is nothing beyond, or behind, the plurality of equally good translations: there is, as he famously put it, no 'objective matter to be right or wrong about' (*Word and Object*, p. 73). And since, for Quine, language is not just a vehicle for the expression of antecedent thoughts but is the very accomplishment of thoughts whose content is given by the sentences which express it, indeterminacy of translation brings with it indeterminacy concerning the identity of the thoughts expressed. There is, again, no 'objective matter to be right or wrong about' as to whether the aliens are having a thought which fits, along with one way of thinking about the world, one translation of a sentence they have uttered or the different thought which fits a different translation, along with its different way of thinking about the world. So indeterminacy of translation implies a radically sceptical doctrine concerning the mind, to the effect that thoughts are not objective elements of the world.

Quine's thesis applies not only to previously unknown speakers, the aliens imagined in the thought experiment of radical translation, but equally to close neighbours with whom we feel entirely familiar, and even to ourselves. For if there is no objective matter as to what the aliens are saying and thinking, there is equally no objective matter as to what our friends and family are saying and thinking, nor even as to what we ourselves are saying and thinking. The alienness of the aliens in Quine's thought experiment is merely a temporary artifice of exposition. At this point it is hard to overcome a sense of vertigo, hard indeed not to feel that Quine has driven us out of our comfortable common-sense conception of meaning into a nightmare in which we find ourselves babbling meaninglessly in a void. But of course if Quine has done this to us, then he has equally done it to himself. Quine likes to contrast his robust realism concerning physics with his scepticism concerning meanings and thoughts; but his scepticism implies that the meaning of any physical theory is itself indeterminate. Indeed his indeterminacy thesis applies to his own statement of it.

In thinking about the indeterminacy thesis an initial issue is that of its relationship to his discussion of analyticity. Quine has observed that the indeterminacy concerning the reference of words such as 'Gavagai' implied by his argument from below goes beyond his earlier position which, while sceptical about meaning, encouraged the view that reference was empirically well-grounded; and many others have felt that the later thesis of the indeterminacy of translation involves a more general degree of scepticism concerning meaning than was implied by the early rejection of synonymy. But in fact the later thesis was implicit in the earlier one. For determinacy of translation implies the possibility of synonymy: if translation is determinate, the possibility of synonymy is implied as a special case of 'translation' within a language. Hence, if synonymy is not possible, translation must be inherently indeterminate. This implication is in fact clear in Quine's claim in 'Two Dogmas of Empiricism' (p. 43) that 'it is misleading to speak of the empirical content of an individual statement'. For this is a formulation of the scepticism characteristic of the later indeterminacy thesis.

Despite these connections between his early and later positions, it is no surprise that the overt scepticism of the later position has attracted most critics. Some (most notably Chomsky) have focused on Quine's inference from the empirical underdetermination of translation to the objective indeterminacy of meaning. For, they observe, in the case of physics Quine rejects the analogous inference from the underdetermination of theory to intrinsic indeterminacy. Quine's defence of this selectivity is that realism with respect to physical entities is internal to physical theory, since physical theory purports to explain observed phenomena by reference to real, though often unobservable, physical structures; but no such realism with respect to meanings is presupposed by the enterprise of radical translation. Quine's linguist seeks to make sense of the alien language, but her project does not commit her to supposing that alien linguistic behaviour is to be accounted for by reference to a domain of real meanings which her translations capture more or less adequately. Instead meanings are at best the outcome of successful translation; they are not presupposed by it.

Quine's critics respond that this position just assumes behaviourism and does not do justice to the structure of explanations in psychology and linguistics which have realist presuppositions comparable to those of physics. It is not possible to resolve this issue here, though related questions concerning the nature of psychological explanation will be discussed in Chapter 9. Instead of taking this matter further, therefore, I want to concentrate on a different criticism of Quine's argument.

This concerns Quine's tendency to concentrate exclusively on behavioural evidence ('stimulus meanings'). The objection here is that Quine's thought-experiment draws on a presumption comparable to that characteristic of the 'first philosophy' he himself repudiates. When we seek to legitimate our knowledge of the natural world, Quine holds that it is vain to stand altogether outside the conception of ourselves and the world which we learn from the natural sciences. But when attempting to legitimate our understanding of each other, he appears to suggest that the only kind of understanding worth having is one that can be reconstructed from the external point of view of a linguist confronting some aliens and drawing only upon the natural sciences. But once we model our understanding of each other on the metaphor of the sailors already at sea on Neurath's boat, we should think of ourselves as already presuming that we share a common world with others, including common standards of rationality.

It seems to me that this point is basically correct and that it undermines the key argument from above for the underdetermination of translation. We have to be persuaded by this argument that there can be distinct schemes of translation which provide a basis for equally good translations of indefinitely extensible and varied types of linguistic evidence, and for equally good explanations of similarly varied types of behavioural evidence. This hypothesis goes beyond Duhem's considerations by demanding that the merits of alternative translations should withstand empirical inquiry in the light of indefinitely extended trials, whereas Duhem's considerations imply only that, in any particular case, there are alternative ways of coping with unfulfilled predictions. And it is here that the point above concerning Neurath's boat can be applied. For once we take it that the linguist can regard the aliens as thinkers like herself, with broadly comparable standards of rationality, our ordinary experience of correcting our misunderstandings of each other gives us every reason to expect that a linguist with unlimited time and resources should be able to discriminate between alternative translations.

No doubt, even after one scheme of translation has proven itself, an alternative scheme can remain 'in principle' defensible thanks to increasingly fantastic auxiliary hypotheses concerning alien systems of beliefs and preferences; paranoid systems of belief, and the 'erotomania' of those who persist in thinking that the object of their obsessive affections returns their feelings show how it is possible to persist with unwarranted interpretations of others. But this should pose no more threat to our certainty that we broadly understand one another than the 'in principle' defensibility of the hypothesis that the earth is flat. In both cases, as thinkers already at sea in the boat of knowledge, we can legitimately dismiss alternatives that would require us to completely rethink our understanding of ourselves and the world just because, from the abstract detached perspective of a 'cosmic exile', these alternatives cannot be decisively refuted. We have no more reason to think, from within our ongoing understanding of the social world, that the merits of alternative translations can be indefinitely sustained in the light of inquiry than we have to think, from within our ongoing understanding of the natural world, that the merits of alternative physical hypotheses can be indefinitely sustained in the light of inquiry. Nothing in Quine's arguments shows that the two cases are not parallel.

Indeterminacy Reinterpreted and Naturalism Revised

Quine's argument for the indeterminacy of translation is, therefore, unpersuasive. This conclusion does not show, however, that the argument is unimportant. For one can reinterpret it as a *reductio ad absurdum* of epistemology naturalized, in the sense that an epistemology restricted to the methods and assumptions of the natural sciences is shown to be incompetent to provide an account of our understanding of language and psychology. Quine's argument suggests instead that epistemology needs to be 'humanized' as well as naturalized, in the sense that it should incorporate an antecedent commitment to our normal standards of rationality and understanding of each other.

As several critics have observed, the dialectical situation here is comparable to that which arises in connection with Wittgenstein's rule-following argument; indeed the alleged underdetermination of translation resembles Wittgenstein's suggestion that, given a certain conception of rule-following, deviants cannot be excluded. Wittgenstein does not use his argument to establish a sceptical conclusion concerning meaning, but to show the need for a conception of 'blind' rule-following which is sustained by the practice of language-games that are normally communal. Similarly, therefore, Quine's argument should be used, not to establish the sceptical conclusion he himself seeks to draw, but to show the need for the humanization of epistemology.

Although this suggestion (which I have adapted from some of Davidson's writings which I discuss in the next chapter) amounts to a reinterpretation of the significance of Quine's indeterminacy argument, it turns out to fit well with an important change in his own position. The reason for this change concerns the account to be given of the 'stimulus meaning' of sentences. Quine argued that since the utterance of a sentence is in fact prompted by excitation of the speaker's sensory receptors, it is just the pattern of the relevant excitation of the speaker's receptors (the 'proximal stimulus') which should, strictly speaking, be identified as its stimulus meaning, and not the feature of the external environment (the 'distal stimulus') which is causally responsible for this excitation. As Quine notes, this implies that sentences uttered by different speakers differ in their stimulus meanings, which appears to undermine any basis for a common understanding of language.

Quine's way out of this solipsist impasse into which his thoroughgoing naturalism led him is remarkable: he invokes the hypothesis of an original 'empathy' between speakers, whereby each imaginatively puts himself or herself inside the other's skin in order to identify the appropriate translation of the other's utterance—i.e. a sentence that they would assent to in the speaker's situation. In effect, therefore, the notion of stimulus meaning is abandoned, and in its place Quine relies on an original empathy through which we are to regard ourselves as living in a shared world concerning whose obvious features we should presume that we are in agreement with others.

This invocation of empathy, whose merits play an absolutely central role in his late philosophy, appears to be a case of the late conversion of a sinner to the cause of the a priori. Furthermore it cannot be regarded as inherent in the naturalization of epistemology; the thesis that we can find out what others mean by imaginatively identifying with them is no part of the methodology of the natural sciences. On the contrary, it is an admission of the need for the humanization of epistemology; and once it is employed, the grounds for accepting the indeterminacy thesis are removed. For empathy is, in effect, precisely the presumption of a shared world which will in principle enable a radical translator to find reasons for preferring one translation of an alien language over others.

It is important, however, to recognize that an 'empathetic' understanding of the language of others does not necessarily bring with it the kind of 'sympathetic' understanding of them which enables us to feel close to them. Wittgenstein put this point in a nice passage which provides a final comment on Quine's argument:

> We also say of some people that they are transparent to us. It is, however, important as regards this observation that one human being can be a complete enigma to another. We learn this when we come into a strange country with entirely strange traditions; and, what is more, even given a mastery of the country's language. We do not *understand* the people. (And not because of not knowing what they are saying to themselves.) We cannot find our feet with them. (*PI* II. xi. p. 223)

Analyticity Reconsidered

How, finally, do things stand on the issue of analyticity? I have suggested that once we humanize our epistemology, there are no reasons of principle why we should not be able to settle on translations of the language of others that are as determinate as considerations of context and of the vagueness of language allow. Since the indeterminacy of translation was implied by the rejection of analyticity, it follows that the considerations of shared rationality inherent in the humanization of epistemology should provide grounds for mitigating Quine's rejection of analyticity.

In 'Two Dogmas of Empiricism' Quine provides a starting point for thinking about this when he writes of the 'recalcitrant' experiences which prompt us to revise our beliefs. For recalcitrance is inconsistency, and since inconsistency makes sense only in the context of a system of reasoning, it follows that some such system is being assumed. Quine will want to add, of course, that the merits of this system of reasoning are themselves in principle revisable in the light of experience, but this does not undermine the fact that, in any given context of inquiry, there must be some principles of reasoning that are not then in question. Thus even Quine has to allow the legitimacy of a distinction between the system of reasoning which guides one's current context of inquiry, and is therefore not currently in question, and other matters which are open to debate, i.e. a contextual distinction between, in effect, what is a priori and what is empirical.

The traditional conception of logic is that of a system of reasoning which is legitimately applicable to all contexts, i.e. as absolutely a priori. As I indicated earlier, Quine holds that, on the contrary, even logic is revisable in the light of experience. I suggested that Quine's claim is questionable, but since it is not important to the present discussion whether or not the absolute status of some system of logic can be vindicated, the matter can be left open. What is more important here is the relationship between the a priori/empirical distinction and the analytic/synthetic distinction.

It is plausible to hold that our understanding of some of our vocabulary is, in part, formed by our knowledge of the ways in which use of this vocabulary is located within a network of implications. If one thinks of logical vocabulary, i.e. the use of words such as 'if', 'all' and 'not', this seems unproblematic; and the point can be readily extended to our understanding of the vocabulary employed in informal conceptual conceptions. Hence the existence of even a contextual a priori/ empirical distinction will support a similarly contextual analytic/ synthetic distinction (though the issue of the possibility of synthetic a priori truths needs consideration). As compared with the logical empiricist position, however, there is an important reversal of priorities here: analyticity is here derived from a priori status, rather than vice-versa. Thus it is considerations of rationality, rather than meaning, which are now taken to be fundamental. (I leave it open whether a necessary/contingent distinction can be supported by a similar association between necessity and the a priori since I discuss post-Quinean debates about necessity and possibility in Chapter 6).

Since analyticity is here taken to be relativized to contexts of inquiry, the position is similar to Carnap's: his 'linguistic frameworks' provide systems of reasoning appropriate to different contexts of inquiry, and one can derive from them a contextual basis for a distinction between a change in meaning and a change in belief. But Carnap misrepresents the resulting position: having observed that external questions concerning the merits and defects of a framework cannot be answered by invoking the forms of reasoning characteristic of the framework which are employed when dealing with internal questions, he maintains that external questions can only be answered by reference to pragmatic criteria such as efficiency, fruitfulness, and simplicity. This makes it sound as though there is a sharp contrast between internal rationality and external pragmatism. But since Carnap accepts Duhem's thesis he has to allow that pragmatic considerations also have an inescapable place in handling internal questions; and it is equally clear that raising and resolving external questions involves bringing forward reasons. This last point merits further attention.

An external question can arise from previously unnoticed inconsistencies within the language (a famous example of this is Russell's discovery in 1903 of an inconsistency within set theory); more often it arises because the language in question fails to capture similarities or distinctions that have become apparent through unanticipated empirical discoveries (such as that of the constancy of the speed of light). Finally, it can arise through philosophical argument: Quine's indeterminacy thesis, in effect, poses an external challenge to the conception of meaning. In all these cases, however, the challenge cannot arise without presupposing implications that are not being called into question. For there cannot be a challenge to the system of reasoning characteristic of the use of a vocabulary which does not arise from other commitments inherent in the use of the vocabulary which are not being called into question at the same time. Thus the challenge raised by an external question is usually one of constructing, in the light of these other commitments, a revised system of reasoning for the vocabulary of the language which, for the time being, best enables speakers to make the distinctions they need to make in order to carry forward their inquiries or other practices. Conceptual revision has to take place 'at sea', in the context of other practices of reasoning (I say more about this in Chapter 7).

Thus although a contextual a priori/empirical distinction does give rise to an analytic/synthetic distinction, the distinction is not sharp. Once the need for conceptual revision in the light of empirical discoveries is conceded, it has to be acknowledged that the 'analytic' implications inherent in our ordinary understanding and use of some terms can have 'synthetic' presuppositions. The most striking example of this comes from logic: standard systems of logic presuppose that there is something rather than nothing, and this is plainly a synthetic matter of fact, even if it is not a point on which we can imagine ourselves revising our beliefs. Hence although an analytic/synthetic distinction can be constructed in the way I have suggested, no great philosophical significance should be attached to it. This conclusion is not, however, a complete vindication of Quine's early scepticism: for the a priori/empirical distinction, which Quine sought to bring down as well, is both defensible and worth defending.

Despite the downgrading of questions about meaning, therefore, the legitimacy of a priori reasoning, even if it is context-dependent, implies that Quine's criticisms of analyticity do not necessitate a complete reappraisal of analytical philosophy. For, as I stressed in Chapters 1 and 3, philosophical concern with language was generally based upon the aspiration to find logical and conceptual analyses which provide a 'perspicuous representation' (to use Frege's phrase) of our patterns of reasoning; indeed, as I observed earlier, Quine himself has been a conspicuous contributor to analytical philosophy in this sense. As we shall see in later chapters this continues to be the case: analytical philosophers who address questions about the limits of human knowledge or challenges to moral responsibility do not set out to find synonyms for the expressions we use in these areas of discourse. Instead they seek to advance our understanding by articulating the principles of reasoning implicit in our talk and thought—though often only in order to make it clear how an external challenge to these principles is to be developed and assessed.

Wilfred Sellars

I have concentrated here on Quine because he has been, without question, the most influential American philosopher of the second half of the twentieth century. It would, however, be quite wrong to imply that all important American philosophers of the early post-war period were followers of Quine, and in order to correct any such impression it is important to discuss, albeit rather briefly, the work of Wilfred Sellars (1912–89) whose name is often linked with Quine's but whose philosophy points in different directions.

Sellars is a surprising and intriguing thinker. Although his father Roy Wood Sellars (1880–1973) was an important member of the American 'Critical Realist' school of philosophy that flourished at the start of the century, and whose 'realism' involved rejection of the idealism of the previous generation of American philosophers, much of Wilfred Sellars' work has involved reflection on themes from Kant's philosophy, which is the classic source of the idealist philosophy his father rejected. But if reflection on Kantian themes concerning the irreducibility of the category of self-conscious rational persons who are free moral agents constitutes one side of Sellars' work, the other side is provided by a characteristically American emphasis on the merits of the understanding of ourselves and the world that is furnished by the natural sciences. To use an idiom from Quine, Sellars' project was to 'naturalise' Kant's philosophy.

This project is best set out in the papers collected in his book *Science, Perception and Reality* (1963) in which Sellars compares the 'manifest image of man-in-the-world' with the 'scientific image' of man. The content of the scientific image is provided by the natural sciences, and Sellars is unequivocal in proclaiming the unqualified status of scientific knowledge: 'science is the measure of all things, of what is that it is, and of what is not that it is not' (p. 173). The 'manifest image', by contrast, is 'the framework in terms of which man first came to be aware of himself as man-in-the-world. It is the framework in terms of which, to use an existentialist phrase, man first encountered himself—which is, of course, when he came to be man' (p. 6). This image is, Sellars observes, not necessarily unscientific: but it is grounded in our conception of ourselves as persons, and, therefore, excludes scientific theories which either make no place for persons or challenge the conception of the world in terms of which persons understand themselves.

Sellars takes it that the conception of the physical world characteristic of the manifest image is incorrect insofar as it conflicts with the scientific image; it is, he says (using a characteristic Kantian idiom), merely 'a world of appearances'. A case in point concerns colours: Sellars takes it that although according to the manifest image physical objects are coloured, the scientific image undermines this impression by explaining away the phenomenon of colour. Yet despite this conflict between these two images, Sellars insists that we should aspire to a 'stereoscopic' point of view which somehow does justice to both of them. The reason for this is that despite the tension between them, each needs the other. Thus insofar as the scientific image does not accommodate the conception of ourselves as rational thinkers, it cannot make sense of its own status as knowledge. For in describing a mental state as one of knowledge, Sellars holds, we are not giving an empirical description of it which might be confirmed by a scientific theory of cognition; instead 'we are placing it in the logical space of reasons, of justifying and being able to justify what one says' (p. 169), and this 'logical space of reasons' is precisely the domain of the manifest image. Equally the manifest image cannot provide any account of the origin of rational thought, for the emphasis within this image on the perspective of the person, the rational thinker, excludes the possibility of any account of the origins of rationality, since a rational thinker cannot conjure her rationality out of that which is non-rational. Hence the manifest image has here to indicate its own dependence upon an evolutionary perspective that belongs within the scientific image.

Yet how is this stereoscopic but unified vision to be achieved? The context within which Sellars gave the clearest account of this unity is provided by his account of the role of thoughts within explanations and justifications of action. Sellars argued, first, that from within the scientific image there is good reason for us to postulate brain states that play an important part in accounting for our behaviour. For human behaviour has a complexity which transcends the capacity of simple stimulus-response theory. Furthermore, Sellars argued, we can elucidate the explanatory role of these brain states through an analogy with sentences whereby we regard the brain states as involving sentence-like structures that represent states of the environment or of the organism. So far we are still working within the scientific image; but, Sellars suggests, once we find that this analogy is genuinely helpful, we can 'translate' the 'sentences' which characterize the causal functional role of the brain states into our own language and, as such, assess the behaviour thus explained as more or less rational, employing now the normative categories of the manifest image. So, as he writes, 'the "relationship" of the logical to the real order is, in the last analysis, a matter of certain items in the real order playing roles' (p. 57).

Sellars' line of thought here, in papers written around 1960, is sketchy, but astonishingly prescient. As we shall see in Chapter 9, Sellars has sketched out some of the main themes of recent philosophy of mind. Where Ryle just assumed the viability of a dual-aspect theory of mind which combines the practical rationality of the manifest image and the kind of causal explanation characteristic of the scientific image, Sellars offers the beginnings of a position which suggests how a stereoscopic vision of these two aspects may be achieved (though, as we shall also see in Chapter 9, there remain many difficulties here).

Sellars is in fact best known today for his attack on 'the Myth of the Given'. In his use of the term 'the Given' Sellars is referring to the position of C. I. Lewis which I described in Chapter 1 (pp. 9–10); but, more generally, Sellars seeks to attack the views of those philosophers who have held that our knowledge of the physical world is ultimately justified by reference to sense-experience conceived of as something that is simply 'given'—i.e. as 'sense-data'. Sellars' objection to this is inspired by Kant and draws, predictably, on the irreducibility of the manifest image. Because knowledge involves justification it belongs within the 'logical space of reasons' characteristic of the manifest image, and it cannot therefore be grounded in something outside this space, in the bare facts of sense-experience, however sophisticated our scientific understanding of these facts may be.

Sellars does not of course deny that sense-experience plays a part in our knowledge of the physical world; the part it plays, however, is first and foremost causal. Although sense-experience cannot give itself a warrant which certifies the authenticity of the information about the world that it provides, what it can and does do is to cause us to form beliefs about the world in a way which ensures that many of these beliefs are both normally and recognizably reliable; and where true beliefs are of this kind we accord them the status of knowledge. As we shall see in Chapter 8, this point connects directly with a central theme of current discussion in epistemology. So in this respect too, Sellars turns out to prefigure contemporary debate.

5

Understanding Language

As we have seen in the preceding chapters, a central theme of twentieth-century philosophy has been the fundamental importance of language, and there was one final major debate concerning the proper understanding of language and its place within philosophy before attention moved to other areas of philosophy. The chief protagonists in this debate were the American philosopher Donald Davidson (1917–), and the British philosopher Michael Dummett (1925–). I shall begin with an account of Davidson's side of the argument, which is largely expressed in the remarkable series of papers which form his *Inquiries into Truth and Interpretation* (1984: though most of the papers date from the 1970s).

Davidson and Truth-conditions

Davidson studied with Quine and has always been closely associated with him; indeed there are significant acknowledgements to Davidson in Quine's writings, especially concerning the indeterminacy thesis. But in important respects Davidson is to Quine much as Quine was to Carnap—disciple, but also decisive critic. A characteristic disagreement concerns the considerations which they take as their starting point for an inquiry into language. Where Quine's scientific naturalism led him to maintain that our understanding of language must be based upon an identification of the stimuli which prompt speakers to speak as they do, Davidson has no similar commitment to 'naturalism' (a term he avoids) and returns to the position proposed by Frege at the start of the twentieth century, to the effect that the route to an account of meaning and understanding must begin from a concern with truth.

In developing this account Davidson makes much use of the concept of the 'truth-conditions' of a sentence, and this requires a brief introduction. The basic conception of a truth-condition for a sentence is simply that of a condition under which the sentence is true and which is also implied by the sentence's truth. Thus the fact that the sentence 'grass is green' is true in English if and only if grass is green shows that grass being green is a truth-condition of the sentence 'grass is green'. As this case indicates, a truth-condition for a sentence S is standardly expressed by a two-way conditional of the form 'sentence S is true if and only C' where C is replaced by a clause which, as it is said, 'gives' a truth-condition of S.

It is obvious that if a sentence of a language means that grass is green, then that sentence is true if and only if grass is green. Truth-conditions can thus be inferred from meaning. Following Frege, however, Davidson proposed that the direction of this inference be reversed, that an account of the truth-conditions of the sentences of a language should be used to provide a specification of their meaning. In order to understand this proposal it is best to consider a situation in which the language under consideration (the 'object-language') is not the same as that used to give the truth-conditions (the 'metalanguage'). We should therefore start by considering a claim such as that 'Gras ist grun' is true in German if and only if grass is green. This claim is surely correct, and appears to display the meaning of the German sentence by giving a truth-condition for it.

But there is a complication here, in that there is a sense in which all true sentences have the same truth-conditions. This follows from the fact that where A and B are any two true sentences, the sentence 'A if and only if B' is also true. This may seem wrong, and the interpretation of 'if and only if' employed here is not the only one possible, so that there are alternative, less permissive, conceptions of a truth-condition; but Davidson himself accepts this one precisely because by itself its application incorporates no potentially question-begging assumptions about meaning. To illustrate the implications of its use let us go back to the fact that 'Gras ist grun' is true in German if and only if grass is green. Since grass is green and Washington DC is the capital of the USA, it follows that grass is green if and only if Washington DC is the capital of the USA, and thus that 'Gras ist grun' is also true in German if and only if Washington DC is the capital of the USA. Yet the fact that 'Gras ist grun' has this truth-condition tells one next to nothing about its meaning.

In order to deal with this point Davidson holds that it is only where the account of a truth-condition for a sentence meets certain further requirements that it provides a specification of the sentence's meaning, and most of the substance of his account of meaning and understanding lies in these further requirements. The first and most important requirement is that the account of a sentence's truth-condition be one which can be derived within a general theory which yields correct accounts of the truth-conditions for all the sentences of the language involved on the basis of 'axioms' which concern the significance of the basic vocabulary and syntax of the language. In making this proposal Davidson invokes Tarski's work in logic in order to support the hypothesis that there can be a systematic 'theory of truth' for a language which yields a specification of truth-conditions for the sentences of a language on this basis. One can think of this feature of Davidson's approach as an acknowledgement of the familiar fact that the meaning of a sentence depends on the meanings of the words it contains.

To revert to the previous example, Davidson's suggestion is that if we think of all the sentences to be constructed in German which employ (along with other words) the words 'Gras', 'ist' and 'grun', and the simple grammatical construction which combines them, and in particular sentences such as 'Das ist Gras' ('that is grass') and 'Dieser ist grun' ('this is green'), we should recognize that the only way we can expect to get a correct description of all their truth-conditions is by identifying the role of 'Gras' as a way of describing grass, the role of 'grun' as a way of describing the colour green and so on—so that we end up with that account of the truth-conditions of the sentence 'Gras ist grun', namely that it is true if and only if grass is green, which, intuitively, we think of as capturing its meaning. Hence although it remains the case that this sentence is also true if and only if Washington DC is the capital of the USA, we have good reason to think that this latter specification of its truth-condition does not capture the meaning of the sentence, since it will not be implied by a theory which systematically assigns truth-conditions correctly across the language purely on the basis of assignments to the basic vocabulary and grammar of the language.

By imposing this structural condition on the selection of that privileged specification of a sentence's truth-condition which is to capture its meaning, Davidson aims to extract fine-grained meanings from coarse-grained truth-conditions. Since the structural condition implies that the meaning of any one sentence in a language is bound up with that of others, it follows that his conception of meaning is 'holistic'. Arguably this is problematic, and I shall discuss below Michael Dummett's criticism of it on this account. But the aspect of Davidson's position that requires attention now is his proposed method of identifying truth-conditions for the sentences of a language in the first place. For on the one hand, this is not covered by the discussion so far and is plainly not just a matter of straightforward anthropological observation; but, on the other, without some such method, his position does not yield an account of our ability to understand each other.

Radical Interpretation

To deal with this, Davidson takes a leaf, or, rather, a chapter, out of Quine's book by characterizing the theorist as someone engaged in the project of 'radical interpretation', thereby integrating the older Fregean conception of sentence meanings as truth-conditions with Quine's empiricist emphasis on the need for evidence from the linguistic behaviour of speakers to justify discriminations of meaning. But there are important differences between Quine's project of radical translation and Davidson's project of radical interpretation. The change in idiom from 'translation' to 'interpretation' is not by itself important: translation involves matching alien sentences with sentences of the linguist's own language, and since the linguist understands her own language, translation will enable her to give an account of the meaning of the alien sentences—which is what interpretation amounts to. But this change is nonetheless indicative of much more important differences: where Quine's radical translator just seeks to provide translations of alien sentences which match, ultimately on the basis of observed stimulus-meanings, sentences in the linguist's own language, Davidson's radical interpreter has to develop a systematic account of the truth-conditions of sentences of the alien language on the basis of her experience of the aliens. Because of the systematic character of such a theory this is a more strenuous undertaking than that of Quine's radical translator, and the central concern with the identification of truth-conditions raises issues that do not arise within Quine's project.

Indeed it may well appear that the rather abstract character of radical interpretation as described by Davidson makes it inappropriate to use it in an account of our ordinary understanding of language. For, as Davidson allows, when we engage in normal conversation we do not explicitly draw on a systematic theory of this kind. Nonetheless, he holds that his account of the matter provides a model which makes explicit the conditions under which our ordinary understanding of each other is possible. For, he maintains, there is nothing more to the meaning of language than is potentially revealed by radical interpretation. In this sense, therefore, he holds that radical interpretation is an inescapable feature of our understanding of language: 'all understanding of the speech of another involves radical interpretation'. (*Inquiries*, p. 125)

But how is radical interpretation possible? How can one understand the behaviour, and especially the linguistic behaviour, of an alien being about whose mental life nothing detailed is assumed to be known in advance? The basic condition, according to Davidson, is that the alien be a thinker much like us, with thoughts and utterances which stand in rational relations to each other and in causal relations to the physical and social environment that are broadly similar to those which inform our own thoughts and utterances. As a result the interpreter should be able to identify, tentatively, features of the physical and social environment in the light of which the aliens take the utterance of certain simple types of sentence to be true there and then; and if Davidson's basic condition is satisfied, the interpreter is entitled to hold that these features are not only conditions under which the aliens take these sentences to be true, they are also likely to be conditions under which the sentences, as then uttered, are in fact true. This does not exclude the hypothesis that the aliens may turn out to be mistaken with respect to some of these matters, nor that the radical interpreter identifies wrongly the relevant features of the situation: for it only creates a presumption of truth. But the claim is, nonetheless, that mistakes of both kinds are intelligible only against a background of general correctness which secures the interpretation of the basic vocabulary. The more an interpretation suggests that the aliens are radically mistaken in their beliefs about their immediate environment and each other, the more it undermines itself as an interpretation of their utterances.

The interpretation of these simple sentences provides an entry-point for the radical interpreter. For the words which occur in them also occur in other sentences whose utterance is not so clearly tied to the speaker's current environment. But in interpreting these utterances a second element of Davidson's method is brought into play: the need to 'rationalize' the alien by interpreting his utterances in such a way that his overall behaviour—the combination of observed utterances and actions together with the implied experiences and thoughts—makes sense as the expression of a reasonably coherent point of view. This requirement reflects the basic presumption that the alien is a rational thinker whose imputed beliefs provide him with reasons for other beliefs, desires, and actions. It also incorporates a holistic thesis which Davidson regards as characteristic of thoughts in general, namely that they exist only within networks. Thus if, say, an utterance of a sentence is to be interpreted as true if and only if the speaker needs a new pen, then, in ascribing to the speaker the thought that he needs a new pen, the speaker must also be regarded as capable of a range of related thoughts—concerning what pens are and how they used, what he needs a new pen for, how new pens differ from old ones, and so on. The connections here are rational, and reflect the fact that thoughts are essentially identified as combining conceptual capacities that must admit of other exercises.

These two key elements of Davidson's method, the presumptions of truth and of rationality, are, for him, basic a priori conditions of the possibility of understanding. They are sometimes described as a presumption of 'charity' towards those whom we wish to understand; but this is misleading since it makes it looks as though these assumptions are an optional extra. Instead, for Davidson, these presumptions are much more like the unavoidable demands of justice. Yet although they are unavoidable within interpretative inquiries, they have no role within the natural sciences; thus they indicate an a priori distinction between the methodology of the natural sciences and that of interpretative inquiries.

We shall return to this distinction in Chapter 9 in connection with Davidson's claim that there cannot be strict laws which connect mental and physical phenomena as such. Here I want to point briefly to connections with the positions of Quine and Wittgenstein. The way in which I drew on Davidson's discussion in suggesting a reinterpretation of Quine's indeterminacy thesis in Chapter 4 (pp. 85–6) will now be obvious. In fact Davidson does not directly challenge Quine's indeterminacy thesis; instead he says that once the distinctive a priori principles of interpretative inquiries (what I called the principles of a 'humanized' epistemology) are brought into the argument, apparent indeterminacies of translation or interpretation arise only from looking for distinctions within the alien language that are not there. But however the matter is handled, it is clear that Davidson is not a sceptic about meaning.

In the case of Wittgenstein, Davidson shares Wittgenstein's view that agreement in judgement is essential if there is to be objective truth (cf. Chapter 2, pp. 21–3). For Davidson, this claim is an implication of the thesis that in interpreting others we cannot avoid presuming that their beliefs are largely true and that they are generally rational; for in our judgements concerning questions of truth and rationality we necessarily rely on our own standards of rationality and our own beliefs. So in presuming that the beliefs of others are largely true we interpret them in such a way that they largely agree with us; but this agreement also makes it possible for us to understand them where we disagree with them. Since disagreement arises where we impute a mistake to another, and there is no possibility of objective truth where there is no possibility of being mistaken, it follows that our fundamental agreement with others is also a condition of the possibility of objective truth.

Thought and Language

Davidson's account of language has been of central importance in recent philosophical debate, and he himself has used it as the starting point for important arguments in other areas of philosophy. As I have just indicated, he connects his methodological distinction between the natural sciences and interpretative inquiries with the claim that mental and physical phenomena cannot be brought together as such within a unified scientific psychology. This bold claim requires the assumption that understanding a language is an essential feature of anything with mental states, and Davidson does indeed argue that there can be 'no thought without talk'—or, rather, that only those things which can interpret others can have thoughts at all.

Davidson's argument for this thesis, which he acknowledges to be counter-intuitive (especially among animal lovers), starts from the claim that among thoughts belief has a central position: one cannot be a thinker at all unless one has beliefs. This seems right: for thoughts of all kinds (fears, decisions, etc.) draw on the thinker's sense of how things are, i.e. its beliefs. Davidson claims next that even though most beliefs must be true, it is the mark of belief that error is always possible, and, he further maintains, one cannot have a belief unless one recognizes that one might be in error. The final step in the argument is that it is only through an understanding of the errors of others that one can arrive at an understanding of the possibility of being in error oneself. So 'a creature cannot have thoughts unless it is an interpreter of the speech of another' (*Inquiries*, p. 157).

This is an ambitious line of argument and the emphasis on the conditions for the possibility of error is reminiscent of Wittgenstein's discussion (see Chapter 2, p. 21). The distinctive and contentious feature of Davidson's argument is that these conditions include the requirement that the thinker possess an understanding of what it is to be in error. His critics object that it makes sense to suppose that a dog can be in error, e.g. concerning the location of a bone it has buried, without having the capacity to understand this aspect of its situation. Davidson's response is that where a thinker is genuinely in error, it must make sense to suppose that the thinker is surprised at the way things are, and that surprise involves a recognition of error. His critics reply that surprise need not be as rational as this: it can be just caused by finding that things are not as one believed them to be without the need for an additional recognition by the thinker of this fact.

What emerges from this debate is that, for Davidson, beliefs are not just dispositions to behaviour, but provide reasons for thoughts and actions; and, he argues, a thinker cannot be a rational agent, responding rationally to the experience of being in error, unless the thinker understands that it was in error, which it can do only if it can understand language. It is clear that the dispute here centres on the issue as to whether there is a viable conception of belief that is less demanding than the rationalist one Davidson employs. Since debates on this matter are prominent within contemporary philosophy of mind, I shall leave this question now in order to return to it in Chapter 9.

Against Scepticism and Relativism

Davidson's account of language also connects directly with epistemological questions: Davidson takes it to refute that form of scepticism which suggests that, for all we can establish to the contrary, it might turn out that the vast majority of our beliefs, especially those concerning what philosophers call 'the external world', are mistaken. For on Davidson's method we are committed to interpreting each other in such a way that this sceptical hypothesis is wrong; hence we cannot coherently take up such a sceptical attitude, either to others or to ourselves.

As such, the method of radical interpretation manifests a commitment to a modest form of 'realism', whereby we can only make sense of human life, including language and thought, when we place it in the context of an objective natural and social environment whose features cause and rationalize our utterances, thoughts, and actions. This kind of realism contrasts with the relativist claim that there is no such shared world which is the environment of different thinkers and cultures, and Davidson has used his account of language as the basis for an influential critical discussion of this claim. His particular target is the relativist thesis that our own way of thinking, our own 'conceptual scheme', is but one of a variety of different ways of thinking, each of which appropriates to itself its own 'world' and between which there is no basis for comparison. This thesis has been perennially popular with anthropologists and sociologists (it is especially associated with E. Sapir (1884–1939) and Benjamin Whorf (1897–1941), and is often called the 'Sapir–Whorf' thesis). It has never been equally popular among philosophers, although Carnap's way of relativizing internal questions to linguistic frameworks might suggest a position of this kind; but Davidson's discussion was especially prompted by the revival of relativism during the 1960s as a result of the influential work in the history and philosophy of science of Thomas Kuhn (1922–96), whose work I shall discuss in Chapter 7 (where we will see that Kuhn is not best understood as a relativist).

Davidson's discussion starts from the hypothesis that we can identify conceptual schemes with languages and then represent the relativist thesis as the claim that there is a variety of mutually untranslatable languages each of which provides, in its own terms, a viable way of thinking about the world and none of which can claim the privilege of distinctively representing things as they 'really are'. Davidson's objection to this thesis is that we should reject the relativist's assumption that there is a plurality of mutually untranslatable languages. For, he argues, any language which provides a viable way of thinking about a world must provide a way of expressing truths about this world; and yet it is of the essence of truth that truths are translatable.

Davidson takes this last point without discussion from Tarski; but since it is the key to his position it merits some attention. As I see it, the basic point is just that there cannot be inconsistent truths. Hence, wherever we encounter in an alien language a putative truth which, on the face of it, we cannot translate into our own language, we incur no threat of inconsistency if we seek to incorporate this truth into our language by adding some new vocabulary and explaining its meaning in whatever way we made intelligible to ourselves, in the first place, the existence of the putative truth that we could not straightforwardly translate. This may well not be straightforward if we also wish to shed some of the assumptions which are associated with the use of this vocabulary; but the consistency of all truths implies that in principle some such accommodation must be possible. So on this way of thinking, what is untenable about the relativist position is the supposition that there are truths which are in principle untranslatable into a consistent extension of our language.

Since the possibility of translation suffices to ensure that, in principle, different thinkers can make sense of each other as inhabitants of a common world, the relativist thesis that there is no such common world is undermined. So far, then, so good: but Davidson, to my mind unwisely, extends his argument into a general critique of 'the very idea of a conceptual scheme' (this is the title of the paper in which Davidson discusses this matter), which he stigmatizes as the 'third dogma' of empiricism (the others being Quine's two dogmas—cf. Chapter 4, p. 72). Davidson's argument for this claim is that all talk of conceptual schemes carries with it a commitment to the kind of relativism he has shown to be untenable. But this is not persuasive. Conceptual schemes are constituted by networks of a priori commitments of the kind described in the previous chapter. Thus Sellars' contrast between the 'scientific image' and the 'manifest image' of man-in-the-world is an example of two conceptual schemes (a phrase Sellars himself uses in this connection) in apparent conflict; and all that Davidson's anti-relativist thesis implies is that there must be a way of bringing the truths inherent in these two images into a coherent view of man, which is of course precisely what Sellars seeks to do. Indeed Davidson's own contrast between the methodology of the natural sciences and that of interpretative inquiries is essentially a reformulation of Sellars' contrast, and is itself a case of two conceptual schemes in tension, a tension which Davidson himself has also sought to resolve.

In considering how such tensions can be resolved there is an important difference between monists and pluralists in philosophy. Monists believe that somehow the conflicts must be susceptible of a resolution within some one ultimate theory which can incorporate all truths; whereas pluralists hold that this is a quasi-theological illusion, and that we should learn to be content with the kind of consistency that is achieved by settling border disputes in a piecemeal fashion. Davidson's argument against conceptual schemes seems to assume that only a monist position is defensible; but where the limits of different subject-matters, or different points of view, are respected there seems to me no objection in principle to a pluralist position. As I mentioned earlier (Chapter 2, p. 23) the development of Wittgenstein's philosophy is instructive here: his early work, the *Tractatus*, has a monist conception of language, but one of the changes characteristic of his later work is the switch to accepting that there is an irreducible plurality of language-games. And in practice Davidson is also a pluralist of this kind. Hence the true implication of his position is just that in philosophy (as in politics) we have to learn to live with a plurality of standards (i.e. conceptual schemes) without becoming relativists.

Semantic Analysis

Davidson links his attack on conceptual schemes (the 'third dogma') with Quine's attack on the analytic/synthetic distinction (the 'second dogma'). Nonetheless, he has also proclaimed the merits of semantic analysis as a method of philosophical inquiry, and this method was extremely influential during the 1970s, especially in Oxford where, as it was said, a 'Davidsonic boom' swept across the philosophical land-scape. The key to it lies in the thesis discussed at the start of this chapter, that our understanding of a language can be modelled on knowledge of a systematic theory of truth-conditions for the language. For such a theory requires that the sentences of the language be assigned a seman-tic analysis which specifies the contribution of the constituent words and syntactic structures to determining the truth-conditions of the sen-tences in which they occur. Davidson's claim has then been that in some cases the resulting semantic analysis yields philosophically sig-nificant conclusions by showing us how the world must be in certain respects if our patterns of talk are to make sense. For example, Davidson argues, causation is shown to be a relation between events, and actions are shown to be events to which we as agents are related by our action.

This 'method of truth in metaphysics', as Davidson has called it, is an up-dating of old-style logical analysis as practised by Russell, and

Davidson argues that his method of semantic analysis is a new way of revealing 'logical form'. The popularity of Davidson's new method is easily understood; unfortunately, however, as with Russell's old method, it turns out that the old metaphysical disputes (about causation, action and so on) can be reformulated as debates about the correct semantic analysis of the requisite area of discourse. So although the questions raised when applying the method of semantic analysis certainly require an answer, the method has turned out to be less decisive than was originally hoped.

Dummett and Understanding

As I mentioned at the start of the chapter, Davidson's writings are one side of a long-standing Anglo-American debate, the other side of which has been provided by the Oxford philosopher Michael Dummett. Their works exemplify very different styles of writing: while Davidson has written a series of short, dense, papers, Dummett has written several large books. I shall concentrate on the position he puts forward in two of his later ones, *The Logical Basis of Metaphysics* (1991), and *The Seas of Language* (1993: a collection of papers, mostly from the 1980s).

Although Dummett studied philosophy at Oxford at the time of the dominance of the ordinary language movement discussed in Chapter 2, he remained detached from that enthusiasm, and much of his early work was directed to furthering a proper appreciation of Frege's writings (which provides an immediate point of contact with Davidson since he also started from a position broadly inspired by Frege). According to Dummett, Frege effected a 'revolution' in philosophy by showing, in principle, how debates about language provide a fundamental forum for philosophical debate. In accordance with this conception of Frege's achievement, therefore, Dummett has developed a philosophy of language of his own through which he has aspired to provide 'the logical basis of metaphysics'.

Like Davidson, Dummett holds that a philosophical concern with language must be based on an account of the understanding of language. But whereas Davidson takes the position of the interpreter, or hearer, as fundamental, for Dummett it is the position of the speaker that defines the primary object of inquiry, which is the speaker's understanding of her language. Dummett holds that a speaker's understanding of her language comprises a fundamental type of knowledge—an ability to make sense of, and thus conceptualize, the world. Some might think that the elucidation of this ability is properly the province of cognitive scientists and linguists, such as Noam Chomsky (1928–) who certainly regards himself as trying to provide an account of a speaker's knowledge of language. But Dummett rejects the suggestion that the kind of scientific enquiry characteristic of psychology and linguistics could provide the theory of understanding to which he aspires. Such theories, he argues, can at best offer a causal theory of language, whereas he aims to exhibit language as an activity of rational agents. Whether Dummett is right to be so dismissive of psycholinguistics is a point to which I shall return briefly at the end of the chapter, but his stress on the essential rationality of language is a point on which Davidson would of course agree with him.

Nonetheless, Dummett argues, Davidson's account of understanding cannot be right; for Davidson's 'holism' implies that understanding one aspect of language is dependent upon understanding of the rest of the language, and this, Dummett holds, is untenable. It implies that a speaker's reasons for using, say, colour words as she does are dependent upon her reasons for using the rest of the language as she does. This is intuitively absurd and makes the learning of language mysterious; it also contradicts the very idea that a speaker's use of language could ever be a rational activity, since the totality of language is never present to us as speakers.

This point leads Dummett to propose what he calls a 'molecular' conception of language according to which a speaker's understanding of her language has a hierarchical structure, involving mastery of a range of distinct 'molecules'—groups of sentences involving interrelated terms (e.g. colour words) whose understanding may well involve understanding some other terms (e.g. the demonstratives which we use to pick things out), but which does not require an understanding of the rest of language. For example, an understanding of colour terms does not require an understanding of political vocabulary (though our talk of 'green politics' implies that in some respects the opposite dependence does obtain).

This position resembles the theory of ideas of classical empiricists such as Locke, whose theory involves a hierarchy of simple and complex ideas; but there are also important differences. For Dummett, the hierarchy is one of different types of sentence and not a hierarchy of words or the ideas they express, since he follows Frege in holding that it is the use of complete sentences that constitutes the fundamental phenomenon of meaning. So words have meaning only insofar as they contribute to the meaning of sentences in which they occur, which is why Dummett insists that his conception of meaning is 'molecular' and not simply 'atomist'. Further, whereas classical empiricists held that complex ideas are constructed from simple ideas, thus implying that explicit definitions should always be possible, Dummett's hierarchy of linguistic abilities does not have this implication.

How then are these hierarchically structured linguistic abilities to be characterized? Dummett's account of this matter is central to his philosophy. He starts by claiming that we are to obtain an account of 'language as representation', of the thoughts expressed in language, on the basis of an account of 'language as activity', the use of language in context. A crucial aspect of this emphasis on use is the requirement that the account should be one which shows how a speaker's use of language *manifests* her understanding. This 'manifestation requirement' rests on the thesis that communication is of the essence of language: unless a speaker's understanding of her language is manifest within her use of language, 'communication would indeed rest on faith' (*Seas of Language*: 187). It is indeed hard to quarrel with this; Davidson's claim that meaning is just what is arrived at through radical interpretation is much the same point in a different idiom (though it is worth adding that some linguists, such as Chomsky, reject it, on the grounds that communication is not an essential feature of the use of language). But much depends on the way in which this manifestation requirement is construed.

Manifesting Understanding

A first thought might be that a speaker manifests her understanding of sentences involving the word 'rabbit' by using them in situations in which they are, by and large, true of rabbits. For Dummett, however, such an account of the way in which the speaker's understanding is manifested is too 'modest': it fails to make explicit 'the grasp which a speaker of the language must have of the concepts expressed by the words belonging to it' (*The Logical Basis of Metaphysics*, p. 108). By contrast, an account which does make this explicit, and which therefore fulfils the manifestation requirement, is said by Dummett to be 'full-blooded' or 'robust'.

The 'modest' approach Dummett rejects is one according to which an account of the truth-conditions of a speaker's utterances is to provide by itself the basis for an account of her understanding of language which elucidates her reasons for speaking as she does. Dummett seems to me right about this: for as we saw in connection with Davidson, there is no immediate inference from truth-conditions to meaning. Admittedly Davidson then showed that if one brings in a good many further considerations, those inherent in the procedure of radical interpretation, one can make a strong case for supposing that the resulting account of a sentence's truth-condition provides a specification of its meaning. Because of these further considerations Dummett in fact regards Davidson's position as robust; but, as we have seen, he also rejects it as excessively holistic.

Instead of an account based upon the truth-conditions of a speaker's utterances, therefore, the approach which Dummett adopts is based upon an account of the features which a speaker regards as evidence for the truth of her utterance. Such an account will be robust, he thinks, because it shows the way in which the speaker's grasp of the concepts expressed in the utterance is manifested by the reasons she gives for the things she says; but it is not, Dummett holds, holistic, because these reasons do not interconnect indefinitely. This point is disputable and I shall return to it; but for the moment I shall concentrate on presenting Dummett's position, according to which a speaker manifests her understanding of 'rabbit'-sentences by her sensitivity to certain types of evidence which speakers of the language standardly take to justify judgements about rabbits.

Although a speaker's understanding of language is based upon sensitivity to appropriate evidence, Dummett also holds that in saying what an indicative sentence means we identify its characteristic truth-condition. He maintains therefore that there is a necessary connection between evidence and truth: the truth of a sentence requires the existence of appropriate evidence for its truth. But what then does a sentence mean? It may seem that the truth-condition which intuitively comprises its meaning should simply state the existence of this evidence. But, as Dummett observes, the meaning of 'I will be in New York next week' cannot be just that there now exists evidence that I will be in New York next week, since the implications of my presence in New York next week are not the same as those of the present existence of evidence for it, and it is the meaning of a sentence which determines its implications. Instead the truth-condition which captures the sentence's meaning must be just the obtaining of that state of affairs for which the appropriate evidence is evidence – i.e. my presence in New York next week.

Anti-realism

Because this position separates the condition which comprises the truth of a sentence from the existence of evidence for it, it is not a reductionist position which identifies features of the world with the evidence we have for them. Nonetheless, the position does give rise to a distinctively 'anti-realist' metaphysics according to which the existence of evidence, and thus the possibility of knowledge, is a prerequisite of truth and thus places a limit on the implied conception of reality. The opposing 'realist' position, according to which reality is not constrained by the possibility of knowledge of it, is therefore rejected by Dummett as an illusory picture. The best we can do in attempting to make sense of it, Dummett thinks, is to imagine ourselves having magical powers such as the power to range backwards through time or to complete infinite calculations; but precisely because we recognize these powers are magical we recognize that nothing is achieved by appealing to them. Instead, we should recognize that reality 'has gaps, much as a novel has gaps, in that there are questions about the characters to which the novel provides no answers, and to which there are therefore no answers' (*The Logical Basis of Metaphysics*, p. 318).

This line of thought is clearly revisionist: our ordinary conception of the past includes the thought that much that has happened is not only unknown but is also now unknowable because all the evidence has been destroyed. But Dummett seeks to support his position by arguing that his anti-realist position is an implication of insights incorporated in the 'intuitionistic' logical theory developed at the start of this century by a group of mathematicians (Brouwer, Heyting) in opposition to the standard, 'classical', logical theory of Frege, Russell, and most logicians (one should not, incidentally, be distracted by the use of the term 'intuitionistic' here: the term 'intuition' is sometimes used in the Kantian tradition to describe verification, and 'intuitionistic logic' is supposed to be the logic of verification). Indeed it is because of this connection with logical theory that Dummett represents his position as one which provides a 'logical basis for metaphysics'. The important point here is that whereas classical logic involves a presumption of 'bivalence', according to which sentences which are not true are false and vice-versa, intuitionistic logic allows that some sentences are neither true nor false. Such sentences are those which can neither be established as true nor as false; so they are, as it is said, 'undecidable', and it is their existence which leads to the apparent 'gaps' in reality characteristic of Dummett's anti-realism.

The fact that it is revisionist makes Dummett's anti-realist position intriguing, but also such that its adoption requires compelling arguments. Dummett, as we have seen, holds that his anti-realism is the logical outcome of an inquiry into language. But Dummett's opponent, the 'realist', will object that there is no difficulty in manifesting a commitment to classical logic: for there are patterns of reasoning which are characteristic of classical logic and where they are employed in some domain, e.g. the past, their use manifests a realist conception of this domain. Despite the activities of narrative historians, the realist will urge, we can show by the logic we use that our conception of the past is not that of a gappy story of the kind told by novelists.

Dummett will reply that there is nonetheless something unsatisfactory about such reasonings, in that they rely on an understanding of negation ('not') which goes beyond that which is strictly required for the purposes of reasoning. The point at issue is the status of the distinctive classical principle of 'double negation' that 'not not A implies A': according to Dummett this principle goes beyond the requirements of a purely logical conception of negation and manifests instead the realist's metaphysical presumption that the world is determinate in ways which transcend our capacity for discovering how, in detail, it is. But the realist defender of classical logic can respond that once negation is understood as grounded in our attitude of denial, and logic is formulated to take account of this attitude along with that of affirmation, the disputed principle can be seen to be essential to its proper understanding and by no means an extra-logical metaphysical assumption.

The details of this dispute are complex and cannot be pursued here, though it seems to me that the realist defender of classical logic has the better of the argument. It is worth noting in passing that Quine's claim (Chapter 4, p. 74) that disputes in logic are answerable to the needs of theoretical natural science is certainly not here confirmed. Instead, the central question is that of the proper understanding of logical vocabulary and negation in particular. Although this is not simply a matter of laying down some 'analytic' truths about negation, the points at issue can be resolved only in the light of a general theory of a priori logical reasoning, i.e. a philosophy of logic.

Assuming that the realist's classical account of logic is preferred, how then should one react to Dummett's general argument for anti-realism? To reassess this we should return to the question of the connection between evidence and truth. Dummett's realist critic will argue that even where it is granted that our understanding of the past depends upon our sensitivity to the relative significance of various forms of evidence (memory, testimony, documents etc.), it is still legitimate to hold that the resulting conception of the past is a realist one. For the conception of the world for which all this evidence is evidence is one which includes the fact that in some cases no evidence for some past event is going to be found because of the contingencies which affect the existence of evidence. Indeed this seems the merest common sense as soon as we think about questions concerning trivial matters of fact, such as the number of times someone now long dead (e.g. Julius Caesar) blinked during the last hour of their life. Our knowledge of the past justifies complete confidence that there is no evidence to provide a precise answer to such a question, but it would seem quite unwarranted to infer that in this respect the past itself, as opposed to our knowledge of it, has a gap.

This objection seeks to detach Dummett's anti-realism from his general account of our understanding of language. The objection is particularly cogent in those domains where our general conception of the facts involved includes an awareness of the reasons for the contingent existence of evidence. These are the domains where Dummett's anti-realism is intuitively most difficult to accept; abstract domains such as mathematics are a different matter which I shall not attempt to address. But the emphasis on the role of evidence in Dummett's account of understanding raises a different problem which must now be addressed.

Meaning, Evidence, and Knowledge

The problem, to which I alluded briefly earlier, is whether Dummett's emphasis on evidence can be combined with his molecular conception of understanding. Dummett's critics point to the way in which Quine, following Duhem, argued that because there are no principled limits to the ways in which one fact can yield evidence about another, the notion of evidence is inescapably holist (cf. Chapter 4, pp. 71–2). So, if understanding is based upon sensitivity to evidence, and evidence is holistic, then understanding must be holistic too.

Dummett's response to this argument is to hold that the Quinean holist fails to appreciate the importance of the distinction between authoritative, 'canonical', evidence, and indirect, 'non-canonical' evidence (the distinction is similar to Wittgenstein's distinction between 'criteria' and 'symptoms'—cf. Chapter 3, p. 28). Understanding is, he holds, based upon sensitivity to canonical evidence alone, and because such evidence is limited, the resulting conception of understanding is likewise limited, i.e. molecular. The further connections which Duhem emphasized involve indirect evidence and therefore do not undermine the molecularity of understanding.

This position depends on the assumption that an account of our understanding of language can draw on a distinction between canonical and indirect evidence. This is an a priori/empirical distinction: the identity of the canonical evidence for the truth of sentences of some type has to be a priori. I argued in the previous chapter, against Quine, that reasoning can take place only in a context in which some principles of rationality are not in question, and are therefore, in that context, a priori. Dummett's position involves a generalization of this thesis across language as a whole.

Dummett's main argument for his position comes from an account of the way in which we acquire concepts as we learn a first language. He maintains that we acquire a concept by learning that certain phenomena provide evidence for the correct use of the appropriate term; for example, a child learns how to use the word 'rabbit' by learning what rabbits look like. Thus the connection between this evidence and the concept (or meaning) is, for the child, a priori.

This argument is rejected by those who hold that concepts are not acquired at all because they are implanted in us thanks to evolution; but the main objection to it concerns the relationship between features inherent in the acquisition of concepts and the structure of justifications in subsequent use of the concept. Dummett's argument implies that the initial evidential relationships retain a privileged 'canonical' status once a thinker develops a broader understanding of the world. But an important feature of concepts such as 'rabbit', which we also learn as we acquire the concept, is that it is the concept of an animal species whose identity is not determined by its outer appearance—its phenotype. Common European rabbits (*Lepus cuniculus*) have a characteristic appearance and habits which we normally rely on to recognize them and in learning what rabbits are we learn the obvious elements of this. But species boundaries are not clearly marked by evidence of this kind—most pet rabbits are of this species but their appearance is often very different, and there are apparently similar rabbits of different species. Instead the evidence that would now be regarded as authoritative concerns the animal's genetic constitution, its genotype. But about this most people know next to nothing.

This point, which was already made by Quine in the 1930s, shows that our understanding of language is rather more loosely related to evidence than Dummett's 'acquisition' argument implies. As our general knowledge develops, our concepts evolve away from dependence upon the evidence by reference to which we acquired them towards an acknowledgement of the existence of further connections about which we usually know little in detail but which, we accept, permits correction of our original evidence. Our grasp of our own concepts is such as to allow us to cut them free from their evidential apron strings.

This conclusion undermines Dummett's molecular conception of understanding and threatens to legitimate the holism he has opposed. But there is a way of modifying Dummett's position which provides a new way of handling this issue. In *The Varieties of Reference* (1982) Gareth Evans argued that the truth behind Dummett's 'robust' insistence that our understanding of language involves a grasp of the concepts expressed in the language is best captured by introducing Russell's thesis that our understanding of a term is dependent upon our having some knowledge of the identity of that to which it applies. For it is when people use phrases ('quark', 'deconstruction', 'Godel's theorem') in a way which manifests complete ignorance about the things in question, that we judge that they do not understand what they are talking about.

Evans' Russellian thesis is distinct from Dummett's position, since the knowledge in question does not require a grasp of the relevant authoritative evidence. My understanding of the term 'e. coli' does not include any ability to recognize it; instead it is, I take it, adequately sustained by my knowledge that e. coli is a type of bacterium which is often present in raw meat, and which is liable to give rise to extremely violent food poisoning when eaten, indeed leading in some recent cases to death. Admittedly, this knowledge has been acquired from sources which are appropriately authoritative (textbooks and newspapers), so my understanding is based upon an indirect relationship with those who possess authoritative evidence. But I do not myself possess this evidence, nor would I be able to recognize it.

On the face of it, this emphasis on the role of background knowledge meets Dummett's requirement that the account of understanding be one which exhibits speech as a rational activity. Since, however, background knowledge can in principle be connected in indefinitely many ways to further knowledge it remains vulnerable to the charge of implying an impossibly holistic conception of understanding. The way around this is to recognize that there are degrees of knowledge, and, similarly, degrees of understanding: my understanding of the vocabulary of a science such as botany is greatly inferior to that of specialists in the field. But understanding does not have to be perfect. A child learns language as it acquires knowledge and it does not have to have perfect knowledge to be able to understand the language it learns. Equally, the child's use of language is rational insofar as it manifests its imperfect knowledge of what it is talking about. So, on this account, holism represents the potential for indefinite improvement in our understanding, not an impossible obstacle to its achievement in the first place.

The resulting position offers the prospect of a partial reconciliation of Dummettian understanding with Davidsonian interpretation. For one does not have to stretch Davidson's account of radical interpretation far to reinterpret it as a way of gaining an understanding of someone's language on the basis, among other things, of a grasp of their knowledge of what they are talking about. Davidson's emphasis on the presumptions of truth and rationality, for example, fits well with the thought that a speaker's understanding is dependent upon knowledge since what is known must be true and one normally has reasons for what one knows. The fit here is not perfect, however, and I want finally to touch on a significant disagreement between Davidson and Dummett concerning the role of convention in an account of language: Davidson holds that conventions have no important role in language, whereas Dummett holds that they are essential.

Meaning and Convention

The chief protagonist of the conventionalist position has in fact been David Lewis (1941–) who, in a brilliant work *Convention* (1969), used game theory to show how regularities within a community can become conventions without any explicit agreement to establish them as such. Lewis's theory implies that a community in which there are regular connections between utterances, and the beliefs and actions of hearers, is likely to be such that these connections become matters of convention; and he further showed that where this development takes place, utterances in which speakers intentionally invoke these conventions involve a distinctive pattern of complex intentions on the part of speakers which H. P. Grice had earlier famously identified as characteristic of meaningful utterances.

Why then does Davidson reject this conventionalist position in his later writings? The reason that he gives is that as soon as we look to our ordinary uses of language, we find all sorts of phenomena—jokes, irony, innuendo, even malapropisms—which we are able to understand perfectly well despite the fact that they violate the rules which the conventionalist takes to be essential to language. There is, he suggests, an 'autonomy of meaning' whereby speakers can distance themselves from the literal meaning of their words in a way which conflicts with the conventionalist's dull prescription that speakers must mean what they say. The conventionalist's response to this will have to be that the conventions of language characterize only this literal meaning which speakers can then play around with in the ways Davidson describes. This implies that these conventions cannot be based upon simple regularities which connect utterances with the actions and beliefs of hearers in the way in which Lewis's theory supposes; for the existence of the well-understood unconventional utterances shows that there are no such regularities. Instead, the conventional meaning of an utterance will have to take the form of an initial specification of the meaning of the words uttered which his hearers are expected to recognize, but can then set aside when the speaker's behaviour shows that it is inappropriate. But quite how Lewis's theory should be adapted to encompass such conventions remains to be determined.

This debate cannot be settled here, but the issue involved is symptomatic of two very different conceptions of language and its importance for philosophy. The conventionalist position connects readily with the view that language is essentially a social phenomenon to be understood by reference to the normative practices of the community within which it is used. Despite his 'robust' insistence on the importance of an individual speaker's understanding of their language, Dummett is a strong supporter of the conventionalist position; thus he takes it that in learning a language speakers internalize conventional rules that are social norms; so their speech-acts cannot be understood fully without reference to this social context. Equally, Davidson's rejection of the very idea of linguistic convention in his later writings shows his rejection of this conception of language as a system of rules. Instead, he now holds, although there has to be a 'community of understanding', i.e. general agreement between speakers, we make sense of each other by applying the method of radical interpretation in such a way that we can deal properly with the idiosyncrasies of each individual speaker. In practice, he accepts, we usually start, especially with strangers, from some general presumptions about the use of language; but these presumptions are not conventions and once we get to know each other we learn how to qualify and, sometimes, disregard them completely.

Davidson has a powerful ally in Noam Chomsky, who has for some time argued forcefully that it is a complete mistake to think of language as an essentially social phenomenon. Yet the dialectical situation here is complex: for Chomsky is also a forthright critic of Quine on the grounds that he fails to do justice to the reality of the knowledge which constitutes our mastery of language (cf. Chapter 4, p. 83)—so that in this respect he is closer to Dummett than to Davidson. But Chomsky rejects Dummett's view that this knowledge is the internalization of social rules; instead he regards it as an essentially innate capacity that has evolved for the expression of thoughts. So he holds that children who are, as we say, learning to speak are in fact just setting certain parameters within their innate internal language system on the basis of their linguistic environment. They are not being initiated into a network of normative social conventions.

On this sceptical view, then, as Davidson puts it, 'there is no such thing as language' ('A Nice Derangement of Epitaphs': 446), conceived of as a network of normative social conventions which speakers have to follow if they are to mean anything. Instead, there are just the general grammatical capacities studied by linguists such as Chomsky, and the individual communicative strategies of speakers whose utterances can be understood through Davidson's method of idiosyncratic radical interpretation. And that is all. So there is no place for a general 'theory of meaning'.

I do not myself accept this new sceptical thesis, but it reinvigorates the philosophy of language precisely by challenging its possibility.

6

Exploring the Possibilities

Empiricists from Hume onwards have been suspicious of the idea of necessary truth since it is not clear how our experience of the world can justify us in distinguishing what is the case but could be otherwise (contingent truth), from what is the case and what could not be otherwise (necessary truth). As I explained in Chapter 4, the logical empiricists sought to legitimate necessary truth as analyticity, but Quine then argued that this conception of analyticity is illegitimate. Although I suggested that Quine's arguments do not preclude a distinction between a priori and empirical truth, we shall see that subsequent arguments make the suggestion that necessary truth is just a priori truth untenable. Hence, much recent philosophy takes it that necessity or, equivalently, possibility, is a primitive feature of the world, though there is also an influential position which propounds an analysis of necessity and possibility in terms of a more general metaphysical conception.

As we shall see, one feature of these discussions is that they illustrate how philosophy has evolved away from concerns primarily directed to logic and the philosophy of language towards an interest in broader metaphysical considerations. Indeed, the conception of a 'possible world' which has been revived in this context has come to provide a vocabulary for this revival of metaphysics.

Quine's Essential Doubts

Quine's writings in the 1950s provide the starting point for subsequent discussions of these matters. Despite his repudiation of analyticity, Quine was content to permit a conception of necessity as the mark of those truths to whose truth we are strongly committed because we take them to follow from some deeper, underlying, regularity. He strongly objected, however, to any suggestion that necessity can also be properly attributed to the properties or relationships of the things described in such sentences. Thus although he allowed that it makes sense to say that '$(2)^2 = 4$' is a necessary truth, he denied that it makes sense to say, concerning the number two itself, that its square is necessarily four. Necessity inheres in some of our ways of speaking of things, not in the properties of things themselves.

The position Quine is here rejecting is one according to which an object's identity is fixed by its 'essential' properties and 'internal' relationships with other objects. According to this position, an object (e.g. the number two) would not be what it is without these essential properties and internal relationships, which are to be distinguished from the 'accidental' properties and 'external' relationships which it has but might have lacked. This position is prominent in the works of Aristotle and his successors, so Quine likes to express his position in the rhetoric of a seventeenth-century empiricist battling against scholastic philosophers who remain entangled in 'the metaphysical jungle of Aristotelian essentialism'.

One of Quine's arguments has become central to later discussion: he argues, first, that the essentialists he opposes are committed to the thesis of the essential necessity of identity which states that

if $x = y$ then, necessarily, $x = y$

where this is to be understood as saying that, if x is the same as y then it is an essential property of x that it be the same as y (and vice-versa). Secondly, Quine argued that this thesis is absurd, in that it has implications such as that it is essential property of the number 9 that there are 9 planets in the solar system (since 9 = the number of planets in the solar system) or that it is an essential property of Bill Clinton that he was the President of the USA in 2000 (since Bill Clinton = the President of the USA in 2000). Quine is clearly right in holding that these consequences are unacceptable. But the rest of his argument has been much disputed: his critics reject either the initial commitment to the necessity of identity or its supposed implications.

Possible Worlds

The first crucial step in the response to Quine has been the revival of Leibniz's conception of a 'possible world'. This revival initially took place in the context of debates concerning the logic of necessity and possibility, i.e. 'modal' logic. Modal logic has been studied since the time of Aristotle, but following the revival of formal logic initiated by Frege, Peirce, and Russell at the start of the twentieth century several different formal systems of modal logic were developed. This gave rise to inconclusive debates as to which system was correct, but in the 1960s several logicians suggested that the way to take matters forward was to introduce reference to a domain of objects which they informally identified as 'possible worlds'. For once one interprets necessity as truth in all possible worlds and possibility as truth in at least one possible world one can show that different systems of modal logic correspond to different assumptions about the relationships between possible worlds.

This talk of possible worlds is liable to arouse suspicion, and I shall discuss their status later in this chapter. For now, however, it suffices to understand claims about the existence of possible worlds as claims about the existence of hypothetical possibilities, which is a conception with which we are reasonably familiar, whatever precise significance we take it to have. What is then distinctive about possible worlds is just that they are taken to be 'maximal' possibilities—possibilities which, unlike all ordinary possibilities, constitute a complete way in which things might be, a way which leaves unanswered no question as to how things would be if this possibility were actual. Indeed, the actual world itself, the way things actually are, is a paradigmatic possible world. For what is actual must be possible.

Though the details of modal logic do not concern us, the value of talk of possible worlds can be illustrated by their role in elucidating the logic of 'counterfactual' conditional sentences such as 'if Bob Dole had won the 1996 election, the USA would not have intervened in Kosovo', where the antecedent is assumed to be false. 'What if' questions involving counterfactuals are familiar in historical speculations, but they also arise in connection with important philosophical concepts such as causation, dispositions, knowledge, and responsibility and for this reason their elucidation is of considerable philosophical significance.

A distinctive feature of the logic of counterfactuals is that by adding clauses to the antecedent of a counterfactual one can switch the consequent from truth to falsity and vice-versa. Thus suppose you have been to a boring party: it may then occur to you that if your lively friend Jane had been there the party would not have been boring, i.e.

> If Jane had come, the party would not have been boring.

But if Jane's dull friend James had also come he would have monopolized her, so—

> If Jane and James had both come, the party would still have been boring.

If, however, James' friend Will had come he would have distracted James, so—

> If Jane, James, and Will had all come, the party would not have been boring.

And so on.

This phenomenon is not a feature of straightforward logical implication: if A logically implies B then (A & C) logically implies B, whatever extra clause C may be. So counterfactuals are not cases of straightforward logical implication. It seems intuitively clear that the phenomenon arises from background assumptions which change as the antecedent is changed. These assumptions are not stated explicitly, but in 1968 Robert Stalnaker (1940–) and David Lewis argued persuasively that they are best identified by interpreting counterfactuals as claims to the effect that the consequent is true in the possible worlds which are 'closest to', or most similar to, the actual world except for the fact that the antecedent is also true in them. Thus the consequent of the first counterfactual above is to be evaluated with reference to the possible worlds closest to the actual world except for the fact that Jane did come to the party; that of the second with reference to the closest possible worlds in which both Jane and James came to the party; and so on. For in each case it is easy to grasp how the consequent, that the party was not boring, switches between truth and falsity as it is evaluated with reference to these different possible worlds.

This possible world account of counterfactual conditionals is widely accepted, and partly for this reason the idiom of possible worlds is now a familiar feature of philosophical discourse. The resulting situation poses a challenge to Quine since the essentialist theses he rejects can be easily formulated in this idiom: my essential properties are those which I possess in all the possible worlds in which I exist. Just to say this, however, is not to rebut Quine's arguments that essentialism has unacceptable consequences; but an influential rebuttal of Quine's arguments was provided by Saul Kripke (1940–), a philosopher and logician who had earlier helped to develop the technical role of possible worlds in modal logic.

Rigid Designators

In his 1970 lectures (published as *Naming and Necessity* (1980)) Kripke accepted Quine's claim that essentialism brings with it a commitment to the essential necessity of identity. He argued, however, that Quine's complaint that this thesis brings with it unacceptable implications, such as that it is an essential property of Bill Clinton that he was the President of the USA in 2000 is mistaken; the thesis has no such implications. His argument starts from the point that a thing's essential properties can be regarded as properties that thing has in all the possible worlds in which it exists at all. Hence, in thinking about putative cases of essential properties, it is important that one should have a way of identifying one and the same thing in the different possible worlds under consideration and this leads Kripke to distinguish between 'rigid' and 'non-rigid' designators. Rigid designators (e.g. '2') are names and descriptions whose meaning is such that they designate, or refer to, the same thing in all the possible worlds in which they designate anything at all, whereas the meaning of non-rigid designators (e.g. 'the President of the USA in 2000') is such that there are possible worlds in which they designate something different from the thing which they designate in the actual world (e.g. there is a possible world in which 'the President of the USA in 2000' designates Bob Dole). Once this distinction is made, it follows that in thinking about a thing's essential properties we must employ a rigid designator to think about it; for with a non-rigid designator we are liable to end up considering different things as we consider different possible worlds.

The application of this point to Quine's discussion of the essential necessity of identity is straightforward. The supposed cases of this which are unacceptable all exploit the use of non-rigid designators ('the number of planets in the solar system', 'the President of the USA in 2000'). Yet it is obvious that it is not proper to rely on them when considering the essential necessity of identity since this precisely involves considering whether identities that obtain in the actual world obtain in non-actual worlds. Equally, it is obvious that where we just employ rigid designators to consider instances of the essential necessity of identity, we will find the thesis confirmed.

At this point it may be objected that Kripke has simply begged the question against Quine, since his distinction between rigid and non-rigid designators assumes the legitimacy of the essentialist distinctions that Quine rejects: the meaning of a non-rigid designator is such that it designates whatever it does only in virtue of that thing's accidental properties whereas the meaning of a rigid designator somehow draws on an essential property of the thing it designates. As with all such disputes, much depends on where the burden of proof is supposed to lie. I take it that Kripke does help to show that essentialist thought is coherent by showing that it does not have the unacceptable implications Quine alleged. Admittedly, in doing so Kripke does not legitimate essentialism *ex nihilo*; but, harking back to Quine's own epistemological standpoint (cf. Chapter 4, pp. 76–7), Kripke can urge that since both ordinary language and scientific thought are thickly permeated with essentialist distinctions, it is neither necessary nor sensible to require an external vindication of essentialist thought. The burden of proof lies with Quine the sceptic rather than with Kripke the defender of common sense essentialism.

Kripke's position implies that if we are to be able to articulate and defend essentialist theses concerning objects of some kind, we must be able to find rigid designators for some of them. It is unproblematic that rigid designators (e.g. '2') are to be found in abstract sciences such as arithmetic. But essentialists maintain that ordinary things—cabbages, kings, and bits of sealing wax—also have essential properties. So these too require rigid designators, and Kripke advanced the striking proposal that ordinary proper names are rigid designators of them: their meaning is such that they designate the same thing in all the possible worlds in which they designate anything.

This seems, at first, a counterintuitive thesis; for ordinary proper names seem very different from the names of numbers. For example, since Mary Ann Evans was in fact George Eliot, the essential necessity of identity implies that Mary Ann Evans was necessarily George Eliot, and this can appear to be incorrect. It is no objection to it that Mary Ann Evans might not have taken 'George Eliot' as her *nom de plume*; for in using the name 'George Eliot' to refer to the person in question the contingencies involved in the choice of this name are set to one side. After all, the fact that the number 4 might not have been called '4' does not show that $2 + 2$ is not necessarily 4. But there is a different, and much more potent, objection: identities such as this are empirical. Mary Ann Evans published her novels under the name 'George Eliot' precisely in order to conceal her true identity. But if it is only an empirical truth that George Eliot was Mary Ann Evans, how can this be an essentially necessary truth about her? Surely necessary truths are truths which can in principle be established by some a priori method of reasoning or calculation?

As we saw in Chapter 4, the logical empiricists held that the answer to this question is affirmative, and Quine largely agreed with them about this. But Kripke disagrees: there is, he holds, an empirical component to necessary truths such as that George Eliot was Mary Ann Evans. This is the second, and most important part, of his critical response to Quine's sceptical argument. One way to understand what is going on here is to see that two different dimensions of the meaning of a sentence are in play, a 'process' and a 'product' dimension. The a priori/empirical distinction concerns the ways in which rational thinkers come to have knowledge of the world; thus it involves a conception of meaning tied to the process of understanding, to the ways of thinking of things characteristic of the words employed. By contrast the necessary/ contingent distinction concerns whether things might be other than they are; so it involves a conception of meaning that looks to the product of understanding, to the truth-conditions of the sentence. It is an empirical truth that George Eliot is Mary Ann Evans, because no thinker could deduce this truth by reason alone from the process of understanding the names separately, since their use belongs to different contexts which give rise to different ways of thinking of the person named; but it is also a necessary truth because the truth thus understood, the product of the understanding, is a truth which could not be otherwise since Mary Ann Evans, and thus George Eliot, cannot divide into two distinct persons.

This last line of thought is not unchallengeable, and we shall later consider the way in which David Lewis has challenged it. Furthermore one should not exaggerate the implied distinction between necessity and the a priori: the thesis of the essential necessity of identity is itself a priori. What remains empirical is just the truth of particular identity-statements such as that George Eliot is Mary Ann Evans. But Kripke reinforces his position by arguing that just as there are empirical necessities, there are also contingent a priori truths. The type of case that he points to here is that in which a name is introduced for someone or something whose existence is postulated as the explanation for some observed phenomenon: thus we are introduced to 'Jack the Ripper' as the man responsible for a series of murders committed in the late nineteenth century in the East End of London and to 'Neptune' as the planet responsible for the perturbations in the orbit of Uranus. Since the reference of the name is fixed in this way, the truth of the resulting identity statement—e.g. 'Jack the Ripper is the man responsible for the East End murders'—is a priori; but it is only a contingent truth, since the man who was responsible for these murders might not have done them at all.

This last point may seem wrong: but one way to clarify it is to distinguish between the descriptions 'the man responsible for the East End murders' and 'the man *actually* responsible for the East End murders'. The first description is, in Kripke's jargon, a non-rigid designator since in different possible worlds these murders are committed by different people; but the second can be understood as a rigid designator, designating in any possible world the very person (if he or she exists in that world) who was in our (actual) world responsible for the East End murders, if there was indeed such a person. The name 'Jack the Ripper' can therefore be treated as an abbreviation of the description 'the man actually responsible for the East End murders', and the contingency thesis is then just a consequence of the fact that the man who was actually responsible for these murders might not have done them at all. Indeed it is now easy to see that truths of the form 'the F = the actual F' are typically both a priori and contingent. They are a priori because the process of understanding each description guarantees that, in the actual world, that which satisfies one description will satisfy the other; but the product of this understanding, the truth-condition, is typically contingent because one description ('the actual F') is rigid while the other ('the F') is not and this implies that even though they are satisfied by the same thing in the actual world they are satisfied by different things in other possible worlds.

An obvious feature of the discussion so far is that what started out as a discussion of necessity and possibility has turned in part into a discussion of language. As the title (*Naming and Necessity*) of Kripke's lectures indicates, he holds that the use of proper names provides ordinary thought with rigid designators which enable us to keep constant the identity of the things under discussion while we engage in hypothetical speculations concerning them, much as our ability to focus visually on physical objects enables us to keep track of our environment while we change our point of view. Quine's objection to essentialism, that it treats necessity as a feature of the structure of things rather than just a feature of our ways of talking about things rests, therefore, on a false opposition: it is because necessity enters into our ways of talking that we can frame thoughts to represent the ways in which necessity enters into the structure of things.

Yet it is a fair question to ask how this is possible—how our use of proper names is such as to provide them with this remarkable, some would say magical, rigidity. Kripke himself suggests that our normal use of names is to be understood as arising from an 'original baptism' whereby a name is bestowed on an object and then handed down by a causal chain to subsequent speakers through a deferential practice whereby speakers pick up names from others and use them with the intention of referring to the object which their source has used it to refer to. This is, I think, too simple (e.g. the speakers need to know something about the thing named—cf. Chapter 5, p. 116); but what is important here is that the account implies that names achieve rigidity in the first place through the original baptism at which an appropriate object is singled out for naming by a demonstrative expression such as 'this child'.

It is certainly true that demonstrative expressions function as rigid designators in a given context: if we engage in hypothetical specula-tions about a child present to us and designated as 'this child' the iden-tity of the child designated remains fixed rigidly in that context by the demonstrative. But what is distinctive about names is that their use is in principle not context-dependent in the way in which that of demon-stratives is. So the question returns as to what it is that sustains their rigidity; and to this, I think, the answer has to be just the essential necessity of identity itself. Thus the situation is like that of launching a satellite into orbit: we need context-dependent demonstratives in order to blast through the general fog of ordinary thought and single out a definite object. But once we have achieved this identification we can use it to launch a name into orbit and, thanks to the essential necessity of identity, the name should then be able to retain its rigid referential function without needing further help from the context of utterance.

Essentialism

So far, the essentialist claim under discussion has been primarily that a thing's identity is essential to its existence. More substantive essential-ist theses arise from claims as to what constitutes the identity of things of various kinds. Kripke and others have made three general proposals here, concerning the essential necessity of origin, of substance, and of form. The essential necessity of origin is exemplified by Kripke's claim that it is essential to a child that it had the (biological) parents that it does have; the essential necessity of substance is exemplified by the claim that it is essential to the identity of my desk that it be made of the pieces of wood of which it is made: a desk made of other pieces of wood, or of plastic, would be a different desk. Finally the essential necessity of form is exemplified by the claim that my dog could not but be a dog: it could not have been a cat or a kingfisher. Its identity is dependent upon the kind of thing it is.

These claims all have considerable intuitive plausibility; but, on reflection, they are also questionable. Kripke's example of the necessity of origin draws on the genetic dependence of a child upon its parents. This is a causal thesis, and the techniques employed in gene therapy show that the genetic links between parents and children can in principle be interfered with. In the case of the necessity of substance, there is certainly a conception of a 'whole' which is just the sum of its parts and therefore something whose identity is dependent upon that of its parts. But the application of this conception to familiar objects is problematic: parts of an organism are continuously replaced without altering its identity, and we do not treat the result of replacing a car's oil filter as a new car. Admittedly, these points primarily concern an object's identity through time; but their extrapolation as grounds for doubt about the essential necessity of substance, which concerns identity through possible worlds, is legitimate, since an understanding of what is essential to a thing's identity draws upon an understanding of what changes to it are possible.

This last point also applies when considering the thesis of the essential necessity of form, but here it supports the essentialist position. For, especially where we are considering the identity of an organism or something similar whose identity over time is not simply given by the identity of its parts, we draw on a conception of the kind of thing we are dealing with in order to provide, as it is said, a 'criterion of identity' which provides a principled way of reidentifying the very same thing at different times or in different possible worlds. This point is even exemplified by fairy stories in which an evil magician turns a prince into a frog. For we make sense of such stories by taking it that the criterion of identity for the prince is provided by his being a stream of consciousness which can be continued within a frog's body. One may well wonder whether the conception of a stream of consciousness does provide a genuine criterion of identity (real streams can divide and unite), but in the present context the essentialist does not need to take a stand on that point. All he will point to is the implied acknowledgement here of an enduring, and essential, kind which underpins the identity of that which also changes as radically as a fairy story character.

This line of thought is not unchallengeable: one can play off a plausible instance of the necessity of substance, where the 'same stuff' is involved, against the necessity of form—e.g. where one has a lump of wax which has been moulded into a statue. For it is not clear in advance whether hypothetical speculations about 'the same thing' include imagining the lump of wax moulded into different shapes (in accordance with the necessity of substance) or imagining the statue with some new wax added to replace a broken part (in accordance with the necessity of form). Abstracted from context both ways of thinking seem coherent, although they pull in different directions. One reaction is then to hold that these different possibilities show that in reality we are dealing with two things, a lump of wax and a statue, which, for a time, occupy the same space, but whose identity is determined in different ways, so that one can be destroyed without destroying the other. Yet this is a strange hypothesis, since these 'two' things—a single lump of wax moulded into a statue—certainly strike us as one and the same: the lump of wax *is* a statue.

There is a large array of puzzle cases of this kind, most of which concern the identity of artefacts such as statues and ships. They do not show that there is no place for a criterion of identity for such things; but they do suggest that in the case of artefacts our conception of their identity is primarily guided by the pragmatic considerations appropriate to the context in which a question of identity arises. Hence, insofar a distinction between their accidental and essential properties has any application, it is dependent on these same considerations.

'Water = H₂O'

Pragmatism concerning artefacts should, on reflection, be acceptable; they are, after all, things created for use by us. This is not true of the 'natural kinds' studied in the natural sciences, and it is widely held that our understanding of their identity has essentialist implications that are rooted in the nature of things, rather than in our pragmatic concerns. This position is reminiscent of Locke's view that natural kinds of thing each have their own unique 'real essence'; but whereas Locke held that this real essence is unknowable by us, Kripke and Putnam argue that it can often now be illuminatingly identified in scientific terms.

As we saw earlier, for Kripke the formulation of an essentialist thesis requires rigid designators; so in this case he and Putnam hold that terms such as 'water', 'gold', and 'tiger' are rigid designators of natural kinds, naming precisely the same kind in all possible worlds in which there are things of the kind at all. Hence, they hold, since chemical terms such as 'H_2O' are also rigid designators, the identity statement

$$\text{Water} = H_2O$$

is a necessary truth which exhibits the real essence of water. This position implies that there is no question of our discovering a different, non-H_2O, type of water; instead any such watery liquid will have to be of different kind—not water but 'fool's water' (comparable to fool's gold, iron pyrites). Is this right? Hilary Putnam used a famous thought experiment to suggest that it is.

He invited us to imagine that when travelling through some distant galaxy we discover a planet, Twin-Earth, that appears at first to be just like our own Earth, including being inhabited by organisms that appear to be human beings just like us. We also discover, however, that on Twin-Earth the liquid that looks, tastes, and superficially behaves just like water is not H_2O, but has a different chemical composition, XYZ. Although the people on Twin-Earth, whose language seems just like ours, call this liquid 'water' this fact does not settle the question whether it is water, and Putnam maintained that it is not water since the reference of our term 'water' is fixed by the fact that it is standardly learnt as a name for the watery liquid back here on Earth, which is H_2O and not XYZ. The fact that there might be a watery liquid on Twin-Earth, which is called 'water' by people there who are apparently like us (though they have XYZ in their bodies instead of H_2O), does not show that there might be other types of water.

Duhem's thesis (cf. Chapter 4, p. 71) applies to thought-experiments at least as much as to ordinary scientific experiments. Putnam's thought-experiment is an intuitively effective way of illustrating the essentialist position, but contains no argument for it, since the fact that we learn to use the term 'water' in H_2O contexts will only restrict proper use of the term to H_2O if it is already granted that our use the term 'water' does not allow for the discovery of other types of water, which is the point at issue. On the face of it, this point can be readily challenged: people have long distinguished between freshwater and seawater; so why should we not also allow for the discovery of further types of (fresh)water? Putnam himself admits that the conception of water within cultures which lack significant chemical knowledge, such as our own until about 1800, does indeed permit this; but, he holds, the use of 'water' in our own culture has by now been regimented by our chemical knowledge in such a way that the essentialist hypothesis applies to it. For, as he puts it, there has been a linguistic division of labour whereby we ordinary folk defer to the scientists concerning the identity of kinds such as water.

In effect, therefore, Putnam appeals to the understanding of natural kinds employed within the natural sciences. If we look to the natural sciences, however, the facts turn out to be more complicated than essentialists suggest. Hydrogen is a case in point: hydrogen atoms normally have a single electron and proton; but there are also hydrogen ions with no electron (H^+) and ions with two electrons (H^-). There are also three isotopes of hydrogen: the normal one whose nucleus is just the single proton, one with with a single neutron as well (deuterium), and one with two neutrons (tritium). Deuterium and tritium are rare, though they are present throughout samples of hydrogen; deuterium oxide (heavy water) has important uses in the nuclear industry as a coolant, and tritium is a potential source of fusion energy. The point here is often obscured by the fact that the term 'hydrogen' is usually contrasted with 'deuterium' and 'tritium'; but there is nonetheless a clear sense in which all three are isotopes of one element, also called 'hydrogen'. And there are further variations as well: 'ortho-hydrogen' differs from 'para-hydrogen' in virtue of the different directions of spin in their atomic nuclei. Thus although hydrogen is a natural kind, there are many different types of hydrogen; equally, therefore, there are different types of H_2O, and thus of water. Nor is this a special case—there are isotopes and ions all through chemistry. Once one actually opens a textbook of chemistry one quickly learns that Mendeleev's famous table of elements, important though it is, tells only a small part of the story.

Do the facts of chemistry (and other sciences) turn out, then, to refute the essentialist position? A position which is suggested by some of the language that Kripke and Putnam use is certainly refuted: their talk of rigid designators for natural kinds suggests a direct extrapolation from individual objects to natural kinds which would preclude the possibility of there being different types of a natural kind; for there cannot be different types of one individual object. What remains true, nonetheless, is that the ways in which sciences such as chemistry identify natural kinds implies that certain properties are characteristic of normal samples under standard conditions—e.g. it is characteristic of normal samples of hydrogen that its atoms have just one electron and proton, even though ions and isotopes also exist in nature. This position can be regarded as one which thereby identifies the essential properties of normal samples of the kind. I am not sure whether much clarity is gained by this redescription; but in this modest sense we can agree with Putnam that it is an essential property of water that it is H_2O.

Once the matter is formulated in this way, however, the important question is not so much the defensibility of the modest essentialist position as its significance. On Putnam's account of the matter, the differences between natural kinds were regarded as distinctions rooted in the real essences of things and the necessity of the laws of nature which concern them was said to be essential necessity. Yet once one observes the diversity that surrounds the identification of natural kinds, this position seems misguided: 'real essences' are only the characteristic properties of normal samples and pragmatic considerations have an important role in selecting them. This is especially clear in the case of biological species; for example when it comes to drawing distinctions between species, sub-species, and local variations among populations of dandelions, the fact that the relevant differences are primarily only differences of degree implies that the distinctions that are drawn inevitably involve pragmatic considerations arising from the context in which they are drawn.

This last point does not, however, imply that the identity of natural kinds is just a matter of the uses we make of the kinds we distinguish. For even where pragmatic concerns are prominent the distinctions that are drawn will still be distinctions grounded in natural facts—e.g. in differences in the genotypes of different dandelions. But these differences are not, in the first instance, 'essential' differences; instead they are causal differences. Unlike the situation with artefacts, therefore, the discrimination of natural kinds is based upon the causal distinctions inherent in their characteristic properties. Since these properties enter into laws of nature which specify their causal significance in relation to other properties, it follows that where the properties concerned are used to identify natural kinds the necessity of the law can be regarded as an 'essential necessity', as Putnam holds. But this is at best an implication of, and not the basis for, the identification of natural kinds. It is causation that provides the real basis for the pragmatically selected natural kinds we attend to.

Modal Realism

So far I have been discussing the new orthodoxy inspired by Kripke's work. The most important alternative to this orthodoxy is the position developed from the late 1960s by Kripke's Princeton colleague, David Lewis, and expounded in his book *On the Plurality of Worlds* (1986). A central feature of Lewis's position has been his uncompromising realism concerning possible worlds. Just as a realist about time holds that past and future times are just as real as the present, Lewis holds that worlds which are merely possible are just as real as the actual world, which is distinguished only by the fact that it is the world in which we live. So there is a 'plurality of worlds', each just as 'concrete' as the actual world. Worlds are wholes whose parts are connected by spatio-temporal relations; the parts of one world, however, have no spatio-temporal relations to parts of another world. So worlds are entirely separate space–times, with the consequence that nothing can belong to more than one world.

For Lewis this last point reflects the fact that things cannot have incompatible properties. Suppose that I myself were to belong to more than one world: in the actual world my hair is short, but since it might have been long, this supposition implies that there is a world in which I have long hair, and since that world is just as real as the actual world, it follows that my hair is really long, just as it is also really short. But this is a contradiction, so the initial supposition must be rejected. The obvious response to this argument is that all that is implied is that my hair is short in the actual world and long in another world, which is no more a contradiction than the changes in the length of my hair from one time to another. But this response is not entirely satisfactory, for it seems to imply that length is a relational property, like that of being a father or a son (which is why there is no contradiction in my being both a father and a son); yet length does not seem to be relational property.

There is more to be said here (arguably it is the predication of length that is time- and world-relative rather than length itself), but it will be apparent that Lewis's position conflicts sharply with the Kripkean orthodoxy that essentialist truths concern the properties things have in all the possible worlds in which they exist. Lewis proposes instead that essentialist claims draw upon similarities between different, but similar, things in different worlds—'counterparts', as Lewis calls them. So the claim that Socrates was essentially a man is interpreted as the claim that all of Socrates' other-worldly counterparts are men; and the claim that he was only accidentally snub-nosed is interpreted as the claim that he has a counterpart in some non-actual world who is not snub-nosed.

This way of interpreting essentialist claims strikes at the heart of Kripke's position by challenging the thesis of the necessity of identity.

This is best seen by considering the equivalent thesis that if things might be different then they are different, i.e.

if it is possible that $x \neq y$, then $x \neq y$.

For Lewis the antecedent here is interpreted as the condition that there is a possible world which includes distinct things, a and b, which are respectively counterparts of x and y in the actual world. It is not so far said that x and y are distinct, but the Kripkean thesis is that since a and b are distinct, so are x and y. For Lewis this thesis is not correct: the counterpart relationship permits situations in which one thing, x, has distinct counterparts, a and b, in another world. This will arise where these 'twin' counterparts are equally similar to x, and it is inherent in the notion of similarity that such situations can arise. Where they do, they are counter-examples to the thesis that different counterparts must be counterparts of different things: for where a and b are twin counterparts they are different counterparts of some one thing which is both x and y.

Once the thesis of the necessity of identity is rejected, essentialist truth no longer depends on rigid designators or any special doctrines about names and reference; instead, essentialist truth just depends on similarity. Lewis argues that there are many different types of similarity, and this, he suggests, explains well the difficulties which arose in connection with the theses of the essential necessity of origin, substance, and of form. For while each of these draws on a kind of similarity, and can be used to support essentialist claims, no one kind is pre-eminent: hence it is not surprising that when they pull in different directions we find that we have conflicting essentialist intuitions.

This implication of Lewis's position is attractive. But the overall acceptability of his position depends on the acceptability of his realism concerning non-actual worlds. Lewis's realism is unquestionably a radical doctrine. Some object to it on grounds of ontological extravagance—that it sins against the principle associated with the English medieval nominalist philosopher William of Ockham that 'entities are not to be multiplied without reason'. But this principle just expresses a presumption in favour of ontological parsimony and one can with equal reason advance the different principle of generic parsimony, that 'kinds of entity are not to be multiplied without reason'. This is a principle which Lewis certainly does not sin against. On the contrary, he argues, one can give an account of many kinds of thing in terms of worlds and their relationships—properties, causes, meanings, and even thoughts. So there is no good objection to Lewis to be obtained from these abstract principles of parsimony. Instead we need to look for ways in which his position conflicts with our ordinary beliefs.

One ground for disquiet arises from the fact that Lewis's theory implies that whatever might be the case is really the case. Thus if there might be some blue swans, then there is a world in which there are some, and since whatever happens in some world really happens, it follows that there really are some blue swans. Hence the common-sense belief, that although there are no blue swans there might be some, has to be interpreted as a belief which just concerns the actual world, that there are no blue swans here. This does not seem right; but metaphysics often demands subtle revisions of common sense, so this point cannot be decisive. A more worrying revision arises from Lewis's dependence upon counterparts to capture essentialist thought. Consider the resentment the victim of an attack feels towards their assailant: an important element of this is the belief that the assailant could have acted otherwise. For Lewis this belief just affirms the existence of a world in which a counterpart of the assailant acted differently. Yet the existence of such a world seems irrelevant to the victim's resentment, which is directed at the person who attacked him. The fact that in another world someone suitably similar to his assailant acted otherwise has no intuitive connection with the victim's feelings concerning his actual assailant.

But the main barrier to acceptance of Lewis's theory is that the theory seems to imply that we have no good reasons for our beliefs about what is possible or impossible. According to Lewis, these beliefs concern the details of worlds that are altogether separate from the actual world. Yet, as Lewis's theory also implies, the actual world is the only world of which we have any experience. So how can we have good reasons for these beliefs about other worlds? Traditional theorists appeal to a priori reasoning (as in mathematics) as one important source of modal knowledge, and despite the complications associated with Quine's scepticism about the analytic and the a priori (cf. Chapter 4, pp. 87–90) and with Kripke's arguments discussed earlier (which, of course, Lewis will in some respects qualify), this source still seems hard to abandon. But it is unclear how Lewis can invoke such reasonings: for how can reasoning alone provide us with reliable information about the structure of worlds that are as real as this world? Given Lewis's theory, such reasoning seems comparable to a priori astronomy or history.

As a guide to what possibilities there are Lewis in fact advances a principle of recombination, to the effect that duplicates of the parts of one world coexist with duplicates of parts of other worlds to form further worlds. Given our ordinary beliefs about what is possible or impossible, one can indeed see the point of this principle: but it is still proper to ask how, in the light of Lewis's modal realist theory, we can have good reason to accept it. Lewis's response is to suggest that we should adapt our epistemology to his position and accept that we can have quasi-inductive knowledge of other worlds. This is hard to swallow, but it raises the question: are there any defensible alternatives to Lewis's position which are not vulnerable to a similar objection?

Modal Fictions

If one rejects realism about possibilities, one will be an 'anti-realist' of some kind concerning them: one will hold that reality is exhausted by the actual world, and that non-actual worlds are unreal. There are many ways to develop this further, but I shall concentrate on a position according to which these unreal worlds are 'fictional'. In the case of straightforward fictions, such as the adventures of Sherlock Holmes, the actual world contains the writings of Arthur Conan-Doyle about Sherlock Holmes, and we do not think it necessary to suppose that in addition to the actual world there is another equally real world of which Sherlock Holmes and Dr Watson are parts. In treating possibilities as fictional, therefore, one holds that they are like stories: the actual world contains real representations of these possibilities, but it is not necessary to suppose that what is thus represented, the possibility itself, is also real but non-actual.

Unlike stories, however, possibilities do not need linguistic representations. Instead they are best represented in a 'Lagadonian' fashion (to use Lewis's nice phrase, which recalls Swift's fiction in *Gulliver's Travels*) whereby objects and properties represent themselves, and possible states of affairs are represented by sequences of properties and objects, which can be assumed to exist if the properties and objects do. Thus the possibility of my living in London will be represented by the sequence of myself, London, and the relation of living in. Possibilities which involve the existence of a non-actual object, such as a son I might have fathered, are represented by sequences which represent the instantiation of properties which this object would have instantiated—the property of being a male human child and of being fathered by me; and by further similar considerations one can make a reasonable case for the view that this Lagadonian method of representation provides representations of all possibilities (though this point is disputed).

For the fictionalist, the actual world is distinguished from all other worlds precisely by not being fictional: it is represented by the totality of Lagadonian representations which represent actual states of affairs. Non-actual worlds are by contrast fictional: they are represented by similar totalities, but in some respect the states of affairs represented within these totalities are non-actual. But there is an important further constraint on these totalities: the representations they include must be consistent—a totality which includes representations of me at noon GMT on 1 January 2000 in York UK, and at the same time in New York USA does not represent a possible world. So possible worlds are possibilities represented by totalities of consistent representations (this is of course another point where stories diverge from possible worlds).

The resulting position is one which fits with Kripkean orthodoxy, at least in respect of the thesis of the necessity of identity. For since objects represent themselves a Lagadonian representation of the distinctness of a and b is just the sequence comprising distinctness, a and b; so if a and b are in fact one and the same, then this representation is equally a representation of the distinctness of a from itself; but this is inconsistent. There, is, nonetheless, a slight terminological shift from the

Kripkean position, in that the fictionalist position is that possible truth is truth according to some consistent representation of a world, rather than truth in some possible world. If one wants one can reinterpret these representations of worlds as surrogate possible worlds and thereby preserve the traditional definition of possible truth as truth in some world. But this reinterpretation undermines the rationale for the talk of representations of worlds in the first place; so I prefer the fictionalist idiom which distinguishes unreal possibilities from real representations of them.

Whatever option one takes, however, the position depends on the notion of consistency. Since representations are consistent where what they represent is possible, this dependence implies that the anti-realist position does not offer an analysis of possibility: hence, as Lewis puts it, according to the anti-realist modality is 'primitive'. By contrast, Lewis holds that his account of possibility does not involve any similar 'primitive' modality, since he analyses possibility in terms of what obtains in some world and his account of worlds as spatio-temporally unified wholes does not depend on any assumptions concerning what is, or is not, possible. One might object that his account draws on the possibility of a merely possible world. But on the face of it this would be a misapprehension: for worlds which are merely possible are simply not the actual world, and this is not a modal conception at all.

Thus according to Lewis there is a trade-off between the theoretical merits of his realist position which provides a reductive metaphysical analysis of possibility in terms of worlds, and the greater intuitiveness of anti-realist positions which respect our common-sense convictions without providing the same theoretical simplification since they have to assume possibility instead of analysing it (Lewis also argues that there are technical deficiencies inherent in anti-realist strategies, but these arguments are disputed). Apparent trade-offs of this kind are common in philosophical debate, and there is no abstract principle to which one can appeal to resolve them. Lewis holds that the balance of argument favours his own realist position; my own view is the opposite.

This is partly because of the epistemological difficulty which I identified earlier, though this only counts against Lewis if anti-realist positions are not in principle vulnerable to a similar difficulty. So far as I can see, they are not: on the contrary, with their commitment to primitive modality but to no special metaphysics of modality beyond that, anti-realists are in a position to draw on whatever plausible reasons there are for modal beliefs. This is not the place to argue the point, but it seems to me that despite the empirical necessities discussed earlier, there are defensible a priori arguments for necessary truths on which anti-realists can draw; equally, there is every reason for them to allow also for natural, empirical, impossibilities of the kind which our everyday experience of causality reveals to us.

My other reason for rejecting Lewis's position is that I believe that his account does involve primitive modality. The way to uncover this is to ask whether there might be worlds other than those which there are. If it is allowed that there might be, then the thesis that something is possible if it is true in a world is not acceptable: for it implies that something is impossible because there are no worlds in which it is true, even though there might be worlds in which it is true. The way to avoid this consequence is to hold that for worlds mere possibility suffices for existence; but then the existence of a world turns out to depend on its possibility. So there is after all a 'primitive modality' at work in the background of Lewis's realist theory; in which case the main reason he offers for preferring it to its anti-realist rivals is undermined.

Despite my eventual disagreement with Lewis, however, I have nothing but admiration for the way in which, by challenging orthodoxy, he has forced philosophers to think through again the implications of their talk of possibility and necessity. If I am right, there remains more to be said on this topic by way of elucidation of 'primitive modality'. But those who are anti-realists concerning possibilities must accept that there is no way to turn the clock back and banish talk of possible worlds from philosophical discourse.

7

The Scientific Paradigm

The influence on English-language philosophy of the arrival of the logical empiricists from central Europe during the 1930s was especially marked in the area of philosophical reflection upon science, particularly with respect to the natural sciences. There was, of course, a long tradition of philosophy of science in Britain and North America, which in the nineteenth century had included major works by William Whewell (1794–1866), J. S. Mill (1806–73) and C. S. Peirce (1839–1914). Within this tradition the philosophy of science was generally conceived as a branch of applied philosophy, involving the application of empiricist or rationalist principles to the critical assessment of scientific claims. But the logical empiricists took it that the extraordinary achievements of early twentieth-century physics necessitated a new 'scientific world-conception', which included a new conception of philosophy as nothing more than the analytical logic of science (cf. Chapter 1, p. 6). This puritanical conception of philosophy did not survive long, but the debates to which it gave rise concerning the logic of science provide the starting point for subsequent, post-World War II discussion in the philosophy of science.

The Three-sided Debate

In this discussion there have been three main positions: (i) the logical empiricist position which Carnap, Hempel, and others brought with them from Vienna and then refined after World War II in the United States; (ii) the 'critical rationalist' position which Sir Karl Popper (1902– 94) also first presented in Vienna and then refined after World War II in London; (iii) the 'historicist' position of the American historian and philosopher of science, Thomas Kuhn (1922–96). The logical empiricist position received its classic formulation in essays by Hempel which were collected in his volume *Aspects of Scientific Explanation* (1965). Popper's major work, *The Logic of Scientific Discovery*, was first published in Vienna in 1934, but its main period of influence dates from the publication of an English translation with substantial additions in 1959, when it caught the attention of the scientific community at large. Kuhn's classic work, *The Structure of Scientific Revolutions*, was published in 1962. It was the last in a series of volumes, intended to comprise 'The International Encyclopaedia of Unified Science', founded in the late 1930s by the Viennese logical empiricists themselves. Significantly, however, the background to Kuhn's work is not Viennese; instead he acknowledges the influence of the writings of the great French historians and philosophers of science of the early twentieth century, especially Emile Meyerson (1859–1933) and Alexander Koyré (1892–1964).

For the logical empiricists, the main aim of science is explanation, and a good explanation of a phenomenon is one that would have enabled the phenomenon to be predicted. Deductive logic plays an essential part in these predictive explanations, for predictions are supposed to be justified when they are logically deducible from the combination of a general theory concerning phenomena of some type (e.g. the solubility of various substances) and data which describe some particular situation to which the theory applies (e.g. the immersion in water of a chemical compound). Hence when things are found not to be as they were predicted to be, and the data has been checked, it should follow logically that the theory is refuted. Equally, when things are observed to be as they were predicted to be, the logical empiricists held that scientists are entitled to regard their predictive explanations as inductively confirmed. So the logic of science is a combination of the deductive refutation of theories whose empirical implications are falsified by observation and the inductive confirmation of theories whose empirical implications are verified.

The distinctive feature of Popper's critical rationalism is his denial that successful predictions confirm a theory which has given rise to them. For Popper this inductive inference is just a case of the notorious logical fallacy of 'affirming the consequent', of arguing from the truth of a consequence of some hypothesis to the truth of the hypothesis itself (supporters of inductive inference will respond that this criticism wrongly imputes to them the view that inductive inference is a form of deductive inference). Thus for Popper the logic of science is exclusively the deductive logic of empirical refutation. This logical *via negativa* is, however, too minimal to be a complete account of science; so Popper adds that theories are 'corroborated' where they have survived attempted refutations, and that scientists are entitled to hold that the better corroborated a theory is, the more it approximates to the truth. Corroboration so conceived is therefore a central element of the 'quasi-inductive' path of science (*Logic of Scientific Discovery*, p. 276). Nonetheless, the disagreement with logical empiricism remains: for Popper the progress of science consists not in the refinement of unrefuted theories which are ever more strongly confirmed as more predictions made on their basis are verified, but in the replacement of refuted theories by theories which are corroborated only by the failure so far of attempts to refute them. According to Popper, in science we learn primarily from our mistakes.

Kuhn's historicism starts from the claim that the logical conception of empirical refutation that Popper and the logical empiricists share lacks straightforward application. This is not because Kuhn disputes the elementary logic of falsification, i.e. that, given not-B and if A then B, one can infer not-A. Rather he observes that, given Duhem's recognition of the role of auxiliary hypotheses in connecting theory to observation (see Chapter 4, p. 71), this pattern of inference cannot be straightforwardly applied to the assessment of scientific theories. In the schema above, if 'B' is to follow logically from 'A', then 'A' will have to include these extra hypotheses along with the relevant theory and data. So unsuccessful predictions do not by themselves refute a theory; one can always blame an erroneous auxiliary hypothesis instead for the failure. Hence, Kuhn infers, logic and observation alone are too blunt for an understanding of scientific reasoning, and to get a better picture one must look to its history. What one finds there is a pattern of alternating activity: sciences alternate between periods of 'normal science', which is the cumulative application of a successful theory to the study of nature, and periods of 'crisis' followed by 'revolution' when an old theory breaks down irreparably and a radically new one takes its place. In effect, therefore, according to Kuhn, scientific thought alternates between periods for which the logical empiricist account is appropriate and periods for which the Popperian account is to be preferred. But to understand and assess the ways in which this takes place, Kuhn argues, one has to understand the contribution made by the judgements of the scientists themselves; so the philosophy of science has to engage with the history of science.

Before discussing the details of this three-way debate, a couple of preliminary points should be made. The first concerns a distinction made by the logical empiricists between the 'context of discovery' of a scientific hypothesis and the 'context of justification' for it. The point of this distinction is that, according to the logical empiricists, one would commit the fallacy of 'sociologism', of thinking that whatever the scientific community judges to be right is right, if one sought to derive critical principles concerning the justification for scientific belief from descriptions of the ways in which scientists make their discoveries. Instead these principles arise within the 'context of justification' and are the proper business of the philosopher seeking to elucidate the logic of science. As we have seen, the logical empiricists and Popper have different accounts of the logical principles appropriate for this context of justification. But the point to be grasped now is that Kuhn does not offer yet a third set of logical principles; instead his claim is that a proper account of the justification of science involves reference to its history and thus to the context of discovery. To his critics this sounds like sociologism. But Kuhn maintains that questions of justification cannot be separated from those of discovery, and thus that there is no absolute distinction between the two 'contexts'.

The second point concerns the emphasis here on the natural sciences. This arises largely because the philosophers whose work I am discussing have themselves concentrated on questions concerning these sciences. During the post-1945 period there have of course also been important debates concerning the status of the social sciences; but most of the important contributions to these debates have been made by French and German theorists, especially concerning the interpretation and assessment of Marx's writings, and not only are these not achievements of English-speaking philosophers, they have not yet penetrated English-language philosophy in the way in which the work of the previous generation of German-speaking exiles from Central Europe did.

Popper and Logical Empiricism

I return now to the debate between the logical empiricists and Popper concerning the logic of science. As I have indicated, the value of inductive inference was the central theme of this debate: the logical empiricists held that the truth of an explanatory theory is supported by the success of predictions made on its basis, whereas Popper held that the main thing to be learnt from a successful prediction was just that this observation did not provide a refutation of the theory. This difference connects with a further disagreement concerning the aims of scientific inquiry: whereas the logical empiricists held that the establishment on inductive grounds of merely probable truth is a legitimate goal of scientific inquiry, Popper maintained that no such inductive probability of truth exists.

When one thinks of the role of scientific inquiry in fields such as medicine and engineering, it is hard to question the role of inductive inference in justifying belief and practice. It might appear that Popper's conception of a well-corroborated theory which has survived several attempts to refute it provides the basis for an alternative non-inductive justification. But if this corroboration is taken to provide a justification for belief and practice, then Popper's 'quasi-inductive' method of corroboration is just a form of inductive confirmation. In fact, however, Popper was not much interested in the justification of belief and practice; he writes instead of the scientist's 'recklessly critical *quest* for truth' (*The Logic of Scientific Discovery*, p. 281). This may be appropriate when one is thinking of a speculative theoretical science such as astrophysics; but when we want advice as to which drug offers the best protection from malaria, or what design for a bridge will best withstand high winds, we do not want unrefuted but recklessly bold hypotheses; we want advice with the highest probability of truth.

Popper's anti-inductive polemic is, therefore, misguided. Some of his points can, nonetheless, be interpreted as sound criticisms of over-simple methods of inductive inference. For example, successful prediction does not always provide much support for a hypothesis: finding more and more black ravens does little to increase the probability of the hypothesis that they are all black. Instead, the hypothesis will be supported much more by finding that it applies in a variety of different situations, and the process of verifying that this is the case will not differ significantly from that of failing to refute it by testing it in these situations. Popperian corroboration is indeed a good method of inductive confirmation.

Logical empiricists can readily incorporate this point in an account of the relative merits of different types of inductive inference. But there is a type of inductive inference which is more problematic for them—'inference to the best explanation'. This familiar type of inference is exemplified by the inference from some observed symptoms of ill-health to the hypothesis concerning the underlying disease which best explains the observed symptoms. The difficulty here for the logical empiricists is that their deductive conception of explanation implies that explanation is symmetrical with prediction, so that for them inferences of this kind turn out to be just inferences from successful predictions, which, as we have seen, do not always add much support to a hypothesis. So, although the logical empiricists were surely right to include inductive inference in their account of the logic of science, in this respect at least their purely deductive conception of explanation precluded them from providing a satisfactory account of it. I shall return to this point at the end of this chapter.

Popper's criticisms of inductive inference are part of his criticism of the empiricism of the logical empiricists, and this general theme is further developed in another, more cogent, line of argument. This concerns the view of the logical empiricists that the predictions whose success or failure confirm or refute a theory should be couched in an 'observation-language' whose meaning is independent of scientific theory so that its understanding can provide the basis for understanding the meaning of theoretical terms. In the writings of the logical empiricists this view was closely allied to a sceptical attitude concerning the ontological status of the unobservable things postulated by scientific theories. It was suggested that these things are to be thought of primarily as fictions with a status comparable to that of the epicycles of Ptolemaic astronomy, and that theories which include apparent reference to them should be regarded merely as 'instruments', i.e. as calculating devices constructed to facilitate predictions formulated in the observation-language.

In advancing this 'instrumentalist' position the logical empiricists were no doubt influenced by the account of theoretical physics put forward in the late 1920s by Nils Bohr and Werner Heisenberg (the 'Copenhagen interpretation'), according to which the only way to understand the strange formalisms of quantum mechanics is by working out its implications for macroscopic, and hence observable, phenomena. Nonetheless, Popper firmly rejected the instrumentalist position in favour of the 'realist' view that the ontological status of the unobservable things and properties postulated by scientific theories (e.g. genes as postulated by Mendel or quarks today) is not intrinsically different from that of ordinary, observable, things and properties. In support of this he argued that the observations and experiments which actually test scientific theories are not independent of scientific theory; hence the logical empiricist's belief that science can be reconstructed on the basis of a pure observation-language is untenable. In which case, he argued, it must also be wrong to regard theories simply as calculating instruments constructed to facilitate predictions expressed in such a language and equally wrong to regard the things and properties postulated by these theories as mere fictions.

This conclusion seems right, though one needs to allow for theories which explicitly employ such fictions as perfectly elastic spheres in order to facilitate calculations. More generally, however, given the vagueness of the distinction between the observable and the unobservable once real instruments such as electron microscopes are taken into account, it seems altogether misplaced to use this distinction as a basis for an ontological distinction between what 'really' exists and what is a mere 'fiction'.

The Kuhnian Revolution

I shall return to the issue of 'scientific realism', but it is now time to assess the challenge to Popper and the logical empiricists which arises from the arguments advanced by Kuhn and Paul Feyerabend (1924–94), who was another critic of the logical empiricist tradition, though with a different positive programme from that proposed by Kuhn. Kuhn and Feyerabend argue that once the myth of a pure observation-language has been abandoned, and the complexities implied by Duhem's thesis are acknowledged, refutation of a scientific hypothesis cannot proceed in the way envisaged by Popper and the logical empiricists. Without a neutral observation-language there will often be ways of arguing that a putative counter-example said to have been observed was not observed at all; and even if it is accepted that it was observed, its falsifying significance can be rejected by rejecting some of the background auxiliary hypotheses involved in connecting the hypothesis with what has been observed. According to Kuhn and Feyerabend, therefore, one cannot just confront a theory with 'the observed facts', for the identity of these facts and the significance of any such confrontation is radically underdetermined.

Both Popper and Carnap had in fact already acknowledged that the assessment of scientific hypotheses is underdetermined by experience and inferred that there is therefore an inescapable role for decision and convention in scientific method. Popper stressed the importance of decisions concerning the significance of particular observations:

Science does not rest upon a solid bedrock. The bold structure of its theories rises, as it were, above a swamp. It is like a building erected on piles. . . . We simply stop when we are satisfied that the piles are strong enough to carry the structure, at least for the time being. (*The Logic of Scientific Discovery*, p. 111)

Carnap, by contrast, had stressed the importance of the analytic conventions which separate off background assumptions from the 'internal' questions that can then be treated as unproblematically empirical. These conventions can be challenged, but when they are, they give rise to 'external' questions that challenge the methods of inquiry (cf. Chapter 4, p. 75).

These are both fair points, but so far from providing materials for a response to Kuhn and Feyerabend, they imply that a proper account of the rationality of science needs to incorporate a recognition of the role of decisions and conventions in the assessment of scientific hypotheses alongside that of logic and empirical inquiry; and it is precisely this recognition which Kuhn seeks to articulate. The central concept of Kuhn's discussion is that of a 'paradigm', and the term has now entered common usage in a way which draws on Kuhn's use of it in *The Structure of Scientific Revolutions*. As he later acknowledged, however, Kuhn here uses this term in two main ways (though one critic alleged that he used it in twenty-one senses!). In one use, drawing on its root meaning as a standard example, he uses it to denote a experiment, technique or calculation that is characteristic of a general type of theory (such as Newton's use of a spectrum in his investigations of light or his derivation of Kepler's laws from his inverse square law of gravitation). But he also uses the term to denote the informal background assumptions, conventions and language which scientists acquire through their education and training and which are needed in order to focus their inquiries. In order to disambiguate the term, I shall call paradigms of this second kind 'disciplinary paradigms', as opposed to the 'exemplary paradigms' described earlier.

For Kuhn it is only when a disciplinary paradigm is established within some field of inquiry that serious science is possible. This is because the disciplinary paradigm, while providing a language within which distinctions can be drawn and calculations made, solves the problem of empirical underdetermination by tacitly restricting the range of possibilities to be considered if a prediction is unsuccessful. If, in practice, there is no great cacophony of conflicting beliefs despite the empirical underdetermination of theory, this is because of the role of a shared disciplinary paradigm. Hence, as Kuhn says, while such a paradigm is in place, the business of 'normal science' proceeds in a generally cumulative manner which largely fits with the account provided by the logical empiricists of confirmation by successful prediction. The only catch is that because success here is largely a matter of the extended application of a disciplinary paradigm that is not called into question, it is not a case of fitting one's theory to the facts, but of fitting nature to one's theory (e.g. by 'mapping' the human genome in the light of the current disciplinary paradigm that guides molecular genetics).

Kuhn holds that the disciplinary paradigms which guide normal science are rather like stars which consume themselves as they give off energy: the paradigms eventually use up their capacity to solve empirical puzzles, and when this happens recalcitrant measurements and other anomalous observations are liable to build up. At this stage the disciplinary paradigm begins to lose its grip and the scientific discipline enters a 'crisis' from which it emerges only when, after a 'revolutionary' period, a new disciplinary paradigm is established. Given the thesis of the underdetermination of theory by logic and observation alone, it follows that when a disciplinary paradigm which has for a time provided for empirical determinacy collapses, the nature of scientific activity is liable to change: there may be a period when there is a cacophony of alternatives, as Kuhn holds that there was at the end of the nineteenth century when it became apparent that classical physics just could not accommodate the new phenomena being discovered (X-rays, photons etc.). According to Kuhn, however, this period is not likely to be particularly fruitful until a new disciplinary paradigm is established which, by providing for empirical determinacy again, makes it possible for serious normal science to proceed.

Incommensurability and Procedural Rationality

A central question raised by Kuhn's position is that of the reasons available in a revolutionary situation to support the adoption of a theory which leads to the development of a new disciplinary paradigm. The issue here has become famous as the challenge of the 'incommensurability' thesis: Kuhn and Feyerabend hold that new theories are likely to be 'incommensurable' with old ones in the sense that there is no uncontested body of evidence which the new theory demonstrably fits better than the old one. That kind of comparison is typically possible only within normal science where there is a stable set of background conventions about the significance of observations. Without these conventions, and in the absence of a neutral observation language in which the relevant evidence can be formulated, defenders of an old paradigm may simply not recognize the validity of new kinds of evidence. In which case, those engaged in a fundamental scientific dispute during a crisis cannot engage with each other in sustained argument without drawing on assumptions which are in dispute.

Feyerabend gives as an instance of this the debate between Galileo and traditionalists such as Cardinal Bellarmine concerning the hypothesis of the Earth's motion. On the one hand, Galileo adduced the observations he had made with his telescope, such as those of the phases of Venus, which he took to imply that Venus revolves around the Sun in the way in which the Moon revolves around the Earth, and thus to support the hypothesis that the Earth also revolves around the Sun. But Bellarmine was not much impressed by this since he could readily question the significance of Galileo's alleged observations with his telescope, a new-fangled device whose workings were not then well understood, even by Galileo. On the other hand, Bellarmine pointed to the fact that when a stone is dropped from a tower it falls directly to the base of the tower, which he took to imply that the tower, and thus the Earth, is not moving. But Galileo responded to this by pointing out that if the person dropping the stone were moving along with the tower one would still expect the stone to fall to the base of the tower, in the way in which a stone dropped from the top of the mast of a moving ship falls to the base of the mast.

This case exemplifies Kuhn's metaphor that there is a 'gestalt switch' when one switches from an old paradigm to a new theory (the comparison is with switches in the visual recognition of shape—*gestalt*— which psychologists such as Wolfgang Köhler had brought to attention in the 1930s with their ambiguous figures). Coming to appreciate the significance of Galileo's discussion of relative motion, and thus learning to think of oneself whirling around in space (relative to the sun) along with all one's earthly surroundings, is performing a gestalt switch concerning the apparent stability of the Earth. Kuhn famously added to this metaphor the thought that 'though the world does not change with a change of paradigm, the scientist afterwards works in a different world' (*The Structure of Scientific Revolutions*, p. 121). Clearly, two senses of the word 'world' are in play here: on the first occasion of its use, Kuhn is talking about the world as it is 'in itself', with things and properties which are not dependent on our ways of thinking about them; on the second occasion, however, the conception of the world is the world in which the scientist works and lives; it is the world as the scientist believes it to be, which does alter once the scientist's beliefs change radically.

As such Kuhn's claim essentially concerns the psychological significance of a scientific revolution; but it has often been interpreted as implying a further relativist thesis. This cannot be a form of metaphysical relativism, since the world in itself is said not to change with a change of paradigm. Instead the thesis said to be implied must be a form of epistemological relativism, that where there is incommensurability of evidence there are two (or more) ways of thinking about some subject-matter with different merits and defects which cannot be ranked in a non-arbitrary fashion. This thesis is indeed suggested by Kuhn's gestaltist metaphor. For in standard cases a gestalt switch occurs where a perceived figure is genuinely ambiguous and can be seen in two equally good ways. So the metaphor suggests that wherever there is incommensurability there are two equally good ways of thinking, just as the epistemological relativist holds.

Someone who was, arguably, a relativist of this kind was Carnap, whose position, I observed earlier, can be regarded as an early version of Kuhn's: Carnap's conventional analytic rules are comparable to Kuhn's disciplinary paradigms and the contrast between internal and external questions closely resembles that between normal science and scientific revolutions. Carnap was always vulnerable to the charge of relativism because of the role of conventions in his position and, for a time, at any rate, he embraced this conclusion as his 'principle of tolerance', according to which 'in logic, there are no morals', i.e. there is no right or wrong—a principle which is to apply to systems of reasoning generally, including scientific theories. So the question is whether Kuhn embraces a similar conclusion, that 'in science, there are no morals'.

The answer to this lies with Kuhn's account of theory-choice. There are, he says, two primary criteria to guide choice:

First, the new candidate must seem to resolve some outstanding and generally recognised problem that can be met in no other way. Second, the new paradigm must promise to preserve a relatively large part of the concrete problem-solving ability that has accrued to science through its predecessors. (*The Structure of Scientific Revolutions*, p. 169)

The rationale for these criteria is obvious: if a new theory is to resolve the crisis engendered by the collapse of an old paradigm it must somehow get around most of the problems which gave rise to the crisis; and yet it must equally preserve the 'concrete' merits of the old paradigm, typically by showing that much of the old theory is in some sense approximately true. These criteria are, however, indecisive; they yield no 'neutral-algorithm for theory-choice' (*The Structure of Scientific Revolutions*, p. 200). In order to give an account of their application, therefore, we have to have recourse to the judgement of the scientific community:

In particular, confronted with the problem of theory-choice, the structure of my response runs roughly as follows: take a *group* of the ablest available people with the most appropriate motivation; train them in some science and in the specialities relevant to the choice at hand; imbue them with the value system, the ideology, current in their discipline . . . and, finally, *let them make the choice*. If that technique does not account for scientific development as we know it, then no other will. ('Reflections on my Critics', pp. 237–8; Kuhn's italics)

It is passages such as this which have raised the ire of Kuhn's critics. They take him to be saying that the rational choice of theory is simply that which is made by the current scientific community, and thus that scientific development or progress is simply the record of the choices made by the dominant community at the time. So a philosophy of science which seeks to understand and critically assess the rationality of science can, in the end, do no more than describe the historical sociology of science. Such a position does indeed amount to a form of epistemological relativism.

Despite Kuhn's acknowledgement that his position is 'intrinsically sociological' ('Reflections on my Critics', p. 238), I take it that it is more complex than these critics recognize. I think the way to understand

Kuhn's position is to compare it with a position which has been famil-iar in ethical theory from Aristotle onwards: sometimes the best way to specify the right thing to do in a complex situation in which there are bound to be conflicting considerations is to specify an ideal procedure for reaching a decision. Obvious examples of this are contracts and other agreements between people: in these cases what makes the terms right was that they have been arrived at by a fair procedure, and there may well be no way of saying in the abstract, without reference to the procedure, what it would have been right for the parties involved to have accepted. The same point applies to some personal decisions: suppose someone has to choose between two very different possible careers, both of which fit reasonably well with their antecedent abilities and interests. Here too, the right decision is that which is the outcome of informed and sensible deliberation, and it is a mistake (though a common enough illusion) to suppose that there was a right answer to be found independent of this process of deliberation. That the pro-cedure was followed properly in these cases is integral to the rightness of the result.

Kuhn's invocation of a role for the judgement of the scientific com-munity in assessing whether the adoption of a new theory was rational is, I suggest, to be seen in the light of this procedural conception of rationality. If this is right, then Kuhn is not the relativist critic of scien-tific rationality that his critics suggest. Instead his thesis is that because logic and empirical observation underdetermine the choice of theory there is an inescapable procedural element to scientific rationality, involving an appeal to the judgement exercised by a scientific com-munity which understands and is committed to the general ideals of scientific inquiry, such as those given in his own two primary criteria for theory-choice. This position can be compared with Wittgenstein's account of the role of the community in resolving the apparent scep-tical paradox thrown up by the rule-following considerations (Chapter 2, pp. 22–5). In both cases there is a recognition that explicit rules do not suffice to answer all questions, and that the possibility of objective truth depends upon agreement in judgement within the relevant community.

Feyerabend has objected that this position prescribes greater scientific consensus than is either necessary or desirable. He argues that whereas Kuhn's picture is one according to which scientific inquiry flourishes only where there is just one dominant disciplinary paradigm within a scientific discipline, science will in fact flourish best when there is a proliferation of different paradigms. This is his method of 'epistemological anarchism', vigorously advanced in his book *Against Method* (1975). It can be seen as a variation on the position of Kuhn's Popperian critics, who hold that the true ideals of scientific inquiry are realized during periods of 'revolutionary' activity when there is no established paradigm, though they have a different political metaphor for their position: borrowing Trotsky's idiom, they advocate 'permanent revolution'.

The substantive question here is whether a procedural conception of scientific rationality is best developed in the context of the anarchist pluralism that Feyerabend and Popper envisage, both of whom commend J. S. Mill's defence of free speech in his essay *On Liberty* as a sketch of the ideal framework for scientific inquiry, or whether, as Kuhn implies, it is only when there is a consensus concerning the disciplinary paradigm appropriate to a given scientific discipline that fruitful inquiry can proceed.

One can easily think of practical reasons for Kuhn's position: scientists working with the same disciplinary paradigm will be able to collaborate and criticize each other, whereas discussion across paradigms is bound to be precarious in the light of the incommensurability thesis. But I think one can use the moral of Davidson's discussion of the possibility of alternative conceptual schemes (cf. Chapter 5, pp. 104–6) to resolve the issue here. Since all truths are consistent, the truths expressed by scientists using apparently different paradigms must either be such that each scientist can in fact capture them within an extended version of their own paradigm, so that what were supposed to be different paradigms turn out to be capable of unification, or else they must be such that they concern different radically domains, or matters of fact, where the same paradigm need not apply. Thus a pluralism of disciplinary paradigms (conceptual schemes, language games) can co-exist alongside the presumption that for each domain just one paradigm is appropriate.

The conception of procedural rationality is also the key to under-standing the way in which Kuhn seeks to blur the logical empiricists' distinction between the contexts of justification and discovery. For on the one hand, the specification of the role of the ideal scientific com-munity belongs within the context of justification; but, on the other, where that role is played by some actual scientific community which meets the standards for rational theory-choice, its actual choice deter-mines what it is then rational to accept. So scientific rationality is fully specified only within the context of discovery. Kuhn is not committed by this position to the Hegelian aphorism that 'all that is real, is rational' (he is, among other things, a historian of the Copernican revo-lution in astronomy and thus of the attempt by the Catholic Church to suppress the Copernican hypothesis). Nonetheless, he is committed to the view that there is an ineliminable historical contribution to be made to the understanding of scientific rationality—a claim which he set out with startling boldness in the famous first sentence of *The Structure of Scientific Revolutions*:

History, if viewed as a repository for more than anecdote or chronology, could produce a decisive transformation in the image of science by which we are now possessed. (p. 1)

Scientific Realism and the Pessimistic Meta-induction

Yet there is still a worry here, which is engendered not so much by the role of procedural rationality as by the memory of past scientific revolu-tions. It was part of the logical empiricist conception of science that a new theory should be able to explain what was right about the theory it replaced. But where the replacement of a theory marks a scientific revo-lution, it is not clear how such an explanation is to be provided, despite Kuhn's requirement that the new theory preserve the problem-solving ability of the theory it replaces. For if the theories are radically different, no part of the old theory itself will be logically deducible from the new one; on the contrary, the new theory will imply that the concepts employed in the old one were fundamentally mistaken in some respects. The resulting anxiety has been nicely captured by the contemporary philosopher Larry Laudan as 'the pessimistic meta-induction': if we reflect on the history of science, we cannot but be impressed by the fact that theories and the broader disciplinary paradigms associated with them in all fields of science have been shown to be mistaken. So it takes only a modest degree of humility to expect that current theories and paradigms will suffer the same fate. Hence, however rational science may be, it cannot legitimately represent itself as a way of securing true beliefs in the way in which scientific realism requires.

This is a somewhat paradoxical argument: the conclusion is broadly Popperian, but the argument is inductive. One intuitive response to it is that the success of contemporary science gives us good reason to take it to be true. Here is the great American physicist Richard Feynman describing the success of quantum electrodynamics:

experiments have Dirac's number (the measure of an electron's magnetic moment) at 1.00115965221 ... the theory puts it at 1.00115965246 ... To give you a feeling for the accuracy of these numbers, it comes to something like this: If you were to measure the distance from Los Angeles to New York to this accuracy, it would be exact to the thickness of a human hair. (*QED: The Strange Theory of Light and Matter*, p. 7)

Yet despite astounding successes such as this, the example of classical physics serves as a potent warning. Here was a theory which was, by the standards of its time, just as astoundingly successful as quantum electrodynamics is today. Furthermore, unlike quantum electrodynamics it was intuitively intelligible—so much so that some philosophers tried to show that it could not turn out to be wrong. And yet it did turn out to be wrong—wrong about the structure of space and time, about the structure of matter, and about the fundamental forces of the universe. So only hubris can inhibit an expectation that contemporary physics faces a similar fate.

But of course, classical physics is still taught and practised: for contemporary theory implies that its laws provide a very good approximation to the truth where one is dealing with things whose speed is low relative to the speed of light, and since its equations are much simpler than those of quantum electrodynamics, there is every reason to use them where they provide all the accuracy one needs (e.g. when constructing a space rocket). This case is typical: where a theory is successful in some domain there is good reason to think it is getting something 'roughly right' in that domain. So can we respond to Laudan's pessimism by saying that although the history of science shows that present success is no guarantee of the absolute truth of contemporary theory, it does give good reason for holding that contemporary theory is roughly true?

I think we can, but the response needs to be clarified in two crucial respects—concerning the notions of 'rough truth' and 'success'. The notion of rough truth here cannot be simply modelled on that of a measurement which is approximately true. For that would imply that old theories can be viewed as successive approximations towards a truth which lies somewhere extrapolated beyond present theory—as if what happens when old theories are replaced by new ones is primarily a matter of the refinement of some laws and calculations to take account of newly discovered disturbing forces. But that is the old cumulative account of science which does not take account of the existence of scientific revolutions. Instead the 'rough truth' of an old theory has to be understood in a way which is compatible with its fundamental falsehood.

We can make a start at a better account by reintroducing the conception of what is observable. In order that an old theory be roughly true it must be possible to reinterpret its predictions concerning observable phenomena in such a way that, according to current theory, they are approximately true within the domain which comprises the situations to which the old theory was standardly applied (while excluding situations which have been only subsequently investigated, such as the extremely small, distant, cold, etc.). An element of reinterpretation will typically be required here because the concepts employed in the two theories will typically differ; nonetheless, it should be possible to achieve a satisfactory interpretation by simplifying distinctions drawn in current theory which the old theory did not make.

By itself, however, this account of 'rough truth' is too thin: it does not add much to the thought that new theories should respect the predictive successes of old theories. To complete it, therefore, more needs to be said about what it is for a theory to be successful.

One part of success is of course predictive success; but what of explanatory success? For the logical empiricists, because of their deductive conception of explanation, this is just predictive success again. But I briefly mentioned earlier that this position is problematic, and it is now time to return to this matter. Intuitively, prediction is neither necessary nor sufficient for explanatory success: we are often able to explain after the event why a car accident has occurred even though we could not have predicted it; and we sometimes predict changes in the weather without being able to explain them. Further examination quickly reveals that the topic of explanation is full of complexities, e.g. concerning the nature of statistical explanations, the role of context in assessing explanations, and the grounds for the comparative evaluation of explanations. We do not need to pursue all these matters, important though they are: it suffices here to differentiate explanation from prediction by noting that prediction sometimes has a symmetry which explanation lacks. Thus, to take a famous case suggested by Sylvan Bromberger, where a vertical pole casts a shadow on the ground in the sunlight: one can predict the sun's direction from the position of the shadow and vice-versa. But one explains the position of the shadow by reference to the direction of the light from the sun, and not vice-versa. Why is this? A plausible suggestion advanced by Nancy Cartwright and Ian Hacking is that the notion of explanation incorporates a requirement that it should identify some feature, or set of them, which is causally responsible for the fact to be explained. Thus in this case, it is because the pole blocks out the sunlight that the shadow is where it is; it is not because the shadow is where it is that the sun is located in a certain direction.

Causal explanations draw on laws which connect changes in the properties of things. There are many types of such laws: but one common type specifies equilibrium conditions, and causal explanations which invoke them draw on the fact that the introduction of a disturbance into a set-up governed by such laws sets up a chain of changes until equilibrium is restored. In a case of this kind the last such change will typically be the phenomenon to be explained, and its explanation will consist in identifying the initial disturbance (perhaps a rise in temperature) which is 'the cause', and the laws which require subsequent changes, such as changes in volume and pressure, in order to restore equilibrium. Requiring that explanations of particular events be causal, therefore, requires setting that event in a context governed by causal laws and finding some initial cause which, in that context, leads in accordance with the laws to the effect to be explained. Explanations of properties, such as the explanation of the solubility of common salt in water, are not in the same way causal, for properties are not changes initiated by some cause. Instead, explanations here typically advert to laws connecting other more fundamental properties of the set-up; for example, in the case of explanations of solubility those connecting the energy input required to form an ionic lattice and that given out during hydration. In this case, therefore, the causal aspect of the explanation arises from the fact that it licenses straightforward causal explanations of relevant changes when they do occur—e.g. when some salt dissolves in water.

There is much more to be said about causal explanation; my aim here has only been to give some plausibility to the thesis that explanation in the natural sciences is causal and a full defence of this would require a proper discussion of functional explanation in biology which is, on the face of it, rather different. But suppose it be granted that explanation is standardly causal: then explanatory success will require more than predictive success; it will also require the identification of an underlying causal set-up, with causally relevant properties and laws connecting them. How is this to be done? In part, of course, by the usual method of conjecture and refutation; but there is no doubt that the ability to use causal hypotheses successfully in the design of experimental techniques and more generally within applied sciences enhances the support for them. For it is in this context that inductive inference to the best explanation is especially plausible: the causal hypotheses which have gone into the construction of some equipment provide the best explanation for why it works as it does (assuming of course that it does).

We can return now to the issue of the relation between the 'rough truth' of a theory and its success. Where an old theory enjoys explanatory success, this will typically be because it employs well-confirmed causal hypotheses. Hence, just as the rough truth of an old theory implied that its predictive merits should be accommodated in its successor, it is reasonable to add that its explanatory merits should also be accommodated, and thus that the well-confirmed causal hypotheses involved should also be captured from within the new theory. This is particularly obvious where the practical application of these causal hypotheses has been successful: the adoption of new theories in chemistry and physics cannot be seriously taken to imply that medicines, machines, chemical processes, etc. that work well have simply not been understood at all in the past. What is nonetheless to be expected is that at some more fundamental level the explanation for these causal hypotheses will itself alter completely, with, no doubt, consequential refinement of the concepts employed in stating these causal hypotheses. So here too the notion of 'rough truth' will need to be employed to capture the way in which old descriptions of causal processes need to be reinterpreted in the light of current theory. But once this is done, then nothing stands in the way of responding to Laudan's pessimistic meta-induction by affirming that where contemporary scientific theories enjoy predictive and explanatory success, we have good inductive reasons for thinking that subsequent theories will show that these theories are roughly true, even if they also show that these theories are also fundamentally mistaken in some respects.

8

Natural Doubts

A central concern of the previous chapter was how the claims to knowledge that are characteristic of the natural sciences are justified. But the issue of the validity of claims to knowledge does not just concern scientific knowledge: traditional sceptical arguments cast doubt on our ordinary claims to knowledge, and the issues they raise are among the most difficult and fundamental of philosophy, since the challenges they pose require us to reassess our self-image as rational beings, capable of giving reasons for what we believe to be true.

The Brain-in-a-vat

The most famous of traditional sceptical arguments is that grounded in Descartes' fiction of an 'evil genius' (*malin génie*) who is supposed to be capable of penetrating our minds so deeply that he can plant within us false beliefs about the things which strike us as most certain, such as the features of our immediate environment and the elementary truths of arithmetic. In contemporary philosophy this fiction has been updated by Hilary Putnam as the 'brain-in-a-vat' hypothesis that our minds are the minds of a brain suspended in a vat of suitably 'life'-preserving liquids with electrodes attached to neural inputs and outputs in such a way that a mad scientist with the right equipment can induce in it experiences, feelings, beliefs, etc. so that he can have it think whatever he chooses it to think—for example that it is now sitting reading a book about contemporary philosophy in English. The challenge that this poses to our ordinary self-consciousness will be obvious: for how are you to tell that you are not now the mind of such a brain? Any test you seek to give yourself (e.g. pinching your leg) can be assumed to be one whose successful accomplishment the mad scientist can replicate. But if you cannot tell that you are not the mind of a brain-in-a-vat, does this not show that you do not have the reasons for your belief that you are reading this book that you previously took yourself to have? Indeed that you do not know that you are doing any such thing?

There are many different ways of responding to this challenge to our confidence, including attempts to show that there is something illegitimate about the description of the brain-in-a-vat hypothesis in the first place. But before considering these responses it is important to recognize that there are other types of sceptical argument. One which has attracted a good deal of attention is the 'new riddle of induction' presented in 1955 by the American philosopher Nelson Goodman (1906–), who has been a colleague of Quine and Putnam at Harvard. Just as the brain-in-a-vat story is a development of Descartes' 'evil genius' story, Goodman's new riddle is a development of Hume's old riddle of induction, and it is worth saying a little about this first.

Hume's Riddle and Goodman's Paradox

Hume's argument concerns the reasons we have for our beliefs concerning the future. Since we do not now have evidence from the future itself, whatever reasons we have for our beliefs about the future are based on what we know about the past and present; but this knowledge only yields reasons for beliefs about the future if there is also reason to believe that what will happen in the future is suitably connected to the past. Hume therefore asks whether there is such a reason. As only a little reflection will reveal, it is very difficult to find a non-circular reason: the fact that, in the past, what was then still in the future was suitably connected to what was then already past only provides a reason for supposing that this connection will obtain in what is now the future if one takes it that what has happened in the past is a reason for supposing that the future will be similar—which is another instance of the belief for which we were seeking a reason.

Hume's argument is the basis of Popper's scepticism about induction which I discussed in the previous chapter. But Hume's attitude to induction is not Popper's: Hume thinks that we cannot avoid inductive inferences and should just get used to the idea that our basic ways of forming beliefs are natural habits for which we can give no non-circular reason. We shall come back later to this important type of response to sceptical arguments, but I want now to lay out Goodman's intriguing extension of Hume's argument.

Goodman focuses on the fact that in any inference from the past to the future we are dependent on the way in which the past has been described; for it is the past as thus described that we 'project' into the future. Thus Goodman's argument exemplifies a way in which here too considerations of language have an important role in philosophical argument, and Goodman's inventive way of imagining a new use of language to set up his argument has been widely copied. He starts from a pair of apparently uncontentious inductive inferences: because all the emeralds so far examined have been found to be green we expect that the next ones we examine will be green; similarly because all the sapphires so far examined have been found to be blue we expect the next ones we examine will be blue. But the facts which constitute the evidence here can also be described in a way which gives rise to quite different expectations. Suppose we introduce the terms 'grue' and 'bleen' as follows:

> At time t, x is *grue* if and only if: either (i) t is before 1 January 2010 and x is green: or (ii) t is on or after 1 January 2010 and x is blue.

> At time t, x is *bleen* if and only if: either (i) t is before 1 January 2010 and x is blue: or (ii) t is on or after 1 January 2010 and x is green.

Then all the emeralds so far examined have been found to be grue and all the sapphires bleen; so, following the same pattern of inductive inference, it seems that we should expect that emeralds examined in the future will be grue and that sapphires will be bleen. After 1 January 2010, however, this expectation conflicts with the expectation that they will then be respectively green and blue.

The immediate rejoinder to Goodman's paradox is that because the terms 'grue' and 'bleen' have been introduced with a built-in change of application at a future time, it is not reasonable to employ inductive inference in connection with evidence described in these terms. But Goodman replies that the question as to which terms have a built-in change of application at a future time is not straightforward. For one can define 'green' and 'blue' as follows:

> At time t, x is *green* if and only if: either (i) t is before 1 January 2010 and x is grue: or (ii) t is on or after 1 January 2010 and x is bleen.

> At time t, x is *blue* if and only if: either (i) t is before 1 January 2010 and x is bleen: or (ii) t is on or after 1 January 2010 and x is grue.

Goodman's critics respond that this formal symmetry between the two pairs of terms is not decisive, since there remains an important epistemological distinction between them: the only way someone can tell whether something is grue or bleen is by using the original definition while keeping track of the time and noticing whether things are green or blue. In which case it remains unreasonable to base inductive inferences on evidence described in those terms.

This response assumes that in order to be using a pair of colour predicates as a 'grue/bleen' pair one has to know in advance of their future change of reference. But we can avoid this assumption by imagining the situation of someone (a 'Goodmaniac') who has learnt the terms 'green' and 'blue' just as we have, and at present applies them just as we do, but who applies them from 1 January 2010 in a way which implies (as we would then say) that by calling something 'green' he has meant all along that it is grue, and by calling something 'blue' he has meant that it is bleen. For on 1 January 2010 it strikes the Goodmaniac that a radical change in nature has just taken place, that emeralds are, as he says, 'blue', and sapphires are 'green'. We will say that no such radical change has taken place and that the Goodmaniac's bewilderment derives only from a deviant understanding of our familiar colour terms; but from his perspective it is we who are failing to respect our previous understanding of colour terms by failing to note the dramatic changes in the colours of things that have taken place.

When Goodman's position is developed in this way, it becomes clear that the sceptical challenge it poses to us is that we might ourselves turn out to be Goodmaniacs, with concepts that somehow fail to capture the unchanging similarities and differences between things. Since, however, Goodman's argument depends on the fact that what we identify as a change depends on the ways in which we describe things, it implies that there is no difference from our own perspective between supposing that the world might change so radically that the future no longer resembles the past and supposing that our language fails to capture the unchanging similarities and differences. Hence his new riddle is essentially an ingenious refinement of Hume's old riddle.

Responding to Sceptical Arguments

Like the 'brain-in-a-vat' story, Goodman's argument invokes a fantastic hypothesis which we have trouble taking seriously. This is an indication of the fact that these sceptical arguments are not intended to give rise to practical doubts which might lead us to seek reassurance through further practical investigations. There is supposed to be nothing you can *do* to show yourself that you are not the mind of a brain-in-a-vat or a Goodmaniac. The role of sceptical hypotheses of this kind is, therefore, distinctively philosophical: they are intended to raise challenges to our sense of our own rationality, and to respond to them we have either to show that they are incoherent or else find a way of living with them.

The position of the logical empiricists exemplifies the first alternative: they held that sceptical hypotheses are empirically unfalsifiable and therefore meaningless. This position is not persuasive: we have no general problem understanding stories about a mad scientist who keeps brain in vats and there is no good reason to hold that in imaginatively applying these stories to oneself one suddenly undermines their meaningfulness. In the early post-war period, however, a more interesting empiricist response to scepticism become popular for a time. The central idea here was that words get their meaning from their use in certain 'paradigm' situations, and thus that sceptical doubts as to whether we have good reason to think that they apply can be set aside by observing that we would not understand them at all unless we were able to use them legitimately in these exemplary paradigm situations (N.B. the term 'paradigm' does not here have the special significance that Kuhn gave it which was discussed in the previous chapter). Anthony Flew provided a memorably ill-chosen example of this line of thought, the so-called 'Paradigm Case Argument', in the following passage:

Thus, since the meaning of 'of his own freewill' can be taught by reference to such paradigm cases as that in which a man, under no social pressure, marries the girl he wants to marry (how else *could* it be taught?): it cannot be right, on any grounds whatsoever, to say that no one *ever* acts of his own freewill. ('Philosophy and Language', p. 19)

The trouble with this argument is that concepts such as free will and knowledge have implications which cannot be uncontentiously manifested in particular situations. One cannot therefore dismiss sceptical arguments by simply bringing forward 'paradigm cases'. This difficulty became apparent in the discussion of attempts by Norman Malcolm and others to use the paradigm case argument in order to reject radical scepticism concerning the possibility of knowledge of the external world. According to Malcolm, G. E. Moore's famous 'proof' of an external world (delivered in 1939 and a frequent point of reference thereafter) in which he held up his hands to his audience and challenged them to deny that he then knew that his hands exist, provides 'a paradigm of absolute certainty' which shows that scepticism concerning our knowledge of the external world conflicts with our understanding of language. But Malcolm's critics responded that, however exemplary the situation of Moore and his audience might appear to be, Malcolm was not justified in regarding Moore as having provided a case of knowledge which undermines the challenge posed by sceptical arguments. For the sceptic's arguments precisely imply that knowledge is not a state which can be uncontentiously manifested in this way.

Moore's hand-waving performance was not in fact intended by him to be a refutation of scepticism (his target was the idealist thesis that there is no genuinely external world). Instead, Moore's response to sceptical arguments was to argue that we are more certain of the truth of the everyday particular things we think we know than we are of the general grounds for doubt concerning them introduced by sceptics. So we are entitled to turn sceptical arguments on their head and regard their unbelievable conclusions as reasons for rejecting their premises. By itself this response appears complacent: it needs further support from an account of certainty. Such an account was offered by Wittgenstein in his notes *On Certainty* (cf. Chapter 2, pp. 34–6) where he argued that Moore's emphasis on our common-sense certainties is an inchoate recognition of the fact that our common-sense understanding of the world and ourselves provides the context within which inquiries and doubts are alone possible. In comparing Moore's common-sense certainties to the hinges on the which the doors of doubt and inquiry are supported, he implies that if the sceptic unscrews the hinges, the doors will just fall uselessly to the ground.

Wittgenstein's position is different both from that of Moore and from that of the adherents of the Paradigm Case Argument: he held that our common-sense understanding is not a matter of intellectual assurance but of practical belief. So his view was that reasons for belief and methods of inquiry are grounded in practical convictions for which no reason is possible or necessary. As a result his position is a form of 'naturalism' in epistemology (cf. Chapter 2, pp. 37–8), reminscent of Hume's invocation of our natural propensities for belief. It needs to be emphasized, however, that this kind of naturalism is very different from that propounded by Quine in 'Epistemology Naturalized' (cf. Chapter 4, pp. 76–7). Quine's naturalism is a naturalism of the natural sciences and his 'naturalization' of epistemology is an attempt to fashion an epistemology in the light of an understanding of the world and ourselves provided by the natural sciences. It will be obvious in the light of Wittgenstein's hostility to attempts to prioritize the natural sciences that he would repudiate Quine's project.

Wittgenstein argues that scepticism is self-undermining because the sceptic's conclusion removes the context which makes possible the reasoning he seeks to employ. A similar strategy has been employed by many philosophers who argue that philosophical scepticism is self-defeating because it undermines the attribution of the very beliefs whose rationality it calls into doubt. One example of an argument of this kind was Davidson's argument (cf. Chapter 5, p. 103) that we are committed to interpreting each other in such a way that the vast majority of our beliefs are correct. For Davidson, to suppose that all these beliefs are mistaken is to suppose that they are not our beliefs at all.

Transcendental Arguments

Arguments of this kind are generally known as 'transcendental arguments'. This slightly unfortunate name has nothing to do with 'transcendental' conceptions of God. It derives instead from Kant's use of the term 'transcendental' in his *Critique of Pure Reason* (1781) to describe a priori conditions which make it possible for us to have thoughts concerning a world of objects which we perceive. 'Transcendental arguments' are, therefore, arguments which seek to demonstrate such conditions, and the revival of transcendental arguments has been a revival of Kant's philosophy. The person primarily responsible for this mid twentieth-century neo-Kantian movement has been the Oxford philosopher Sir Peter Strawson.

We first encountered Strawson as a youthful critic of Russell in Chapter 3 (pp. 59–61), objecting that Russell's theory of descriptions does not account properly for our ability to refer to particular objects. Strawson's discussion then was of course couched in the idioms of ordinary language philosophy, but in retrospect it is apparent that when criticizing Russell he was already drawing on Kantian themes. Strawson's revival of Kantian themes became overt in his 1959 book *Individuals* in which he develops a series of transcendental arguments which are intended to establish some essential features of our 'conceptual scheme' and thereby show that philosophical scepticism is self-defeating. He writes here:

This gives us a more profound characterisation of the sceptic's position. He pretends to accept a conceptual scheme, but at the same time quietly rejects one of the conditions of its employment. Thus his doubts are unreal, not simply because they are logically irresoluble doubts, but because they amount to the rejection of the whole conceptual scheme within which alone such doubts make sense. (*Individuals*, p. 35)

The central thesis of *Individuals* is that if we are to have thoughts about certain objects, we must be able to give some substance to questions about the specific identity of these objects, in particular to the ways in which we can legitimately suppose ourselves to reidentify the very same object on different occasions. One intriguing argument concerns space and connects with Kant's thesis that any series of experiences which make the presence of objects apparent to us will be one in which these objects are perceived as located in space. To assess this thesis Strawson takes the case of hearing (auditory experience), precisely because it is the mode of experience which we are best able to imagine, at first at least, as not involving essential reference to space. Strawson argues that in order that a series of auditory experiences be legitimately regarded as perceptions of audible objects, i.e. sounds, which one might reidentify after an interval during which they were absent from experience, there must be a way of making sense of the persisting but unheard existence of these sounds. This, he argues, requires that our experience should include a representation of a quasi-spatial dimension, a 'Master Sound', along which these sounds are as it were located and through which we can think of ourselves as moving as our auditory experience changes. So, he concludes, a qualified version of Kant's thesis is correct: any conception of auditory experience which provides auditory representations of reidentifiable sounds must include a representation of a dimension which functions as an analogue of space.

This argument was famously criticized by Gareth Evans who argued that the apparent presence of the Master Sound amounts only to a simple regularity in auditory experience, and as such is insufficient to legitimate the characterization of auditory experience as experience of sounds capable of existing unheard. Instead, Evans argued, Strawson's reidentification requirement can be met only where one's experience provides one with a way of understanding the structure of one's auditory experience by reference to one's location in a physical space which includes the sources of the sounds heard. Evans described how our experience normally enables us to meet this requirement, stressing the importance of proprioception as our way of locating ourselves in space and discussing the conceptions of space employed by the blind. There is no space here to discuss this intriguing material, but Evans helped to open up a dialogue which continues today between philosophers attempting to articulate transcendental arguments concerning the presuppositions of objective experience and psychologists investigating the basic structure of human thought and experience.

Another of Strawson's arguments in *Individuals* revolves around the notion of self-consciousness: he asks what is presupposed by a thinker's ascription of thoughts to herself. Again the concept of identity is central: Strawson argues if a thinker is to be able to identify herself as a particular thinker, she must allow for the possibility that there are other thinkers—'if *only* mine, then *not* mine at all' (*Individuals*, p. 109). Hence, Strawson argues, our experience must provide a basis for the identification of other thinkers on the basis of their perceptible characteristics. So they must have 'material' properties which provide 'logically adequate criteria', largely involving behaviour such as speech, for the identification of their psychological properties. Beings which combine connected psychological and material properties are 'persons'; and since others are persons, and we identify ourselves as a thing of the same type as these others, each of us must be a person too. Thus although we do not ascribe our thoughts to ourselves by observing our own behaviour, we must nonetheless manifest the kinds of behaviour which provide others with logically adequate criteria to ascribe thoughts to us.

In a later discussion of Kant's philosophy, *The Bounds of Sense* (1966), Strawson takes matters further by arguing that 'for a series of diverse experiences to belong to a single consciousness it is necessary that they should be so connected as to constitute a temporally extended experience of a unified objective world' (*The Bounds of Sense*, p. 97). Again, the argument concerns the presuppositions of self-consciousness: in this case Strawson argues that one can think of one's experiences as one's own only where one is able to contrast them with objects whose existence and properties are independent of one's experience of them:

What is meant by the necessary self-reflexiveness of a possible experience in general could be otherwise expressed by saying that experience must be such as to provide room for the thought of experience itself. The point of the objectivity-condition is that it provides room for this thought. It provides room, on the one hand, for 'Thus and so is how things objectively are' and, on the other, for 'This is how things are experienced as being'; and it provides room for the second thought *because* it provides room for the first. (*The Bounds of Sense*, p. 107)

These are ambitious arguments in which Strawson treats self-consciousness as a veritable Aladdin's Lamp of conceptual truths, and not surprisingly his arguments have attracted many critics. Some focus on the way in which Strawson seems to move uneasily between arguments which suggest that a condition is sufficient for some distinction to a conclusion which states that it is necessary. Thus in the passage quoted just now, the claim that the objectivity-condition 'provides room' for a way of thinking about one's experience as one's own surely means that it is sufficient for this way of thinking. It will not follow that this condition is also necessary for this way of thinking, which is the conclusion Strawson wanted to reach, without a further demonstration that it is the only way of legitimating this way of thinking; and this Strawson does not provide.

But much the most influential criticism, due to the American philosopher Barry Stroud (1935–), has been that Strawson's arguments draw on a verificationist assumption, similar to that employed by the logical empiricists, that if we are to be able to make sense of a distinction, we must be able to discover that in some cases it really obtains. This can be easily seen in the argument concerning the existence of other persons: for Strawson here maintained that, given that self-consciousness requires the ability to make sense of a distinction between ourselves and others, our experience must be such that we can in principle discover that others really exist. Stroud inferred that transcendental arguments are therefore of no great use in confronting philosophical scepticism: for if we accept the verificationist assumption, then of course scepticism about other minds and the like can be dismissed; but that is not news and the intelligibility of sceptical doubts is a good reason for rejecting the assumption. It does not follow that transcendental arguments are of no merit: Strawson's arguments show us what we need to be able to make sense of if we are to enjoy self-conscousness—e.g. that there are other persons like us; but the arguments themselves are compatible with sceptical doubts as to whether there really are good reason to believe these things at all.

Among others, Strawson himself was sufficently impressed by Stroud's arguments to retract the claim that transcendental arguments provide good reasons for repudiating sceptical doubts. So, in his later book *Scepticism and Naturalism: Some Varieties* (1985), he withdrew to the naturalist response to scepticism to be found in Hume and Wittgenstein. From this revised perspective the role of transcendental arguments is that they point to unobvious connections within our conceptual scheme—a task which fits well with Strawson's long-standing commitment to 'descriptive metaphysics', the internal elucidation of our conceptual commitments. But, he now holds, the basic structure of our conceptual scheme lies so deep in our thought and practice that its legitimation is neither possible nor necessary.

Despite Strawson's retraction others have persisted in the hope that significant conclusions about ourselves or the world can be reached by the method of transcendental argument. Usually they seek to establish that, despite the possibility of mistakes, the capacity for thinking thoughts of various kinds is dependent upon the thinker's existence within a world which is largely as it is believed to be. The difficult stage is always that of vindicating the dependence of thought upon the world without relying on verificationist assumptions. Davidson's method of radical interpretation, to which I alluded earlier, provides one argument of this kind. A different approach was developed by Hilary Putnam in his book *Reason, Truth and History* (1981) and it merits attention as an influential example of this form of anti-sceptical argument.

Putnam's Brain

Putnam argues that the sceptic's brain-in-a-vat hypothesis can be undermined by showing that a brain-in-a-vat cannot think such things as that, for all it can tell, it is a brain-in-a-vat. For if this is granted, the thought which the sceptic seeks to commend to each of us, that for all I can tell, I am a brain-in-a-vat, is one which we do not need to worry about. For if I can think it, I am not a brain-in-a-vat. But why can the brain-in-a-vat not think that it might be a brain-in-a-vat? In the sceptic's story the brain-in-a-vat is supposed to have the types of neural activity that are characteristic of ordinary human brains when people think such things. Putnam argues, however, that the capacity for thinking such thoughts is also dependent upon the 'external' situation of the thinker.

In developing this position Putnam draws on his account of the reference of terms such as 'water' which I discussed in Chapter 6 (pp. 133–4). I suggested there that his essentialist thesis is questionable; but it does not follow he is mistaken in holding that the external context of our use of language helps to fix its reference, and he relies on this thesis in his discussion of the sceptic's brain-in-a-vat hypothesis. He argues that our use of the term 'brain-in-a-vat' with the meaning that the sceptical argument requires, draws on our use of the simpler terms 'brain' and 'vat' to refer to actual brains and vats, and that this requires the presence of brains and vats in situations which underpin our learning and use of these terms. Thus, the position replaces the implicit verificationism of the older transcendental arguments, with the 'externalist' thesis that by and large the basic terms of a language refer to those features of its real world context which explain their use, so that 'one cannot refer to certain kinds of things, e.g. *trees*, if one has no causal interaction at all with them, or with things in terms of which they can be described' (*Reason, Truth and History*, p. 16).

Putnam takes it that this thesis applies to thought as much as to language. So in attributing thoughts to a brain on the basis of its neural processes one must take account of those features of its actual context which explain these processes. Hence, he holds, in the case of the brain-in-a-vat, insofar as it has thoughts at all, these concern features of the neural inputs which give rise to them, and not such things as brains and vats, which play no part in explaining the occurrence of these neural processes.

Is this persuasive? I shall discuss Putnam's externalist thesis in Chapter 9 (pp. 222–4). But one obvious point to make here is that Putnam's argument does not rule out the sceptical implications of a case in which a mad scientist sets up his equipment in such a way that real brains and vats play an explanatory role in generating the neural input for a brain-in-a-vat. To deal with this objection more needs to be said about the presuppositions of reference and thought, and Putnam points in one such direction when he remarks that his argument resembles Wittgenstein's discussion of meaning in his *Philosophical Investigations*. For Wittgenstein's arguments imply that the content of any thoughts a thinker might have is dependent upon the integration of the actions and speech they give rise to in a language game (cf. Chapter 2, pp. 20–5). Since involvement in a language-game requires agency, and this is incompatible with the situation of the brain-in-a-vat as envisaged by the sceptic, it follows that, for Wittgenstein at least, its brain processes can have no meaning, even if their production is dependent in some way upon features of the external world.

This last line of thought can be queried, and some of the issues involved will be discussed in the next chapter. But I want now to turn to scepticism concerning the possibility of our having reasons for beliefs about the future. This type of scepticism is associated with the arguments of Hume and Goodman described at the start of this chapter and is not in any obvious way amenable to transcendental arguments. For the sceptic's hypothesis of a radical change in nature does not undermine patterns of thought and reasoning to whose merits he is himself committed. Nonetheless, there have, of course, been many attempts to show that there is a legitimate justification of inductive inference. Several of these involve considerations of probability and statistical inference and quickly become somewhat technical; so I shall not discuss them here. But I do want to introduce a line of thought proposed by Frank Ramsey which has subsequently become central to a new way of thinking about epistemology.

Reliable Belief

Ramsey's proposal is that justification is primarily a matter of reliability: a belief is justified if it was obtained by a process which is in fact reliable, i.e. by a process which ensures that there is a good chance that the belief is true (even if it is not). Thus beliefs which are arrived at by inductive reasoning are justified insofar as that way of forming beliefs is reliable, i.e. insofar as 'the world is so constituted that inductive arguments lead on the whole to true opinions' ('Truth and Probability', p. 99). Admittedly, our reasons for thinking that induction is reliable include the fact that it has thus far proved itself to be so: so the familiar circularity is still here. But our belief in the reliability of induction is justified by the reliability of the reasoning that leads us to form this belief, and this depends on the actual constitution of the world, and not on our thoughts about it. So by making justification a matter of 'external' fact, and not one of 'internal' reasoning, Ramsey is able to legitimate an appeal outside the familiar circle of inductive reasonings to suggest why beliefs obtained by inductive reasoning are justified.

It may seem that there is a trick here, that Ramsey is somehow committed to supposing that we can slip outside our own skins to check up on the reliability of our reasoning. But this is not so: he simply holds that the justification of belief is dependent on the world's being such as to ensure that the belief was acquired through a reliable process and not, in the first instance anyway, on our being able to show that it was reliably acquired. Whether this 'externalist' conception of justification is fully satisfying when we wonder whether our beliefs are justified is a question to which I shall return, but for the moment I shall concentrate on developing the position.

Ramsey points to the fact that this externalist conception of justification is well-suited to memory, where again there is a threat of apparent circularity in the use of reasoning concerning the past as a way of justifying beliefs based on memory. It is also easy to apply it to perception by holding that it is primarily the reliability of our senses within a suitable range which implies that perceptual beliefs which concern matters which fall within that range are justified. So this externalist approach to justification can be applied quite widely, and it has obvious similarities with Putnam's externalist theory of reference. Indeed given the familiar connections between meaning and justification it is no surprise to find similar developments in both areas, though the connections here are not inescapable: some philosophers reject Putnam's externalist theory of reference while accepting an externalist account of justification while others maintain the opposite combination.

Externalism and Internalism in Epistemology

The traditional conception of the justification of belief has been 'internalist': the basic thought has been that a thinker's belief is justified where, but only where, the thinker is able to justify it by providing good reasons for it. Though this seems at first barely disputable, it quickly gives rise to difficult questions; in particular, since the thinker's reasons will be further beliefs, we can ask whether these beliefs are themselves justified. If they are not, then it seems that they should be regarded as mere presumptions or prejudices and the thinker's justification of the beliefs in whose support they were invoked is called into question; yet if they are justified, we can just repeat the question concerning the thinker's reasons for these beliefs. So it looks as though internalist justifications are like irritatingly persistent children in that they give rise to an unending regress of reasons for reasons. The regress will, however, halt if there are beliefs whose truth is so obvious, where they are true, that they need no further justification and are therefore 'self-evident'; or if circular patterns of reasoning can provide justifications. The first of these alternatives is called 'foundationalism' since self-evident beliefs can provide foundations for other beliefs; the second is 'coherentism' since beliefs which fit together, or cohere, involve large-scale circular patterns of reasoning. Much recent debate in epistemology concerns the relative merits of foundationalism, coherentism, and Ramsey's reliabilism, which avoids the 'regress of reasons' thanks to its reliance upon external justifications that do not involve the thinker's reasons.

The standard objection to foundationalism is that our inescapable fallibility implies that not even the most obvious beliefs are such that no further justification of them is ever appropriate; and the standard objection to coherentism is that merely circular patterns of reasoning cannot justify beliefs. Though these objections are effective against simple versions of the doctrines in question, more complex positions which involve a combination of them are not so easily refuted. Wittgenstein's position is a case in point: he takes it that our lives are built up around practical beliefs which may on occasion turn out to be mistaken, but which nonetheless normally provide a basis for the justification of other beliefs by providing us with 'a *picture* which forms the starting-point of belief for me' (*On Certainty*, sect. 209). Thus there are credible accounts of justification which give an initial presumption of truth to normal perception and memory, but also require that the resulting beliefs should be capable of combination and refinement through inferential practices to provide a coherent understanding of the world and ourselves.

Externalists maintain that the status of these presumptions and practices is underpinned by a reliabilist account of the epistemic merits of the capabilities involved (perception, memory, inductive inference). This seems to me right, but some further element of explicit reasoning is required to provide responses to sceptical arguments. For the fact that a method of acquiring belief is justified because it is generally reliable provides by itself no response to sceptical doubts since such facts cannot literally speak for themselves. So the question arises as to how one is to do justice to the merits of externalist considerations when responding to sceptical arguments which demand a response that is, on the face of it, internalist.

My own view is that the way to bring things together here is to start from the response to scepticism to be found in the later work of Wittgenstein and Strawson. On this view, as thinkers, we start out from a common-sense picture of the world which we acquire as we learn a language. The elements of this common-sense picture and the practices of reasoning associated with it are not initially justified; but our reflective affirmation of them in the face of sceptical argument requires that it be possible to construct, by a combination of transcendental argument and externalist theorizing, an understanding of the world and our place within it which confirms that the common-sense picture is broadly correct and that these practices are reliable. Indeed the fact that our fundamental presumptions and practices are only externally justified manifests itself in the fact that the cognitive dispositions and capacities which constitute them are, for us, an initially ungrounded source of beliefs. Thus this response to scepticism, though necessarily conducted by means of internalist reasoning, seeks to confirm retrospectively its own foundations by showing how they are externally justified. The resulting position, therefore, involves a combination of the foundationalist, coherentist, and reliabilist accounts of justification that are opposed to each other in much contemporary discussion.

Knowledge

I have been discussing the justification of beliefs in the light of the anxiety that sceptical arguments might show that they are not justified. These arguments are often taken to show that we do not know the things which we normally take ourselves to know. The connection here is that according to the standard account of 'knowing that', e.g. knowing that the cat is on the mat, someone who knows this is someone who believes that the cat is on the mat, where this belief is also both true and justified. Thus in showing that such a belief is not after all justified one shows that the person lacks this knowledge. This account of knowledge has, however, been much criticized. One line of criticism concerns the assumption that knowledge is just belief which satisfies the further conditions of truth and justification. For this suggests that, in order to tell whether or not someone knows something, we should first find out whether they believe it, and then check to see to see if their belief is true and justified. But this cannot be right: it implies that we can settle questions about what someone believes in advance of determining what they know—whereas in fact one can only have beliefs about, say, Alexander the Great if one has some knowledge about him (cf. Chapter 5, p. 116).

This point shows that belief and knowledge are interdependent (for it is also clear that one cannot have knowledge about Alexander the Great without some beliefs about him). But it does not follow from this that knowledge is not belief, and although there are further arguments for this claim, I shall set that issue to one side in order to concentrate on the issue of the kind of justification required for knowledge. This issue was given special prominence following a brief paper (1963) by Edmund Gettier (1927–) in which he showed that it is all too easy to find cases of beliefs which are true and in a way justified, but which we would not regard as cases of knowledge.

Here is one such case: suppose that I am regularly encountered by my students driving to work in a BMW. My students therefore believe that I own this car, and thus that someone in the Philosophy Department owns a BMW. By our ordinary standards, these beliefs are justified. Nonetheless, suppose that I do not in fact own the BMW I drive—I have simply hired it; but suppose also that one of my colleagues in the Philosophy Department does own a BMW. She, however, keeps it at her villa in France and has never talked about it to the students; so they know nothing about it. In this situation the students have a belief, that someone in the Philosophy Department owns a BMW, which is both true and apparently justified. But surely they do not know this.

One can object that the fact that the students' belief that I own a BMW is mistaken shows that this belief was not, after all, justified. But the justification of belief has to allow for human fallibility: if a belief is to be regarded as justified only where the justification strictly implies that the belief is true, it will follow that very few, if any, of our beliefs are justified and thus that the sceptical thesis that we have little, if any, knowledge is correct. Furthermore, it is intuitively clear that in this case what undermines the attribution to the students of knowledge that someone in the Department owns a BMW is the fact that their belief that this is so rests on a belief which is false, namely that I own the BMW which I am regularly seen driving. So this problem is plausibly solved by the different 'no false lemma' principle that where a person's justification for a belief depends on another belief which, however justified, is false, the derived belief, even if it is itself true, is not knowledge.

Before considering further complications, it is worth noting the procedure followed in discussing this case. It involves a quasi-experimental procedure of invoking 'intuitions'—judgements not dictated by a general theory—concerning the acceptability or not of claims to knowledge in various imaginary situations. These intuitions are intended to make it possible to identify the considerations which guide our use of the concept of knowledge and thereby assemble an 'analysis' of knowledge. As we shall see it remains an open question whether such an analysis can be attained. Nonetheless this topic has generated a large literature in which extraordinary fables ('Gettier-cases') are concocted as part of this quasi-experimental procedure. Exercises of the imagination of this kind can be found throughout the history of philosophy, especially in the discussions of personal identity that run from Locke to the present day. But there is no doubt that the industry that has sprung up around Gettier-cases has taken this kind of writing to new extremes.

In the case discussed above the 'no false lemma' principle provided a plausible diagnosis of what is wrong with the attribution of knowledge. But the application of this principle is often difficult: for example, where a historian's evidence for some hypothesis includes a mistaken belief, must discovery of the mistake lead at once to the conclusion that he lacked knowledge, even if he was right in his hypothesis? This is surely the wrong verdict if his other evidence was strong and the mistaken belief relatively unimportant. One can argue that, precisely for this reason, the 'no false lemma' principle does not require the verdict that he lacked knowledge, since the historian's justification for his belief did not depend on the mistaken belief. But the matter is not clear-cut since it involves counterfactuals as to what the historian would have believed had he discovered his mistake. So although the principle is defensible, it does not provide the basis for a sharp distinction between genuine knowledge and mere 'opinion'; on the contrary, it suggests that the application of this distinction in the all-too-familiar situations where mistakes are intermingled among well justified beliefs is an inherently vague matter.

The cases discussed so far involve internal justifications of belief, but similar issues arise where the justification is external. Ramsey's account of knowledge as true belief acquired by a normally reliable method is the result of combining an external, reliabilist, account of justification with the standard account of knowledge as true justified belief. An initial difficulty is shown up by the following case. Suppose I see a bird on my bird table and correctly judge it to be a blue tit: so I have a true belief produced by the 'normally reliable' method of eyesight. But suppose I cannot distinguish blue tits from the coal tits which are also common in the locality; in this situation it would surely be wrong to hold that my true belief counts as knowledge that the bird on the table is a blue tit. For I would have had the same belief even if the bird had been a coal tit.

This case ilustrates the rationale for Robert Nozick's (1938–) influential theory of knowledge (*Philosophical Explanations*, 1981), according to which knowledge is true belief which 'tracks the truth'. The basic thought here is that the intuitive reliability of the beliefs of someone with knowledge arises from the fact that their beliefs satisfy the counterfactual requirement that, had things been different in respect of the subject matter of the belief, their belief would have changed accordingly (e.g. they would not have believed that there was a blue tit on the table had there been a coal tit there). For Nozick, then, to have knowledge of some fact, one's understanding must be such that one's beliefs 'track the truth' by varying in accordance with the state of things in 'close' possible worlds (this way of putting the point draws on the 'possible world' treatment of counterfactuals; cf. Chapter 6, pp. 123–5). Knowledge does not, however, demand perfect reliability—i.e. that one's belief should track the truth in all possible worlds. This level of understanding is unattainable and, as ever, it is important to allow for human fallibility. Instead it is sufficient that our beliefs should track the truth in those close (i.e. similar) worlds which are relevant to the case in hand. The reference here to relevance introduces the vagueness inherent in the distinction between knowledge and true belief which we encountered above in connection with internalist theories, but it is now associated with the thesis that in particular cases this distinction is fixed by considerations of context. Thus the resulting position is reminiscent of Austin's claim that in judging whether some bird is a goldfinch 'enough is enough'—we do not have prove that it is not a stuffed goldfinch (cf. Chapter 3, p. 56).

For Nozick, as for Austin, this contextual aspect of knowledge provides a response to sceptical arguments. For our knowledge of everyday matters of fact requires only that we track the truth with respect to alternatives which are relevant to everyday considerations, and these do not include the sceptic's fantastic possibilities. Thus we can have common-sense knowledge while not knowing that we are not having the delusive experience of a brain-in-a-vat. So common-sense knowledge is not threatened by sceptical arguments, which can be regarded much as most people do in fact regard them: namely as peculiar exercises of the intellect which attract our curiosity but do not demand serious attention.

This is an attractive position to take. But it cannot remove the threat posed by sceptical arguments once they have been introduced into a discussion without conflicting with the compelling principle that knowledge is 'closed' under known implication, i.e. that someone who knows that A and that if A then B is in a position to know that B. For suppose that the sceptic shows me that I do not know that B (e.g. that I am not now having a brain-in-a-vat's delusive experience): then it would be just disingenuous to insist that I still know both A (e.g. that I am sitting at my desk at home) and that if A then B (i.e. that if I am sitting at my desk at home then I am not now having a brain-in-a-vat's induced experience). Thus although knowledge has a contextual aspect, Nozick is wrong to rely on this to defuse sceptical arguments. In fact the element of fantasy that is characteristic of sceptical arguments shows that the appropriate context for assessing them is that of achieving a self-consciously coherent understanding of human rationality and its limits; and in this context, one cannot rely on the limited scope of ordinary concerns to protect claims to knowledge from sceptical doubts.

It is, I think, no great objection to Nozick's account of knowledge that it does not suffice by itself to defuse the challenges posed by sceptical arguments. But the account is also unsatisfactory in that it does not always allow adequately for an inability to discriminate between similar relevant alternatives. For example, suppose similar symptoms are produced by two different diseases to which different groups of people, of roughly equal numbers in the population, are susceptible; but suppose also that only one of these diseases has been identified. Then, when someone is correctly diagnosed by a physician as having this disease, the physician's belief will satisfy Nozick's counterfactual test, since if that patient did not have the disease he would not exhibit the symptoms observed, and the physician would not therefore believe that he has the disease in question. But since the physician does not discriminate between a case of this kind and another where the diagnosis would be incorrect (because the person with the symptoms has the other, as yet unidentified, disease), getting the diagnosis right for the first person should not count as knowledge.

This case suggests that passing Nozick's counterfactual test does not guarantee that a thinker has the ability to discriminate reliably from among relevant alternatives which knowledge requires. Although there

are revised proposals which circumvent this problem, a general difficulty has become increasingly apparent: it is very difficult to find an
analysis which is both sufficient for knowledge (and therefore not
exposed to new Gettier-cases) and yet allows for human fallibility (i.e.
allows that one can have a false justified belief). One radical response to
this situation, advocated by Edward Craig (1942–) (1990), has been
to argue that instead of looking directly for an informative analysis of
knowledge we should start from an account of what is distinctive about
the position of a person who knows something. But the topic remains
open and at this point in the debate there is no consensus concerning
the best approach to it.

The Absolute Conception

For some contemporary philosophers (e.g. Alvin Goldman), the prominent role of externalist considerations in recent epistemology is a stage
in the fulfilment of Quine's project of 'naturalizing' epistemology by
founding it within cognitive psychology (cf. Chapter 3, pp. 76–7).
Most philosophers have not been persuaded of this, but in his book
Descartes: The Project of Pure Enquiry (1978) Bernard Williams (1929–)
put forward a striking argument whose conclusion broadly supports
Quine's position.

Williams argued that Descartes' attempt to achieve a vindication of
the possibility of certain knowledge is linked to his belief that the
knowledge thus vindicated will have a kind of ideal purity, such that its
content comprises what Williams calls an 'absolute conception' of the
world (I explain this below). Williams further maintains that although
the theological vindication offered by Descrates of the possibility of
such knowledge is not credible, Descartes was right to think that the
possibility of knowledge of any kind is dependent upon the possibility
of this ideal form of knowledge, and, according to Williams, the way
for us to attain this ideal is by natural science. Since this ideal, the
absolute conception, is to provide an understanding of the way in
which knowledge of any kind is possible, the resulting position implies
that knowledge is possible only if its possibility can be scientifically

comprehended, which is tantamount to its naturalization in the way proposed by Quine.

It will be clear from this sketch of Williams' argument that the central claim he makes is that 'if knowledge is possible at all, it now seems, the absolute conception must be possible too' (p. 65). Williams's 'absolute' knowledge is to be understood by means of a contrast with 'perspectival' knowledge. Taken literally, perspectival knowledge is spatial knowledge which is dependent upon the thinker's location and orientation; Williams, however, applies the term much more generally to knowledge which is dependent upon the thinker's situation, status, species, etc. The 'absolute conception', therefore, is conceived of as the content of a type of knowledge that is in no way dependent upon facts about the thinker. It is to be, as Williams puts, knowledge of 'what is there *anyway*'.

Once the absolute conception is understood in this way the affinity between it and the results of scientific inquiry fits with the traditional thesis that the validity of a scientific theory is not dependent upon facts about the theorists who proposed it. It should be said, however, that this thesis is called into question by Kuhn's refusal to isolate questions of justification from those of discovery (cf. Chapter 7, p. 159). Williams likes to cite the authority of the great American philosopher-scientist C. S. Peirce (1839–1914) who held that truth is the 'final opinion' on which inquiry is 'fated' to converge. But this is precisely the kind of teleological conception of science that Kuhn has persistently opposed. So Williams' confidence that he can appeal to scientific method as a way of substantiating a post-Cartesian (and post-Hegelian) absolute conception is disputable. But what still requires examination is his claim that perspectival knowledge depends upon the possibility of absolute knowledge of the facts known which, together with absolute knowledge of a thinker's situation, yields an explanation of the thinker's perspectival knowledge.

If one starts from the case of spatial knowledge, the claim is that perspectival spatial knowledge depends upon the possibility of non-perspectival knowledge of the spatial facts involved which enables one to explain the original perspectival knowledge, taking into account the thinker's location and orientation. It is not at all obvious that this claim is correct, since our understanding of space is fundamentally perspectival and one can have a perspectival understanding of a space without a non-perspectival understanding of it (as when one finds one's way around the corridors of a strange hotel). But a qualified version of Williams' claim is, I think, defensible. It starts from the thesis that a non-perspectival representation of spatial facts, such as a map, captures their identity better than any perspectival representation of them because it is unaffected by changes in the location of the thinker involved. If this is right, as I think it is, it follows that spatial facts are best represented in absolute terms, and thus that perspectival spatial knowledge is best understood by reference to an absolute representation of the spatial facts involved which also takes account of the thinker's location.

What is much more problematic is Williams' extrapolation of this case to other types of knowledge, such as knowledge of colour. Because colour involves a distinctively human visual sensitivity to complex patterns of electromagnetic radiation, Williams holds that it cannot be comprehended as such within the absolute conception, which will contain instead representations of the supposed underlying facts, characterized as the physicist and psychologist characterize them. Yet this case is very different from the spatial case. The relevant 'colourless' facts cannot be identified except by looking back to our judgements of colour, since the boundaries between colours are located within the electromagnetic spectrum in complex ways which have no intrinsic electromagnetic significance. Hence the situation in this case is the reverse of that which obtains in the case of spatial judgements; in this case the identity of the relevant facts is fixed by our 'human perspective'. So there is no reason in this case to accept that the validity of our ordinary knowledge of the colours of things is dependent upon an ideal form of knowledge which draws on colourless facts about them and us to explain why they look coloured to us. For it turns out that this latter knowledge is itself answerable to our ordinary knowledge.

This point can be extended to all those ordinary forms of knowledge that constitute our 'life-world'—such as my knowledge that I am sitting at a desk in a room in a house, etc. Williams' thesis implies that knowledge of this kind is dependent upon the possibility of some 'absolute' understanding of the relevant facts, potentially available to non-human scientists, which will include the everyday concepts that structure our life-world only as items to be explained within an abstract theory which explains why such ways of thinking are appropriate for us humans. Once again, however, any such abstract physical representation of the facts is answerable to our ordinary human understanding of them which fixes the identity of things like desks. Like colours, desks are not 'there anyway' as desks; what makes something a desk is only intelligible in relation to human life, and there is no reason to expect it to be possible to explain knowledge of desks from outside a human perspective. The possibility of knowledge of desks does not depend upon the possibility of absolute knowledge.

Williams at one point suggests that the point of the incorporation of our ordinary knowledge into the absolute conception is that it vindicates the objectivity of our ordinary knowledge. This line of thought is developed by Thomas Nagel (1937–) in his book *The View from Nowhere* (1986): Williams' non-perspectival absolute conception of the world is the content of Nagel's 'view from nowhere' (the same visual metaphor is in play). But Nagel does not tie the view from nowhere as closely to scientific method as Williams does; instead, it is conceived as the limit of a process of objectification whereby we progressively detach ourselves in thought from our limited spatio-temporal, historical, cultural, ethnic, speciesist, etc. perspectives, and fit these limited understandings within successively broader forms of knowledge. As described by Nagel, however, this task is doomed to failure since 'however often we may try to step outside ourselves, something will have to stay behind the lens, something in us will determine the resulting picture' (*The View from Nowhere*, p. 68).

Nagel's position rests on the presumption that the objectivity of our ordinary knowledge can be vindicated only through a process of detachment whereby we abandon the 'subjective' modes of thought characteristic of our ordinary points of view. His pessimism arises from his recognition that, if we are to be subjects of knowledge at all, we cannot altogether abandon our subjectivity. But the example of our familiar life-world again shows the implausibility of his presumption: once we detach ourselves from the modes of thought characteristic of our ordinary concerns and language-games, we will simply not be able to recognize the elements of the life-world which are rooted in these language-games, in our human point of view. Objective knowledge requires, not a detached, inhuman, point of view, but simply respect for the norms inherent in our ordinary language-games.

These positions of Nagel and Williams stand in sharp contrast to one of the liveliest new movements in epistemology—'feminist standpoint epistemology'. This is just one element of the broader feminist movement in recent philosophy, and it might at first seem odd that feminism has a distinctive contribution to make to epistemology since traditional epistemology has been sufficiently abstract to be, one might think, neither masculine nor feminine. Even though it is shamefully easy to point to the existence of distinctively masculine presumptions in many areas of theory the traditional view would be that such presumptions are unrecognized prejudices and that objectivity requires an understanding purged of any dependence on a gendered perspective, masculine or feminine. The claim of 'feminist standpoint' theorists such as Sandra Harding, however, is that this kind of Nagelian detachment fails to do justice to facts that are distinctively apparent from within a feminine standpoint—such as, for example, facts concerning the sexual harassment of women.

It is not Harding's view that these facts are only available from within a feminine standpoint—that would be a kind of epistemic relativism which she rejects. Instead her view is that because these are facts which are, in the first instance, thrown up within the experience of women, the epistemic position of women with respect to them is privileged; although men can come to recognize them, they do so primarily by imaginatively adopting a feminine standpoint. So objectivity with regard to these facts is not a matter of occupying a gender-free standpoint and thereby taking a step towards the view from nowhere; instead it demands a critical evaluation of judgements which takes into account the situation of those whose judgements they are. Such an evaluation need not endorse these judgements; the Wittgensteinian thesis that objectivity is available only where mistakes are possible applies here as elsewhere. But the evaluation has to start by taking seriously the 'perspectival' 'subjective' standpoint of those whose lives and language-games employ the judgements in question.

9

Aspects of Mind

'Naturalism' in one form or another was a prominent theme of the previous chapter, and since 1980 or so the 'linguistic turn' of twentieth-century philosophy has been supplanted by a 'naturalistic turn'. Nowhere is this more true than in the philosophy of mind, which has become increasingly central to general philosophical debate as philosophers have turned from conceptual inquiries based on an examination of our uses of language, to critical investigations of the conceptions of human 'nature' that are implicit in our language and practice, especially in the light of developments in the biological sciences.

As we saw in Chapters 2 and 3, an important concern of early post-war philosophy was to repudiate the Cartesian conception of the mind as a domain of phenomena that are different in kind from anything physical. In different ways, Wittgenstein and Ryle argued that this conception is untenable, though they also held that the natural sciences have little to offer towards an understanding of the mind. Quine took much the same view of our ordinary ways of thinking of the mind, but (as we saw in Chapter 4) because he also held that genuine knowledge is to be found only within the natural sciences, he looked forward to the elimination, or replacement, of our ordinary talk of thoughts and feelings in favour of concepts drawn from a properly scientific psychology; and in recent years this position has been supported by increasing numbers of American philosophers who like to think of our ordinary talk as a pre-scientific 'folk psychology' which is overdue for replacement, just as the 'folk' astronomy in which we talk of the 'sunrise' and 'sunset' has been replaced by scientific astronomy. One can, however, seek to reconcile science and ordinary thought and the philosopher who led the way in this respect was Wilfred Sellars (cf. Chapter 4). This chapter will, I think, confirm that in pursuing this project Sellars, more than anyone else, sketched out in advance the issues and positions which have come to dominate contemporary philosophy of mind.

Intention and Action

During the 1950s and early 1960s, however, the dominant influence was still that of Ryle and Wittgenstein. An important and characteristic work of this period was Elizabeth Anscombe's book *Intention* (1957). Anscombe (1919–2001) had studied with Wittgenstein and was responsible for editing and translating his *Philosophical Investigations*. It is worth noting in passing that, setting aside the more recent work of Sandra Harding mentioned at the end of the previous chapter, Anscombe is the first woman to figure in my discussion. She is, of course, not the first woman to contribute to English-language philosophy (that honour probably belongs to Anne Conway (1631–79)), nor is she the first English-speaking female philosopher to hold an academic position (I believe Constance Jones (1848–1922), who was an early Principal of Girton College Cambridge, merits this description). Nonetheless throughout her career, based first in Oxford and then in Cambridge where she held the professorship held earlier by Wittgenstein, Anscombe set an influential example to other women (such as her Oxford colleague Philippa Foot whose work I discuss in the next chapter).

Anscombe's aim in *Intention* is to clarify what is special about action by explaining the central contribution which an account of the intentions with which we act makes to the understanding of action. She approaches this issue by considering the answers we give to the question 'Why did you do that?' and starts from the case of actions where the answer provides a reason which exhibits the action as appropriate— e.g. where a boy who has just struck his sister answers the 'Why?'-question by saying 'because she hit me'. According to Anscombe, the boy's answer identifies his action as intentional, for it shows the intention with which he did what he did, namely to retaliate against his sister. Anscombe contrasts this case with that where the answer to the 'Why?'-question provides only what she calls a 'mental cause' of the action. For example, suppose the boy's answer had been 'because that loud bang made me jump': in that case his answer would not provide a reason for his action. The standard case, however, is that of intentional action; and in many such cases an answer to the 'Why?'-question will itself be a description of an action concerning which the 'Why?'-question can be asked again: e.g. when asked 'why did you wave your arm?' one might respond 'to signal to my wife', and one can then ask 'why did you do that?'. In such cases it may as a result appear that the agent is performing several actions at once (waving his arm, signalling to his wife, reminding her that it is time to leave, etc.). Anscombe argues, however, that there is in fact just one action: the series of intentions elicited by successive 'Why?'-questions just generate different descriptions of it.

Despite the existence of mental causes, Anscombe maintains that actions are standardly to be identified and understood by reference to the intentions with which they were performed; as she puts it, when we confront an initially puzzling action, 'my order of questions "Why?" can be looked at as a device which reveals the order that there is in this chaos' (*Intention*, p. 80). The order that is thus revealed, she suggests, is that which exhibits the action as rational: for when an agent reveals his intentions he exhibits his action as the conclusion of a piece of practical reasoning. The resulting 'practical knowledge' of action we obtain, she argues, is different from the 'contemplative' knowledge characteristic of scientific inquiry. For in the scientific case we seek to make our beliefs fit the world, whereas in the practical case the agent shows how she acts to make the world fit her intentions. Anscombe illustrates this point nicely by contrasting the normal practical role of a shopping list which lists the items to be purchased with the role of a list constructed by a detective observing the shopper's purchases: the lists may be the same, but the difference in the direction of fit is shown by the different ways in which a mistake would be made—the shopper makes a mistake by failing to buy something on the list, whereas the detective makes a mistake by failing to list something that has been bought.

This contrast between scientific explanation and the rational understanding of action is also central to the argument of Peter Winch's book *The Idea of a Social Science* (1958). Winch (1926–97) argued that the study of society is essentially a study of the logical relationships between the beliefs and intentions of agents and the rules which inform the practices of social institutions. Such a study, he argued, cannot be a causal inquiry: causal inquiries deal with regularities, not rules, and there cannot be logical connections between cause and effect (I return to this point below). So the title of the book is deliberately ironic: though there can be social studies, there cannot be a 'social science'.

Winch's position does not commit him to supposing that social studies involve only the uncritical exposition of existing understandings of social relationships. On the contrary a critic who argues that, say, the employment practices of contemporary capitalism do not live up to the official understanding of them within liberal culture, is engaged in finding contradictions between this official understanding and that implicit in the practices of employers, and contradictions are of course logical relationships. The type of position which Winch is nonetheless committed to rejecting is that exemplified by Marx's famous thesis of historical materialism, to the effect that there is a causal relation between the relationships in a society which determine a person's access to the material necessities of life (food, shelter, etc.) and the political, legal, and other normative institutions of that society which institutionalise these relationships and offer a legitimation of them.

Winch's position can be briefly summarized as the thesis that reasons are not causes. This thesis was discussed in detail by A. I. Melden in *Free Action* (1961) (like Winch's book, this book appeared in a series of 'little red books', most of which pursued neo-Wittgensteinian anti-scientific inquiries into mental concepts). Melden argued that Winch's thesis provides a new way of dissolving the old free will/determinism debate. That debate arises from the threat which the causal determination of action is thought to pose to the freedom of the will: for if acting of one's own free will requires an ability to have acted otherwise and the causal determination of one's action implies that one could not have acted otherwise, there is a direct conflict here. As we shall see later in this chapter, there are many responses to this debate; Melden's basic claim, however, is that the debate should not arise at all since, properly understood, actions simply cannot be causally determined. For if (as Anscombe had argued) actions are fundamentally identified and understood by reference to the intentions which specify the agent's reasons for acting, and if (as Winch had argued) reasons are not causes, then the issue of the causal determination of action simply cannot arise: as Melden put it:

It is futile to attempt to explain conduct through the causal efficacy of desire—all *that* can explain is further happenings, not actions performed by agents. (*Free Action*, p. 128)

Reasons and Causes

The thesis that reasons for action are not causes of action was challenged by Donald Davidson and David Pears (1921–) in the 1960s. A preliminary point they make is that our ordinary talk of reasons for action does not support this thesis. Anscombe, it will be recalled, says that reasons for action are among the answers agents give to the question 'why did you do that?'; other answers cite what she calls 'mental causes', such as the sudden occurrence of a loud noise. One can see the point of her distinction—mental causes are not reasons; but it does not follow that reasons are not causes, and the apparent unambiguousness of the original 'Why?'-question suggests that they are. Furthermore there is a familiar distinction which strongly suggests that reasons are sometimes causes: we distinguish between (i) Tom's having a reason to get up early (e.g. he intends to walk his dog) and (ii) Tom's getting up early for that reason. This distinction appears to be causal: the intention which gives him his reason for action is present in both cases, but it is causally operative only in the second case. This distinction is of great importance to us: for example, when questions of blame and punishment arise, we want to be sure that the alleged offender acted 'with criminal intent', which requires not just the presence of criminal intentions but also the fact that the offender did what he did *because* of these intentions.

What, however, of the arguments for the thesis that reasons are not causes? Anscombe's 'different direction of fit' argument shows that, insofar as an agent's action is a 'logical' conclusion of her reasons, there are logical connections between reasons and actions which are very different from those between ordinary causes and their effects. But her argument does not show that in describing an agent's reasons for action we do not also have to satisfy the opposite direction of fit by matching our description to the facts. Winch's main argument, however, was that the existence of these logical connections between reasons and actions is actually incompatible with a causal connection between them, and this argument merits careful attention.

The argument starts from a point emphasized by Hume, that where cause and effect are described in terms which give the essential identity of the events or states involved, it must not be the case that the effect follows the cause as a matter of conceptual necessity; for the events in question must be such that there is no contradiction in holding that one occurs without the other. Hence, Winch, Melden, and others inferred, the logical connection between reasons and actions precludes a causal connection between them.

In thinking about this, it is important to grasp that Hume's point does not rule out the existence of descriptions of causes and effects for which the connection between them is conceptually necessary: one can correctly, though unhelpfully, remark that the cause of the Great Fire of London caused the Great Fire. All that Hume's point implies concerning this case is that the description of the cause of the Great Fire as such does not capture its essential identity. Furthermore it does not follow from Hume's point that the same concepts cannot be employed in the description of both cause and effect where no necessary connection between them is implied: for example it does not prohibit causal claims such as that it was Jack's fear of falling off the mountain path which caused him to fall off the path. These qualifications do not, however, defuse Winch's argument as long as one accepts the claim, central to the positions of both Anscombe and Winch, that actions are fundamentally identified by reference to the intentions of their agents. For if the features of an action which give it its identity are dependent upon the agent's intentions in so acting, then intention and action are not 'distinct existences' and Hume's requirement is violated.

In response to this, the causal theorist must take over Anscombe's own observation that actions admit of a variety of descriptions, and hold that the essential specification of an action's identity is provided by a description of it which is not dependent upon the agent's intentions. The obvious candidate for such a description is one which characterizes it in terms of the agent's movement of their body: for such a description is independent of the agent's intentions (even if the agent intended to move their body in just that way). The Anscombe–Winch thesis concerning the central role of intentions in the understanding of action now becomes the claim that there must also be a description of an action under which it is intentional, and that an account of an agent's intentions in so acting contributes a central element to the explanation of the action. This is not quite the original claim, and, as we shall see below, it is not uncontentious; but by providing a central explanatory role for intentions it remains reasonably faithful to it.

This is not the end of the matter, however, since Winch and others advanced a further argument for the thesis that reasons are not causes: namely that whereas a hypothesis concerning the cause of some particular effect carries a commitment to the general claim that similar causes have similar effects, an account of an agent's reasons for action in a particular case does not have a similar commitment, either about the behaviour of the agent on other occasions or about the behaviour of other people: the agent can be moody or idiosyncratic. This turns out to be an argument which raises deep and difficult issues, and there is no consensus about the proper response to it.

The common-sense response to it is that a fuller understanding of those who act differently even though they seem to have the same reasons for action will reveal further differences among their reasons. Thus common-sense principles of rational action, such as that an agent who wants X and believes that he has the opportunity to do something Y which will lead to his getting X will try to do Y, are standardly qualified by the condition that 'other things are equal' in order to allow for situations where the agent has stronger reasons for doing something else; and there is a theory, decision theory, which seeks to identify the relative strengths of an agent's motivations in order to improve predictions about her behaviour. Many philosophers are, however, sceptical about this theory, since they hold that there is no robust way of determining the strength and stability of an agent's motivations which is independent of her actions (it is clear, for example, that phenomenology—how things feel to the agent—will not do the required job).

Anomalous Monism

One of the chief critics of decision theory has been Davidson himself. This is partly because of scepticism concerning the explanatory value of talk of the strength of someone's reasons for action, but also because he takes the view that the existence of a causal connection implies the existence of a strict unqualified law of which this causal connection is an instance. This matters because the holistic constraints of rationality which, he holds, inform our attributions of beliefs and desires to others (cf. Chapter 5, pp. 100–1), are, he thinks, not compatible with the hypothesis that these states enter into strict causal laws.

Equally, however, Davidson remains strongly committed to the thesis that the motivations which specify an agent's reasons for his action are causes of the action. The way in which he has managed to square this apparent circle is ingenious. While maintaining that the existence of a causal connection implies the existence of a strict unqualified law, he observes that the implied strict law need only draw on one description of a cause and its effect. If a hurricane is described at the top of page one of today's *Times* and the damage caused by the same hurricane is described at top of page ten of the same newspaper, then the event described at the top of page one of today's *Times* caused the event described at the top of page ten; but this truth brings no commitment to the existence of a strict law that events described at the top of page one of the *Times* have effects described at the top of page ten. It suffices that there is a physical law which connects the forces inherent in the hurricane with a physical description of the damage thereby caused. Similarly, therefore, Davidson maintains, despite the fact that there are no strict laws involving reasons and actions as such, reasons and actions can still be causes and effects as long as there are other descriptions of them which enter into a suitable strict law.

Davidson claims that descriptions which satisfy this requirement can be provided by physics, and physics alone. For the laws of physics are genuinely strict, exceptionless, laws, since physics, being the fundamental science of the universe, applies to absolutely all events and processes. Whereas sciences such as biology have to allow for interventions in biological processes which are not themselves susceptible of explanation in biological terms (such as changes in the earth's climate) there cannot be interventions in physical systems which do not admit, in principle, of a physical explanation, even if we do not currently possess it. In this sense physics forms a 'closed' system which does not admit of non-physical exceptions. Hence, the causal theorist should accept that reasons and actions are themselves physical states or processes, connected by the only strict laws that there are, the laws of physics.

This is a remarkable argument, whereby Davidson derives a metaphysical conclusion concerning the physical nature of mental states from premises which concern their causal role. Davidson calls the resulting position 'anomalous monism'; it is 'monist' in that by acknowledging that mental states are physical it avoids the metaphysical dualism of Descartes. But it is 'anomalous' in that it holds that psychology lacks strict laws, so that there cannot be strict laws connecting physical descriptions of states with mental descriptions of them, even though every state which satisfies a mental description is a physical state and thus has a physical description. So the 'anomalism' of the mental amounts to an irreducible dualism of descriptions of states (mental vs. physical) despite the monism of the states themselves (mental states are physical).

The resulting position is intriguing but has not attracted much support because it suggests that in order to understand the causal role of reasons for action we should concern ourselves primarily with the physical descriptions of these reasons which alone enter into the strict laws which explain their causal relationships. Yet a description of someone's beliefs and intentions as such does not seem irrelevant to a causal explanation of his actions in the way in which a description of a hurricane as the event mentioned at the top of page one of today's *Times* is irrelevant to a causal explanation of its effects. Davidson's position, it is often said, is reminiscent of the old 'epiphenomenalist' doctrine that the mind is only a surface appearance, not really integrated into the causal structure of the universe.

Davidson's response to this criticism has been to insist that he has always acknowledged that the mental description of a state depends on its physical description. He calls this the 'supervenience' of the mental on the physical; the details of this are complicated, and I shall return to them later. What matters here is that Davidson holds that it implies that the mental descriptions of mental states are implicated in their causal connections, and thus that the charge of epiphenomenalism is unwarranted. But the fact that Davidson in this way allows for the causal relevance of mental descriptions, and thus for non-strict generalizations which connect physical and mental descriptions, calls into question his claim that the causal role of mental states depends upon the existence of strict laws concerning them which are couched only in the terms of physics—a claim for which he has never provided much argument. So Davidson's defence against the charge of epiphenomenalism calls into question his argument for anomalous monism.

The Mind/Body Identity Theory

Debate on Davidson's position continues, and I shall return to the issue of the 'supervenience' of the mental upon the physical, but I want to turn now to other accounts of the 'mind/body' relationship, beginning from an argument advanced in 1966 by David Lewis which seeks to draw out the implications of mind/body causation. Lewis starts from the observation that actions involve physical events, such as the movements of limbs and other body parts. Hence, insofar as our mental states are causes of our actions, they have effects which can be characterized in purely physical terms. But, as we have seen, physics is a 'closed' science; so where there is an explanation at all of a physical event there must a purely physical explanation of it. Thus the causal significance of mental states has to accommodate itself to the existence of physical explanations of the physical events which are among their effects. The conclusion that Lewis draws is that mental states are themselves physical or 'material' (in this context, for historical reasons, these terms are treated as interchangeable).

This simple argument lies at the heart of most subsequent discussion of the mind/body relationship. I shall return to it later, but I want first to describe in more detail the materialist hypothesis propounded by Lewis and others. Lewis is an American but he calls himself an 'Australian materialist' because the materialist philosophy of mind was first revived in Australia, beginning with papers in the late 1950s by U. T. Place (1924–2000), and J. C. C. Smart (1920–), before it finally received a full statement by David Armstrong (1926–) in his book *The Materialist Theory of Mind* (1968). It is, I think, no accident that this revival of materialism took place outside Britain and North America, where the dominant Wittgensteinian approach to the philosophy of mind in the 1950s and 1960s was distinctly hostile to materialism. Armstrong and Lewis had in fact both studied with Ryle at Oxford, and their materialist philosophy of mind starts off from a mixture of agreement and disagreement with Ryle. They agree with him that connections between mental states and behaviour are central to our ways of thinking about the mind; but they reject the way in which Ryle uses the comparison between mental states and dispositions such as fragility in order to disparage the reality of mental states. On the contrary, they argue, dispositions such as fragility point to the existence of underlying physical structures which explain why fragile objects behave as they do; so mental dispositions similarly require the existence of underlying structures which explain why people with those dispositions behave as they do (my own, slightly different, views on this matter were set out in Chapter 3, pp. 48–50).

The resulting mind/body identity theory involves a combination of conceptual claims and scientific identifications. The central conceptual claim is that our conceptions of mental states are conceptions of causal roles; the scientific element is the identification of the physical states of the body which play these roles. The causal role analysis draws on the thesis that mental states such as perceptions, beliefs, desires, intentions, emotions, feelings, and so on are to be identified by their potential causes and effects. These causes and effects typically involve other mental states (including beliefs about them) so that mental states occupy nodes in a network of potential causal connections between perceptual inputs, behavioural outputs, and intervening mental states. The details of this network are, it is said, provided by folk psychology, which draws on common-sense principles of rational action concerning our tendency to do things which we believe will enable us to get what we want.

When stated as abstractly as this the general idea of a causal role analysis may well not be persuasive. There is no space here to enter into details, but subsequent discussions in this chapter should provide some further indications of the way in which the causal role analysis is supposed to work. In particular, the later discussion of 'intentionality' includes an outline of a causal role analysis of one central aspect of our conception of mental states.

The causal role analysis by itself incorporates no materialist commitments. Lewis's simple argument, however, implies that mental states are physical; otherwise the 'closure' of physics would be in jeopardy, given that both input and output involve physical changes. But it is then a task for science, and not philosophy, to take further the task of their identification. We know enough about ourselves to know that the only serious candidates for states apt to play these roles are neural states, and the materialist philosopher looks forward to a further identification of these states in purely physical terms, so that their mental causal roles are securely accommodated within physics alone.

Functionalism

The 'mind/body identity theory' faces an objection (due to Hilary Putnam) from the possibility of 'multiple realizations' of the causal roles of mental states. This possibility is inherent in the very language of 'causal roles'; for 'roles' are typically positions that can be occupied or 'realized' by more than one person. A familiar computational analogy illustrates the point: the same software can run on radically different types of hardware. Likewise, then, in the case of mental 'software', radical differences between different people and species strongly suggest that we should allow for different ways in which these roles can be realized in the physical 'hardware'. So the relationship of these different realizations to the type of mental state in question cannot be identity.

The obvious response to this point is to adapt the conception of mental states to allow for their realization in a variety of ways. The resulting position is standardly called 'functionalism' and it has become the dominant position in recent philosophy of mind. Nonetheless Lewis, Armstrong, and other Australian materialists object to it on the grounds that it implies that the properties of mental states are not causally efficacious. For, they argue, functionalism implies that the causally efficacious properties are always properties of the physical states which realize a mental state and are not therefore properties of that mental state itself. So, unlike the identity theory, functionalism ends up disallowing mind/body causation.

In order to deal with the phenomenon of 'multiple realization' which gives rise to functionalism, Lewis and Armstrong propose a different modification of the identity theory, namely that the identities involved should be restricted to species or even, where appropriate, particular organisms. So whereas, let us suppose, the functionalist might say that science demonstrates that pain is realized in humans as the firing of 'C-fibres' (some physical structures of the human brain) and in dolphins as the firing of 'D-fibres' (a different physical structure of the dolphin brain), Lewis and Armstrong say that the correct conclusion to draw is that pain-in-humans is the firing of C-fibres and pain-in-dolphins is the firing of D-fibres. This position is, I think, coherent; but once restricted terms such as 'pain-in-humans' are introduced, the functionalist can readily reinterpret them to suit his own purposes: he can take 'pain-in-humans' to denote pain-as-it-is-realized-in-humans, which is a state which certainly does have causally efficacious properties. So the Lewis–Armstrong strategy of restricting identities provides the functionalist with an easy response to their own objection to functionalism.

Furthermore, there is a further variant of the 'multiple realization' argument which the functionalist can, I think, deploy against the Lewis–Armstrong position. This argument starts from the fact that it is contingent that a physical state of an organism is connected to other physical states in such a way as to enable it to fulfil a particular causal role: if the organism had been 'wired up' in different ways the physical state would not have had that role. Given the Lewis–Armstrong position, this implies that it is contingent that a physical state which is in fact a mental state of some type is of that type. Despite the 'necessity of identity' thesis we encountered in Chapter 6, this contingency is not by itself problematic; for (using Kripke's terminology from that chapter) according to the identity theorist the mental description of the state in question (e.g. as 'the intention to dig the garden') is 'non-rigid', and identity statements involving a non-rigid designator (e.g. 'George W. Bush is the present president of the USA') are contingent.

What is nonetheless problematic here is this very thesis that mental descriptions are non-rigid. Just as the non-rigidity of the description 'the present president of the USA' implies that the present president of the USA might not have been the president of the USA, the supposed non-rigidity of mental descriptions implies that my present intention to dig the garden might not have been an intention to dig the garden. But this seems plainly wrong: even when one thinks through the way in which this is supposed to arise, e.g. via the hypothesis of someone with a radically different neural system from that which humans normally have, there is no inclination to conclude that this hypothesis should modify the identity of intentions themselves. Armstrong himself is plainly embarrassed by this point: having declared in his main contribution to a debate with Norman Malcolm on *Consciousness and Causality* (1984) that his intention to paint his bathroom might have been an intention to write a poem (p. 147) he backs off under Malcolm's criticisms and concedes that 'I agree that intentions with different objects are *ipso facto* different intentions' (p. 209). But this concession is simply not compatible with the identity theory he there propounds and defends. It is, however, readily compatible with the functionalist position which distinguishes the functional properties that fix the identity of types of mental state from the physical properties of the states which, in a given species, realize that mental state. For once this distinction is made, it is obvious that the possibility of different causal environments for these physical states does nothing to undermine the identity of the type of mental state involved since its identity, for the functionalist, simply consists of the causal role which is summarized as, for example, the intention to dig the garden.

It seems to me, therefore, that the general consensus in favour of a functionalist version of this causal-cum-materialist approach to the conception of the mind is sound. It does not, however, follow that the resulting position is satisfactory. The standard criticism of it is that it is too 'reductive' in that it implies that our conceptions of mental states are just conceptions of the causal roles of the physical states which realize them, and thus that explanations of action or thought which invoke mental properties of mental states are in principle reducible to explanations which invoke only physical properties of the physical states which realize them.

Functionalists often reject this criticism on the grounds that the multiple realizability of mental states obstructs any simple, non-disjunctive, characterization in purely physical terms of the causal relationships between mental states. But this is not persuasive: the functionalist is committed to the possibility of an account in purely physical terms of the realization, for a given species or whatever, of the mental states of that species; and these accounts must enable the derivation, for that species, of the causal connections between its mental states. An analogy from chemistry is relevant here: there are two very different types of bonding between atoms whereby the atoms of a molecule are bound together—covalent bonding and ionic bonding. As a result, there are two different physical accounts of the structure of molecules and of the ways in which molecules behave in reactions. But this case of the 'multiple realization' of the phenomenon of atomic bonding does not imply that in this respect chemistry is not reducible to physics.

It seems to me, therefore, that the characterization of functionalism as 'reductive' is legitimate. But why is this a criticism? Functionalism certainly does not imply that the mind is inefficacious. On the contrary it is an account of the mind which lays out in general terms how it is that mental states interact with the physical world. But what remains true is that functionalism does imply that mental concepts have no irreducible, or ultimate, causal or explanatory significance, and it is some such ultimate significance that functionalism's critics yearn for. They feel that the presence of mind within the world should matter not just because mind is itself a form of matter. Just to say this, however, is not to demonstrate its truth. To take this issue further it is necessary first to find a defensible alternative to functionalism.

Dual Aspect Theory

There are of course many alternatives, including Cartesian dualism. But most contemporary philosophers are materialists at least to the extent of holding that everything mental has a physical constitution, and once this point is granted a metaphysical dualism of substances is ruled out. Hence the plausible alternative to functionalism is a 'dual aspect' theory of mind (sometimes the phrase 'attribute dualism' is also used, but for a reason which will become apparent later I think this phrase should be avoided). The basic thesis of this position is that human life has both 'physical' and 'mental' aspects, and that the latter, though aspects of something unquestionably physical, a human being, are irreducible to that being's physical aspects. This position harks back to Spinoza's response to Descartes; more recently, Strawson proposed a dual aspect theory in *Individuals* (1959; see Chapter 8, p. 174) and the position was given a detailed development by Brian O'Shaughnessy (1925–?) in *The Will* (1980).

Plainly it is not enough just to postulate the distinctness of these two aspects of our lives. The difficulty is to ensure that the resulting position is coherent with both our physical constitution and the closure of physics. The challenge arises, as ever, from Lewis's simple 1966 argument: our physical constitution implies that all changes in which the mental aspect of our lives is operative bring with them physical changes; and the closure of physics (which the dual aspect theorist should accept) implies that these physical changes are susceptible of explanations exclusively in physical terms. But what then is the supposedly irreducible role for mental properties? Consider a case of someone deliberately waving their hand. The closure of physics implies that their limb movements had physical causes; and if these causes are sufficient to explain the movements, what is the further role of the mental properties of the hand waving? We seem to have too many explanations on the table.

A preliminary response of the dual aspect theorist will be that different things are being explained: the mental properties contribute to the psychological explanation of acts and thoughts, whereas the physical properties explain just the physical processes involved. But this does not by itself defuse the difficulty: for the inescapable involvement of physical processes in the acts and thoughts being explained implies that the explanations are not independent; and since the physical explanations are autonomous, the suspicion is that the psychological explanations which draw upon them are just derivative.

In response to this the dual aspect theorist has to maintain that to be dependent is not necessarily to be derivative, that the involvement of an autonomous domain of physical processes in our acts and thoughts does not preclude the possibility of psychological explanations of them which draw essentially upon mental properties of the persons involved. The best way to make this plausible is, I think, to invoke Strawson's thesis that the concept of a person has a fundamental role in the understanding of human life as the concept of something with both aspects (mental and physical) which provides an irreducible reference point for all psychological inquiries and explanations. If, like Hume and those contemporary philosophers who seek to 'deconstruct the subject', one thinks of persons as just 'bundles' of mental states (e.g. beliefs and desires), and then concentrates simply on these states, it is not easy to resist a merely functional analysis of these concepts, especially once their physical constitution is brought into the account. By contrast, as long as these mental states are conceived as the thoughts and acts of a person, a unified consciousness capable of rational deliberation and action, so that an explanation of them adverts to other features of the same person, it is easier to resist the functionalist approach. For the dual aspect theorist can hold that the explanatory role of the mental aspects of a person's life remains consistent with the closure of physics because, despite their physical constitution, persons themselves do not enter as such into physical theory.

Supervenience

Yet there is a further challenge to be considered—that from the 'supervenience' of the mental upon the physical. The basic idea here, which came up briefly in connection with Davidson, is that our mental states depend upon our physical constitution in the sense that there cannot be a mental difference between people without a physical difference between them. The thesis is usually now expressed in the idiom of possible worlds (see Chapter 6): any world which is a minimal physical duplicate of our world is a psychological duplicate of it, where a 'minimal' physical duplicate is one which duplicates just the physical constitution of our world. This thesis is put forward as an intuitively plausible claim which should be acceptable to dual aspect theorists among others, and it seems at first quite a weak claim. But Lewis and others have argued that, weak though it is, it suffices to establish a reduction of the mental to the physical, contrary to the dual aspect theory.

The argument goes as follows: first, consider a true mental statement M (e.g. 'TB has a toothache'). The supervenience thesis implies that M follows from a complete characterization of the physical constitution of the actual world, which I shall abbreviate as '$Phys_@$'; for supervenience implies that any world in which '$Phys_@$' is true is a world in which M is true. This gives us a physical condition which is sufficient for M; reduction requires a necessary condition as well. To obtain this we have to consider the other worlds in which M might be true. There are many of these and we can abbreviate complete characterizations of their physical constitution as '$Phys_1$', '$Phys_2$' etc. Each of these is sufficient for M, as is any disjunction of them ('$Phys_1$ or $Phys_2$ or . . .'). It now follows that the disjunction of all of them, including '$Phys_@$', is necessary for M. For if materialism is true, one of them has to be true if M is true. Hence this disjunction, which is stated exclusively in physical terms, is both necessary and sufficient for the truth of M: we have

M implies and is implied by '$Phys_@$ or $Phys_1$ or $Phys_2$ or . . .'

So, say Lewis and others, the supervenience of the mental on the physical guarantees the reduction of the mental to the physical; a God seeking to create worlds which include both physical phenomena and mental phenomena such as toothaches need create only worlds with physical phenomena. Once She has done this She has done enough: TB's toothache is already included, thanks to the equivalence stated above.

This argument is not unchallengeable (e.g. perhaps the conception of a complete characterization of the physical constitution of a possible world is illusory), but I am not inclined to challenge it. So I accept the conclusion that a metaphysical dualism of properties, or 'attributes', is untenable, and thus that a defensible dual aspect theory should not seek to base itself upon a metaphysical 'attribute dualism'. What should then be the distinctive thesis of a dual aspect theory? The supervenience argument certainly establishes no reduction of mental concepts to physical concepts. But this point will not differentiate a dual aspect theory from the positions of functionalists and identity theorists who also do not provide a conceptual reduction of the mental to the physical. The crucial point, therefore, has to be that of explanatory reduction: the dual aspect theorist has to hold that despite the metaphysical reduction of mental properties to physical properties implied by the supervenience argument, the causal significance of these properties is in some respects captured by their mental rather than by their physical description.

Lewis introduces another example of supervenience which, conveniently, can be used to bring out the point here: consider, he says, the ways in which pictures of a human face can be created by using a grid of light or dark spots, pixels, on a screen. The resulting pictures supervene upon the patterns of pixels, since similar patterns are such that if one is a picture of a face, so is the other. Hence, as Lewis maintains, it should be possible to provide a disjunctive definition of the property of a pattern's being a picture of a face by reference to all the different patterns of pixels which are pictures of a face. But it does not follow that this property does not have a causal significance which is not dependent on this definition. For example, a picture of a face is easy for humans to recognize and remember; but this fact is explained by its being a picture of a human face, and not by the fact that it is constituted by some suitable pattern of pixels.

This case provides a model for the dual aspect theorist's claim that, despite their physical constitution, the mental aspects of personal life— a person's thoughts, feelings and acts—have a causal significance as such. Yet the difficult point to be sure about is whether this does not clash with the closure of physics. This matters for it seems mad to suppose that the fundamental laws of physics admit of violations once they are applied to human beings (or organisms generally). As suggested earlier, the way in which dual aspect theorists will seek to negotiate this issue is by insisting that the phenomena explained by reference to mental properties are events in the lives of persons, and thus not events conceived of in terms of physical events at all. Whether this suffices to defuse the issue here, given the metaphysical reduction of the mental to the physical, remains disputed, but I shall not pursue this issue further. Instead I shall look at recent discussions of other topics in the philosophy of mind which, in addition to their intrinsic interest, cast further light on the debate between functionalist and dual aspect theories.

Free Will

I begin with the issue of the freedom of the will. This can be introduced by considering a passage from John McDowell's (1942–) influential book *Mind and World* (1994):

We need to recapture the Aristotelian idea that a normal mature human being is a rational animal, but without losing the Kantian idea that rationality operates freely in its own sphere . . . [W]e need to see ourselves as animals whose natural being is permeated with rationality, even though rationality is appropriately conceived in Kantian terms. (p. 85).

McDowell here connects freedom, rationality and our 'natural being'. By this last phrase McDowell has in mind the possibility of our developing through education and practice what he calls a 'second nature' which is manifested in free rational agency. Since such a 'second nature' is conceived by McDowell as an aspect of human life irreducible to our physical 'first nature', the resulting position is a dual aspect theory.

As these remarks indicate, a dual aspect theory interprets the freedom of the will by taking it that an agent's rational deliberations have an irreducible role in directing their thoughts and actions. To put the matter in traditional terms, such an account is therefore broadly 'libertarian' in its sympathies, but because it is not formulated in the context of traditional Cartesian dualism, it does not require the traditional libertarian's 'panicky metaphysics' (as Strawson put it in his famous essay 'Freedom and Resentment' (1962)), according to which the vindication of free will requires that free agents have the power to violate the closure of physics by intervening *ex nihilo* in the causal order of the physical world. A functionalist theory, by contrast, brings with it a determinist conception of freedom. For although a functionalist theory of mind also provides a role for rationality within the understanding of human life, it implies that the causal significance of the rational connections incorporated in the functional analysis of mental concepts is discharged through the physical systems which realize these rational connections. Hence, this position does not legitimate a conception of the efficacy of rationality as such which libertarians take to be essential to our status as free rational agents. Thus the choice between a dual aspect theory and a functionalist theory brings with it a choice between sophisticated libertarian and sophisticated determinist conceptions of freedom.

It may well seem that this question of the understanding of the place of rationality in human life is not central to questions about the freedom of the will. Instead, it may be thought, these questions concern instead the conditions under which an agent 'could have done otherwise', for the reason that this requirement is both necessary for the freedom of the will and threatened by determinist accounts of human life. It is certainly true that for the first half of the twentieth century debates about free will revolved around the interpretation of this requirement; in 1969, however, the American philosopher Harry Frankfurt (1929–) showed that these debates were largely misguided: one can act freely even where one could not have done otherwise. Frankfurt's demonstration of this point involves a typically philosophical thought-experiment with a cast of three characters: Jane, Charles, and Blake. Jane is plotting to kill Charles; Blake also desires Charles's death;

but Blake prefers not to get involved and, unknown to Jane, has the ability to monitor her intentions and revive her determination to kill Charles if he finds that her commitment is flagging. In the event, Frankfurt supposes, Blake does not need to intervene: Jane's determination to kill Charles does not weaken and she bumps him off successfully.

Jane's situation is such that she could not have done otherwise: for Blake would have brought her back to her project had her commitment to it weakened. Yet it seems clear that, in the case as envisaged, Jane acted as a free agent and is responsible for her action. So free action does not require that an agent 'could have done otherwise'; what is important is the way in which their action depends upon their intentions. The first thought here will be that freedom just requires that action should be caused by the agent's own intentions. But this, Frankfurt argues, sets the standard too low: someone subject to psychological compulsions such as an addiction acts intentionally, but where their intentions are not freely formed we do not regard their will as free. Hence he suggests that what is characteristic of a free agent is that the 'first-order' intentions with which she acts are in harmony with her reflective 'second-order' intentions concerning her own habits and motivations. Thus he distinguishes the 'willing addict', whose habit accords with her second-order intentions, from the 'unwilling addict', whose habits conflicts with them: the former acts freely, even though it is also true that she could not act otherwise; but the latter is not now free.

Frankfurt's thesis that action in accordance with second-order intentions is an important test of the freedom of the will is widely accepted; but his critics argue that since second-order intentions are susceptible to psychological compulsions of the same kind as ordinary first-order ones, their efficacy cannot be by itself decisive for questions of freedom. Instead, they argue, the relevance of an agent's second-order intentions is due to the fact that they involve reflective assessments of reasons for and against one's conduct, and it is this fundamental susceptibility to the efficacy of reasons which is central to the freedom of the will. If this is right, it is then easy to see how it leads back to the issue which I identified earlier as central to contemporary debates concerning freedom, and in particular to the different accounts of the efficacy of reasons provided by the libertarian dual aspect theorist and the determinist functionalist.

Knowledge of Self and Others

There was a sharp contrast between the traditional Cartesian dualist and the behaviourist on the issue of knowledge of ourselves and others: according to the dualist self-knowledge is straightforward (too easy in the opinion of dualism's critics), whereas knowledge of others is inherently problematic; for the behaviourist knowledge of others is in principle straightforward, but reflective self-knowledge is problematic. So it is worth considering how far these points resurface in the context of the debate between dual aspect and functionalist theories.

Consider first the dual-aspect theorist. She holds that our thoughts and feelings provide the reasons which enter into our conscious deliberations. Thus she takes it that thoughts and feelings are rational dispositions with a conceptual structure which normally makes them available to reflective inquiry. Hence the possibility of self-knowledge, albeit fallible and limited (since wishful thinking and self-deception always threaten), comes with this essentially rationalist conception of mental states.

But what about knowledge of others? The traditional dualist proposed that our understanding of others proceeds 'by analogy' with our own case. This was inadequate in the context of a metaphysical dualism that detached thoughts completely from bodily states; but the dual aspect theorist does not share that metaphysics and has no reason to deny that thoughts and feelings are often observable in the lives of others. Thus she will hold that actions, and especially speech, permit rational interpretation in accordance with Davidson's conception of radical interpretation (cf. Chapter 5). In this context the old idea of arguing by analogy is replaced by the idea of 'replicating' others: in our understanding of others we imaginatively 'replicate' their reasonings in order to arrive at an understanding of their actions which exhibits them as rational. So although our understanding of others is limited by the inescapable ambiguities of human life, it looks as though the dual aspect theorist can deal reasonably satisfactorily with the issue of our knowledge of 'other minds' which was a perennial bugbear for the old-fashioned dualist.

For the functionalist the imputation of mental states to others is a causal hypothesis involving connections between these states, perceptions, and behaviour. So knowledge of others is unproblematic in principle. What, however, of self-knowledge? Because the functionalist is not a behaviourist there is no reason for him to reject our own experience of ourselves; instead he will regard this as the product of a further causal connection inherent in the conception of mental states. Yet there remains a doubt as to whether the functionalist does justice thereby to the first person experience of rational deliberation. He regards our reasonings as a way in which we manifest ourselves to ourselves as bearers of complex dispositions which, in the circumstances, have an effect upon us in leading to new thoughts or actions. Although it would be unfair to say that, under this description, we are alienated from our own deliberations, for we experience the relevant dispositions as our own, it remains true that the experience of drawing a conclusion or making a decision on the balance of reasons provides for the functionalist what is at best an incomplete understanding of what is involved, since the changes involved are all to be fundamentally explained in third-person physical terms.

Intentionality

The Austrian philosopher Franz Brentano proposed at the end of the nineteenth century that it is the mark of psychology that it involves acts or states which are 'intentional' insofar as what they are about need not exist or be the case: for example, people are afraid of ghosts, have tried to find El Dorado, and of course have many false beliefs. Brentano's use here of the term 'intentional' comes from medieval philosophy, but it is a little unfortunate since it wrongly suggests an immediate connection with ordinary intentions. In fact ordinary intentions are intentional in Brentano's special sense, but mental states such as beliefs which are intentional in Brentano's sense need not be intentional in the ordinary sense.

It is disputed whether absolutely all mental states are intentional in Brentano's sense—e.g. whether simple sensations are—but this dispute is not important here. What matters is that the fact that mental states are typically intentional in Brentano's sense sets them apart from any ordinary physical relationships: one cannot be hurt by ghosts nor can one live in El Dorado. Hence intentionality is an intriguing and challenging phenomenon, especially if one starts from a presumption that all truths are somehow grounded in physical truths. The obvious suggestion is that intentionality should be accommodated within a physical conception of the world by regarding mental states as representations realized by neural, and ultimately physical, structures, and then explaining how these physical structures can represent what does not exist or is not the case. The intuitive models for such representations are pictures and sentences, both of which are physical and yet can represent the false and the non-existent, and the American philosopher Jerry Fodor (1935–) has indeed argued that the way to understand the intentionality of thought is precisely to postulate the existence of a 'language of thought'. What Fodor means by this is that thought draws upon the existence of brain states which function as sentence-like representations with a content comparable to that which we attribute to particular thoughts (beliefs, desires, etc.). Fodor thinks of these brain states as comparable to the states of a computer and capable of representing aspects of the world in virtue of causal connections between them and features of the world.

This bold position is broadly functionalist in its approach, but includes many details which other functionalists reject. Some argue on empirical grounds that discoveries about the structure of the brain's neural networks undermine Fodor's hypothesis of sentence-like neural representations and support instead a different 'connectionist' hypothesis concerning the way in which states of the brain represent aspects of the world. Others argue that it is anyway more plausible to adopt a pictorial model for mental representation, whereby many different features of a situation are represented together through the structure of the representation instead of being separately represented on a sentence-by-sentence basis. But a crucial issue throughout is whether Fodor provides a satisfactory account of intentionality. Fodor holds that the content of the brain's neural 'sentences' is fixed by causal considerations; but since causes are invariably real, there is then a tricky question as to how what is unreal can be represented.

There is no consensus as to how this matter is to be handled and I cannot discuss here the numerous complex suggestions, including Fodor's, which have been proposed to deal with it. My own view is that it is sensible to start by adopting the pragmatist idea that beliefs involve dispositions to action: thus to believe that Paris is north of London is to be in a state which disposes one to act 'as if' Paris is north of London, e.g. to head north from London if one wants to get to Paris. The great merit of this position, as the example shows, is that this idea readily accommodates false belief. Since this proposal makes reference to desires, however, it also requires an account of their intentionality. The basic idea here must be that desires motivate actions to fulfil them: someone who wants to get to Paris from London is someone who is motivated to try to get to Paris from London. Hence although what someone then does in order to satisfy a desire depends on their beliefs, an account of the underlying disposition, that to desire that X is to be disposed to bring it about that X, does not make reference to beliefs. So the contribution of a desire to the explanation of action is not dependent upon what is believed; and this makes it possible in principle to characterize also a separate role for beliefs. In practice, of course, the evidence available will often underdetermine the identification of the desires and beliefs operative in a given course of action. But the functionalist has further resources upon which to draw in seeking to determine the contents of beliefs, desires and other thoughts by reference to their causal role. Beliefs are dependent upon perception, memory, testimony, and inference; desires connect with needs, with sensations such as pain and pleasure, and indeed with beliefs about what is attractive or repugnant. So the attribution of mental states in accordance with a functional analysis is constrained by these further causal relationships to which it is answerable

A prima-facie plausible functionalist position is, therefore, that the intentionality of mental states arises from the action-guiding roles of physical brain-states, though the question of just what mental state they realize is also dependent upon their causal connections with physical brain-states which realize other mental states. So far as I can see, nothing specific follows about the intrinsic structure of these physical brain-states, whether they are sentence-like, map-like, or altogether different from any system of representation with which we are familiar. Conceptual analysis can stop at a point which leaves that question to be answered by scientists in the laboratory rather than philosophers in their armchairs.

Functionalism's critics object, not surprisingly, that considerations of this kind are insufficient to provide a determinate specification of intentional mental states such as beliefs, desires, and intentions. Dan Dennett (1942–) is a particularly influential critic of this type; his position is similar to Quine's (cf. Chapter 4) insofar as he also takes it that indeterminacy arguments show that meanings and thoughts do not show up within the conception of the world that is apparent when a thinker adopts what he calls 'the physical stance'. But, unlike Quine, Dennett does not privilege physics; so he is content to characterize meanings and thoughts as objective insofar as they are apparent once one adopts an 'intentional stance' towards the behaviour of complex systems such as ourselves. But this, Dennett holds, involves presumptions about rationality (and perhaps purposiveness) which go beyond the causal considerations characteristic of the physical stance on which the functionalist ultimately relies.

The functionalist may complain that Dennett overlooks the role of common-sense principles of rationality in the functionalist's causal role analysis of mental states. But since the functionalist is committed to the thesis that these principles can be substantiated by an account of the physical realizations of the mental states involved, there is a commitment here to determinacy from within the physical stance. Thus what emerges is that the issue here comes back to the functionalism/dual aspect theory dispute: Dennett's claim that there is an irreducible distinction between the intentional stance and the physical stance is an instance of the dual aspect theorist's insistence upon the irreducibility of rationality, and thus intentionality.

The dual aspect theorist's position on this matter is well illustrated by reconsidering Davidson's response to Quine's indeterminacy arguments. Davidson's claim was that as long as we regard others as rational thinkers like ourselves, to whom we can extend the 'charitable' presumptions of truth and rationality, no serious indeterminacy should in principle arise in the course of a radical interpreter's project (cf. Chapter 5, pp. 100–1). But for Davidson these presumptions of truth and rationality are not just plausible causal principles; instead they have an a priori status as conditions for the possibility of interpretation. By giving them this status Davidson implies that our understanding of others as rational thinkers and agents is irreducible to the kind of understanding which informs the functionalist's approach. So Davidson's anomalous monism includes, along with the questionable claims about causation discussed earlier in this chapter, a dual aspect theory: the kind of understanding of thought and language that is characteristic of radical interpretation is irreducible to that which can be found within the physical sciences.

Brutes

At this point the status of non-human animals becomes important. For an obvious functionalist response to the previous argument is to point to the situation of brute animals: our ascription to them of thoughts which, however simple, are still intentional in Brentano's sense seems legitimate, even though, without language, their lives do not manifest the kind of rationality on which the dual aspect theorist concentrates. Davidson's reply will of course be to deny that brute animals have thoughts at all (cf. Chapter 5, pp. 102–3); but common-sense declares this unbelievable. A different option would be to concede that functionalism is a satisfactory account of animal thoughts, but to hold that things are very different for beings with a language like ours ('functionalism for animals; rationalism for humans').

This compromise position implies (contra-Dennett) that there is a form of intentional mental representation for which functionalism provides a satisfactory account; it is only the exercise of rationality which language makes possible that requires the further explanatory resource of a dual aspect theory. This position implies, however, that there is a radical difference in kind between the thoughts and lives of language-speaking people and those of other animals. But we know that in very many respects, including those involved in human language-learning, the differences here are only differences of degree. Hence this objection suggests that one should move from a dual aspect theory that contrasts the mental and the physical, to a 'plural aspect' theory that introduces intermediate biological categories and then enriches the understanding of brute animal thought by reference to their species-specific forms of life. Within the framework provided by such a theory, even 'functionalism for animals' might well be found to be an unsatisfactory doctrine.

Externalism

One initially unexpected objection to functionalism is that it is a neo-Cartesian theory of the mind. The basis for this objection is that functionalism is a theory about mental representations, with inner physical states substituting for Cartesian ideas as intermediaries between the world and the mind. At a rather abstract level this description is indeed fair enough; the objection is then that such a position assumes that the mind is 'in the head', whereas, it is argued by 'externalists', thoughts are inescapably dependent upon the external worlds inhabited by their thinkers.

We encountered this externalist position earlier in connection with Putnam's response to scepticism (cf. Chapter 8, pp. 177–8). It also connects with Strawson's old debate with Russell concerning vacuous names (cf. Chapter 3, p. 60); for the radical version of Strawson's position advanced by Gareth Evans rests on the externalist thesis that our ability to think about a particular object is dependent upon our coming into some cognitive relationship, direct or indirect, with the object in question, and thus upon its existence. According to Evans, where there is a name in use which is taken to be a name of a real non-fictional object, but is not in fact a name of anything, those who use the name not realizing the mistake involved do not thereby express the 'singular' thought concerning a particular object which they suppose themselves to be expressing (though they do show that they have other thoughts, for example that the name in question is a name of an appropriate object). This is a radically anti-Cartesian thesis, since it implies that where thinkers are mistaken about the world they are also liable to be mistaken about the thoughts they are having.

A good case for assessing Evans' thesis concerns the use of the name 'Vulcan' for a large asteroid with an orbit between Mercury and the Sun whose existence was hypothesized by Le Verrier in 1859 in order to account for anomalies in the observed orbit of Mercury as compared with that which is predicted by Newtonian celestial mechanics. It turns out that there is no such asteroid (the anomaly disappears within Einstein's General Theory); hence, according to Evans, the astronomers of the time who speculated about the mass and position of Vulcan were not having the singular thoughts they supposed themselves to be having. Since, however, they were clearly having thoughts about the mass and position of an asteroid in the specific location, Evans' critics maintain that these are just the thoughts which the astronomers would have had anyway, had Le Verrier's Vulcan hypothesis been correct. So, according to these critics, who inherit Russell's side of the Russell–Strawson debate, Evans' externalist conception of 'object-dependent' singular thoughts is a myth. Their position may seem vulnerable to the objection that, by blurring the distinction between names and descriptions, they overlook Kripke's distinction between rigid and non-rigid designators (cf. Chapter 6, pp. 125–7) which remains applicable even in a case of this kind since the astronomers can speculate that Vulcan might have had a very different orbit from that postulated by Le Verrier. But by using 'rigidified' descriptions (cf. Chapter 6, pp. 128–9) such as 'the asteroid actually located between Mercury and the Sun' to specify the content of these speculations, Evans' Russellian critics can in fact readily accommodate Kripke's distinction, and thereby challenge defenders of Evans to show that a similar treatment of thoughts concerning real objects omits anything from the content of these thoughts.

Debate on this issue continues, but most externalists base their case on a slightly different claim, namely that the identity, rather than the existence, of many of our thoughts is dependent on their external context. This claim is standardly supported by an argument similar to that which we have encountered before—Putnam's 'Twin Earth' fable (Chapter 6, pp. 133–4). The basic story in this case is that in a parallel counterfactual universe (rather than a distant galaxy, as before) there is a planet, Twin Earth, which differs from Earth only in that wherever on Earth there is water (= H_2O) there is a different, though superficially very similar, liquid on Twin Earth, twater (= XYZ). We are now to concentrate on the implication that we humans have exact physical duplicates on Twin Earth (though we have to bracket the fact that, as humans, we are largely composed of water!), and ask ourselves about the thoughts we and our twins express when using the word 'water'. Putnam's claim is that whereas we express thoughts about water, our twins express thoughts about twater despite the fact that we are physical duplicates and employ the same descriptions in our 'water'-thoughts. So the identity of our 'water'-thoughts is affected by their worldly context.

Putnam's fiction is supposed to pose a challenge to functionalism, and materialist conceptions of thought in general, because it involves physical duplicates with different thoughts. The dialectical situation here is, however, complicated. I argued in Chapter 6 that the fact that twater is not H_2O does not by itself show that it is not a kind of water—that depends on how different from H_2O the basic physical properties of twater are. But even where twater is assumed to be so different from H_2O that it is not a type of water, the issue is not straightforward, since the functionalist can maintain that, on this assumption, his position implies that we and our twins have different thoughts even though we and they are physical duplicates. For the inner physical states of the twins are being assumed to be normally connected by perception and action to a different type of liquid, and since the causal role analysis which determines the intentional content of these states takes account of the actual normal causal connections which involve these states, the requisite difference between our thoughts and those of our twins will emerge. On the other hand, the functionalist will have to admit that, as far as the psychology of the twins is concerned, this difference is not causally significant, since the underlying physical states which realize the thoughts are precisely similar. So even if functionalism can accommodate a difference between our thoughts and those of our twins, it implies that this difference has no psychological significance.

Is this a substantial objection to functionalism? Only if we are persuaded that Putnam's argument reveals the existence of an important difference between our thoughts and those of our twins. But this is questionable: the case is one in which the descriptions that we and our twins give involving 'water' are exactly similar, though they include the hypothesis that 'water' is a natural kind term which identifies a substance which, in the actual environment, has a single basic structure (a single 'essence', if that language is to be used). It is then added that whereas we are dealing with water (= H_2O) our twins are dealing with twater (= XYZ) (though in neither case is this point known to us). But does this reveal an important difference between our thoughts? Externalism's internalist critics will deny that it does: although our thoughts and those of our twins are about different substances, this does not point to a psychological difference between us. Here is a parallel case: suppose that in the actual world Jack the Ripper was in fact William Gladstone, though no one ever discovered this fact; and that on Twin Earth Jack the Ripper was Benjamin Disraeli, though again no one ever discovered this fact there. Then the 'Jack the Ripper'-thoughts we and our twins express are about different people; but it seems unwarranted to suppose that this difference marks a psychological difference between us.

The internalist thesis that there is no psychological difference between us and our twins faces, however, a straightforward objection: our 'water'-thoughts are true or false of H_2O, those of our twins are true or false of XYZ. But if there are no psychological differences between us, how can our thoughts have different truth-conditions? The internalist's reply to this takes as a model the thoughts which each of us has concerning ourselves—e.g. thoughts such as 'I am tired'; for different people, each thinking 'I am tired', thereby have thoughts with different truth-conditions. This is not an intrinsically challenging phenomenon: it just exemplifies our capacity to employ 'indexical' concepts whose truth-conditions are inherently context-dependent, and functionalism certainly has no difficulty in accommodating concepts of this kind. To apply this model to 'water'-thoughts, the internalist will just point to the implicit presence of the indexical concept 'actually' in the descriptions which we and our twins employ; for this concept 'locates' our 'water'-thoughts in the actual world in which they are true of H_2O and locates the 'water'-thoughts of our twins on Twin Earth in which they are true of XYZ.

The externalist arguments so far considered have failed to make a strong case for a thesis which is incompatible with functionalism. There are, however, many variations of Putnam's fable; as with the Gettier-cases discussed in the previous chapter, there is by now a rich variety of Twin Earth fantasies. An important type, created by Tyler Burge (1946–), involve parallel worlds in which it is the social context constituted by authoritative uses of language that is different. A typical Burge case runs as follows: for us the term 'arthritis' is restricted to painful inflammations of the joints, normally caused by deposits of uric acid there, so that one cannot have arthritis (as opposed to rheumatism) in one's thigh muscles, although uric acid deposits there are also very painful. But one can well imagine a Twin Earth just like ours except that there the term 'arthritis' is taken to be properly applicable to painful inflammations anywhere in the body that are caused by deposits of uric acid. Burge then argues that whereas in our world someone, Oscar, with an inflammation of his left thigh caused by uric acid who utters the sentence 'I have arthritis in my left thigh' expresses a thought which is false, his twin on Twin Earth, TwinOscar, who utters the same sentence, expresses a different thought which is, in his context, correct.

This case involves many assumptions concerning the role of experts in determining the meaning of language and the relationship between thought and language. These assumptions connect with the issues raised at the end of Chapter 5 concerning the extent to which language is a practice which rests on social norms, but if one accepts these assumptions and also that the repertoire of thoughts available to a thinker is constrained by the language he uses, the difference Burge points to will arise. The obvious strategy for an internalist response is, as before, to find an indexical element in the situation, so that the thoughts expressed by Oscar and his twin can be shown to be essentially similar. Thus one can argue that, on the assumptions Burge makes in setting up his case, Oscar and TwinOscar both express the thought that in their left thigh they have the condition which their local experts describe as 'arthritis'; the fact that their local experts then differ concerning what counts as 'arthritis' does not make a psychological difference to Oscar and TwinOscar, even though it gives their thoughts different truth-conditions.

Although this response is, I think, plausible, it seems to me that Burge's case does nonetheless point to a problematic issue for functionalists. For it is far from clear that a functionalist could plausibly accommodate the assumptions Burge makes concerning the social environment of thought within a causal role analysis of the thought realized by a physical state of the thinker. Somehow the functionalist's account of the causal connections which connect an individual's physical states to the world will have to encompass the normative structure of the individual's linguistic and social environment, including, for example, Oscar's deference to experts concerning the identification of diseases. It is not, I think, unduly sceptical to hold that no such account is seriously conceivable—and thus that someone who wants to hold on to a functionalist, or broadly materialist, conception of thought must reject some of the assumptions inherent in Burge's case. In this they will have a potent champion in Chomsky, whose view of these matters (cf. Chapter 5, p. 119) is altogether different from that of Burge. My own sympathies are with Burge, but debate on this matter remains unresolved.

Hence, although there is here a problem for functionalism, the issue is not one which specially concerns the alleged externalist dimension of thought nor, indeed, is it in the end, a new issue. For the question of the importance of the normative structure of our social environment is closely related to the criticisms of functionalism considered at the end of the last section. Functionalism's rationalist critics will argue that Burge's example points back to the fundamental status of language-games as conceived by Wittgenstein (cf. Chapter 2), and to the distinctive principles of rationality inherent in Davidson's conception of radical interpretation (cf. Chapter 5), and thus to considerations which are central to a dual aspect theory of mind, but incompatible with functionalism. This complaint is, I think, serious. But it just reiterates one side of the previous debate concerning intentionality. So externalism poses no extra challenge to functionalism.

Consciousness

I turn finally to the topic of consciousness. This topic is inseparable from that of subjectivity, since to be a 'subject' is to be a subject of consciousness. In a famous paper 'What is it like to be a bat?' (1974) Thomas Nagel argued that however much objective knowledge we might have of a bat's behaviour and of the ways in which its brain works we cannot form an adequate conception of its subjective consciousness:

So if extrapolation from our own case is involved in the idea of what it is like to be a bat, the extrapolation must be incompletable. We cannot form more than a schematic conception of what it *is* like. For example, we may ascribe general *types* of experience on the basis of the animal's structure and behavior. . . . But we believe that these experiences also have in each case a specific subjective character, which it is beyond our ability to conceive. (*Mortal Questions*, pp. 169–70).

It will be clear that, if Nagel is right, the 'subjective character' of experience is very mysterious; indeed Nagel's main aim is to awaken a sense of this mystery. But is there a real mystery here?

Nagel's remarks show that he takes it that the mystery of consciousness concerns bats as well as humans. It is, nonetheless, simplest to deal with ourselves and our own experiences. Philosophical discussion of this topic has focused on the case of visual experience, in particular the experience of colours, and I shall follow this practice (Nagel of course chose bats because their perceptual experience is primarily auditory and not visual). During the first part of this century, especially in the writings of Moore and Russell, sense experience was regarded as awareness of certain distinctive objects, 'sense-data', which, in the case of visual experience, were taken to be patches of colour. But from the start this position was criticized as involving a fallacious inference from the description of a visual experience as one in which something, a ripe tomato perhaps, appears red to a description of the experience as an awareness of the tomato's red appearance. As we saw in Chapter 3, the position was also criticized on other grounds by Ryle and Austin in the early post-1945 period, and by the 1960s it had few supporters .

An alternative position, developed in the 1940s by C. J. Ducasse (1881–1969) and then refined by R. Chisholm (1916–99), takes it that where, on some occasion, a tomato looks red to me this is because the tomato's visible presence causes me to sense 'redly'. Ducasse and Chisholm invent an adverbial form ('redly') of what are usually just adjectives ('red') because they take our visual experience of colour to be constituted by the different ways ('redly', 'bluely' etc.) in which we experience regions of the visual field. This talk of different ways of experiencing can be re-expressed by saying that our experience has different 'phenomenal' qualities and C. I. Lewis's use of Latin terminology ('*quale*'/'*qualia*') when talking of such qualities (*Mind and World Order*, p. 60 (op. cit. p. 278)) has become standard: '*qualia*' are phenomenal (or 'phenomenological') qualities so conceived, and those who believe in them are often called '*qualia* freaks'.

This derogatory term indicates that many philosophers regard *qualia* as weird; they hold that if we think seriously about the metaphysics involved we will see that there could not be any *qualia*. Where a tomato looks red to me, they say, the tomato appears visually to me to be red. But this does not imply either that it is itself red or that there is something else which is red in some further sense—its appearance or my visual experience. Our sense experiences do not need to have an intrinsic phenomenal character in order to represent to us the objective qualities of things, such as their colour. Instead, it is argued, causation provides all that is needed: the fact that a ripe tomato looks red to me just is the fact that my visual experience of it is of a physical type which is normally caused in human beings by a red object in the visual field.

For the *qualia* theorist, of course, such an account is like *Hamlet* without the Prince: it provides a schematic characterization of sense experience, but omits what is distinctive, important and challenging—an understanding of what it is like to experience something as red. There are many attempts to substantiate this complaint, of which the best is the tale of Mary, first told by Frank Jackson (1943–) in 1986.

Mary is a brilliant scientist, living at a time of much greater knowledge of physics and neuroscience than at present, and is an expert in these fields. She knows all the physical facts about the way in which the brain works and about the causal roles of its states. The catch, however, is that Mary has lived so far in an entirely black-and-white environment; so although she knows that things have chromatic colours and that humans have visual experiences in which these colours are apparent to them, she has never had such an experience herself. But one day Mary leaves her black-and-white environment, sees a ripe tomato and learns for the first time what red things look like. Clearly Mary has learnt something; but since she already knew all the physical facts, it seems that she must have learnt something else—which of course the *qualia* theorist will identify as the distinctive phenomenal *quale* of a human visual experience in which a tomato looks red.

The challenge for the critic is, therefore, to provide a plausible alternative account of what Mary learns. David Lewis has proposed that what Mary learns is not a further fact but a new skill—a new ability to recognize experiences in which things look red and to imagine further experiences of this kind. Before she left her black-and-white environment she could use her knowledge of neuroscience to identify the characteristic physical states involved in such experiences; but by actually having experiences of this kind, she acquires a new way of recognizing them. The position can be put in Ryle's terminology: Mary's additional knowledge is 'know-how', not 'knowing-that'.

Is this enough? Mary certainly does acquire these new abilities. But the *qualia* theorist will say that she is able to recognize her experiences in this new way precisely because, in having them, her consciousness now manifests for the first time their characteristic phenomenal quality which she learns to recognize.

To take this debate further it is, I think, helpful to set it in the context of the functionalism/dual aspect theory debate developed in this chapter. For one can certainly speak of the further 'aspect' of experience which Mary discovers when she leaves her black-and-white environment. But as we saw earlier, the supervenience of the mental upon the physical implies a metaphysical reduction of mental facts to physical facts; so this new aspect of Mary's life is not to be conceived as the

discovery of some new and distinctively non-physical subjective qualities. That would amount to an untenable attribute dualism; instead the
importance of this new aspect must lie primarily in its occupying some
irreducible explanatory role. Mary's new abilities do indeed suggest a
role of this kind, but first more needs to be said about the way in which
this aspect is to be conceived.

A central point is to introduce Frege's conception of the 'sense' of a
term as the characteristic 'mode of presentation' of that to which the
term refers (cf. Chapter 3, p. 59) and apply it in an account of the
structure of perceptual experience. For what a reformed *qualia* theorist
needs to do is to abandon altogether the conception of *qualia* as special
phenomenal qualities of experience, and replace it with a conception of
special sensory modes of presentation of the sensible qualities of things
such as colours. The existence of these 'qualitative senses', as I shall call
them, is, by itself, consistent with the position of the functionalist
critics of *qualia* who offer the causal account of them mentioned earlier.
But the ground is now cleared for a critical comparison between this
functionalist approach, with its commitment to a physical realization
of qualitative senses which underpins their causal role, and a dual
aspect theory which assigns an irreducible explanatory role to qualitative senses.

The standard way of arguing for a dual aspect theory in this area is to
maintain that there is an 'explanatory gap' which separates an understanding of experience in purely physical terms from one which
involves the qualitative senses inherent in experience—as the tale of
Mary can now be reinterpreted to show. As we saw above, however,
functionalists have a way of accommodating Mary's new knowledge,
namely as the acquisition of a new skill which enables her to recognize
the type of her own new experiences. So the issue here is comparable to
that confronted in the previous discussion of intentionality; indeed, in
effect, we are dealing here with the intentionality of experience. But the
arguments will have to be somewhat different: dual aspect theorists
cannot draw here on considerations concerning rationality to support
their rejection of the functionalist thesis. For there need be nothing
especially rational about Mary's new ability. Instead dual aspect theorists will, I suspect, need to demonstrate, first, that it is an essential

feature of our experiences, with their qualitative senses, that they are the experiences of a subject who recognizes himself or herself as a subject of experience; and, secondly, that this 'subjective' aspect of experience is one that cannot be satisfactorily accommodated within the purely objective perspective of a functionalist account of experience. In effect, an appeal to subjectivity has to achieve for the irreducibility of the qualitative senses inherent in experience what the appeal to rationality was supposed to achieve for the irreducibility of thought. But whether such an appeal can be substantiated remains, I think, an open question; and, even supposing it can be substantiated for us, there is a further question as to how one might substantiate it for animals such as bats.

10

Questions of Value

Moral philosophy within the English-speaking tradition was still dominated in 1945 by two theses inherited from the first half of the twentieth century. One was G. E. Moore's thesis, expounded in *Principia Ethica* (1903), that there is a mistake, which he rather misleadingly called the 'naturalistic fallacy', in all attempts to provide a foundation for morality which involve a reductive definition of moral concepts. Moore inferred that morality presupposes instead the existence of an irreducible domain of distinctive facts concerning the intrinsic value of many different kinds of things. Although most of his contemporaries and successors agreed with him concerning the existence of the naturalistic fallacy, many held that there is no such domain of distinctive facts concerning value. Instead, and this was the second thesis still prevalent in 1945, they held that our moral judgements just express certain fundamental moral attitudes which are not dependent upon beliefs about the value of the objects of these attitudes.

Taken together, these theses implied that philosophical reflection and discussion had little to contribute to moral debate. Hence all that was left for moral philosophy was the 'analysis' of moral concepts, conceived as a way of clarifying their implications and presuppositions, but without any expectation of validating significant moral judgements. A. J. Ayer gave a succinct statement of this position in 1954:

There is a distinction, which is not always sufficiently marked, between the activity of a moralist, who sets out to elaborate a moral code, or to encourage its observance, and that of a moral philosopher, whose concern is not primarily to make moral judgments but to analyse their nature. ('Editorial Foreward' to *Ethics* by P. Nowell-Smith)

It is indicative of the transformation of moral philosophy during the subsequent half-century that almost no philosopher would now agree with Ayer. For although contemporary philosophy still distinguishes between 'metaethical' debates concerning the nature of moral judgement and 'normative' debates concerning substantive moral theory, it is widely agreed that there is no sharp distinction between the two and that issues of substantive moral theory fall within the scope of philosophy. Indeed the most striking contrast with the situation in 1945 (or 1954) has been the explosion of writing in the area of so-called 'applied ethics', in fields such as business ethics, medical ethics, and environmental ethics.

The emergence of these new areas of inquiry is indicative of a growing confidence in the possibility of ethics. It is, however, important not to misunderstand the term 'applied ethics': it may suggest that, as with pure and applied mathematics, there is a well-established 'pure' ethics that is here just being 'applied' to real life situations. But this is misleading: although there are general theories in ethics such as utilitarianism, the issues that arise within applied ethics typically involve a variety of conflicting considerations, and finding the right balance between them involves an exercise of judgement which is not just a matter of applying some established 'pure' principles to new situations. Indeed, one of the most important features of these new areas of ethical inquiry is that they direct attention to questions that have received little or no attention within traditional general ethical theories, such as the reasons for preserving endangered species or for prohibiting human cloning.

The emergence of these new areas of ethical concern reflects changes in our culture; but the confidence that philosophical reflection about them can suggest anything worthy of attention owes a great deal to debates in political philosophy, particularly in the United States of America. During the 1960s opposition there to the Vietnam War and support for the Civil Rights movement led to sustained debates concerning civil disobedience and human rights, and in *A Theory of Justice* (1971) John Rawls (1921–) showed that philosophical argument can contribute to these debates by combining the analysis of moral and political concepts with substantive moral and political theory. Drawing explicitly on the work of his Harvard colleague Quine (cf.

Chapter 4), Rawls argued that moral and political philosophy have no place for a rigid analytic/synthetic distinction, and thus that the distinction drawn by Ayer in the passage quoted above cannot be sustained: conceptual analysis and moral theory have to proceed together.

The subsequent development of applied ethics is, in part, the result of the application of Rawls' philosophical method to other areas of ethical concern. Though I say more below about the method involved, there is, unfortunately, no space here to discuss either his political philosophy or recent developments in applied ethics. Instead I shall concentrate on the development of debates in moral philosophy from a narrow analytical concern with moral concepts to the revival of debates concerning the place of values in the world and the merits of competing moral theories.

Hare and the Language of Morals

The starting point for these debates was Richard Hare's (1919–) book *The Language of Morals* (1952). In the preface Hare declares his commitment to an analytical conception of moral philosophy : 'Ethics, as I conceive it, is the logical study of the language of morals' (p. v). The central theme of this 'logical study' is the supposed logical distinction between 'facts' and 'values'. Hare's approach to this is based on a thesis taken from Kant, that because morality essentially concerns the choice of action, moral judgements essentially take the form of imperatives: in telling us *what we ought to do* they tell us *what to do*. Matters of fact, by contrast, give rise to no such imperatives: they are typically expressed by sentences in the indicative mood, and the logical distinction between facts and values arises from the impossibility of deriving an imperative conclusion from premises that are exclusively indicative. Hare expresses this point by distinguishing between 'prescriptive' and 'descriptive' language: the language of morals, he maintains, is essentially prescriptive, and it is a mistake to think of morality as a domain of moral facts to be investigated and described.

It is obvious that not all imperatives are moral. Hare follows Kant in taking it that one treats an imperative as a moral requirement when one regards it as an instance of a principle one is prepared to 'universalize': to accept that one is morally obliged to tell the truth here and now is to hold that a principle of truth-telling in circumstances of this kind is of universal application. Kant seems to have assumed that this require-ment of the 'universalizability' of moral principles issues in a unique set of principles, but few have been convinced by his discussion; hence Hare's adoption of a Kantian conception of morality raises the ques-tion as to how he takes it that the content of morality is determined. In *The Language of Morals* Hare seems primarily concerned to emphasize the fact that each of us should make our own choice of principles: ' "Ought"-sentences . . . can only be verified by reference to a standard or set of principles which we have by our own decision accepted and made our own' (p. 78). This test is essentially one of authenticity (resembling the 'existentialist' position famously pro-pounded in 1945 by J-P. Sartre) and seems not to provide any basis for an objective standard of morality. Nonetheless in his second book, *Freedom and Reason* (1963), Hare maintained that the position does provide a basis for serious argument when one encounters moral disagreements.

The resource Hare invokes is his requirement that moral principles be universalizable, which he takes to imply the familiar Golden Rule—'do as you would be done by'. The case which he takes is that of a fanatical Nazi (an all-too-frequent character in post-World War II works of ethics) who holds that Jews ought to be exterminated. Hare argues that if the Nazi regards this as a moral imperative, he is committed to accepting that it applies to hypothetical as well as to actual situations, and thus to hypothetical situations in which the Nazi himself turns out to be Jew-ish. Hare allows that the fanatical Nazi can stick to his principle and agree that, were he himself to be Jewish, he ought to be put to death as a Jew. But Hare thinks that the more we press the Nazi to explore imaginatively such a hypothetical situation, to consider what he would think and feel if it were to turn out that he himself and his children were Jewish, the less likely it is that the Nazi will continue to assent sincerely to his principle.

The history of the twentieth century teaches us that the facts are rather darker: Arthur Koestler's famous novel *Darkness at Noon* accurately explores the actual psychology of principled self-condemnation with reference to Stalin's show trials. So Hare's dialectical strategy does not provide a firm basis for constructive moral debate. But in his third book *Moral Thinking* (1981) Hare provided a further interpretation of the requirement that moral imperatives be universalizable which changes the argument: he here takes it that the imaginative identification with others involved in universalizing an imperative implies that in accepting a general principle one holds that it provides the best way of fulfilling the preferences of all those who might be affected by its implementation. As Hare recognises, despite its Kantian provenance the resulting position is a form of utilitarianism, since it implies that the principles we ought to live by are those which maximize welfare (conceived as the fulfilment of preferences). As such it provides an objective standard of morality, and there is now no difficulty in providing a reason for rejecting the position of the fanatical Nazi, whether or not one can persuade him to change his mind.

Hare's work exemplifies the transformation of moral philosophy from an approach which concentrates on 'the language of morals' to one which attempts to provide a reasoned defence of a substantive ethical theory, utilitarianism in this case. What is distinctive, but unpersuasive, about Hare's work is his attempt to unify it by holding that the later endorsement of utilitarianism can be justified on the grounds of the earlier study alone.

Hare's Critics

Hare's early work provoked several important critical responses. His Oxford colleague Philippa Foot (1920–) argued that Hare's original attempt to characterize morality in purely formal terms was a mistake. Imperatives whose fulfilment has no relevance to the satisfaction of human interests, such as that one ought to clap one's hands three times an hour, do not become moral requirements simply by being universally prescribed. She also argued that Hare's sharp distinction between description and prescription obscures the way in which value-judgements enter into our descriptions of human life. In the case of dispositions such as rudeness, she argued, it is not that we first learn how to describe rude behaviour without reference to any value judgement and then, separately, prescribe that one ought not to be rude. Instead what leads us to group together the varied forms of behaviour we call 'rude' is that they are insensitive or offensive: so a value-judgement enters into their description as rude. Since this is a general feature of virtues and vices, anyone like Hare who holds that description and prescription (and thus evaluation) are mutually exclusive will be unable to do justice to that large part of moral thought in which we think in terms of virtues and vices.

Hare's sharp distinction between description and prescription was central to his account of the 'fact/value' gap. Foot's discussion suggests, therefore, that where virtues and vices are concerned there is no such gap. This question of the fact/value gap was also debated in the context of a different attempt by the American philosopher John Searle (1932–) to bridge it. Searle argued that if we start from facts which concern human institutions, it is possible to derive an evaluative 'ought' from a factual 'is'. The case Searle took concerns promises, and the supposed derivation runs as follows:

1. Jones uttered the words 'I hereby promise to pay you, Smith, five dollars'.
2. Jones promised to pay Smith five dollars.
3. Jones placed himself under (undertook) an obligation to pay Smith five dollars.
4. Jones was under an obligation to pay Smith five dollars
5. Jones ought, other things being equal, to pay Smith five dollars.

Searle acknowledged that, as stated, the argument needs further elaboration—e.g. the step from (1) to (2) requires further details concerning the way in which by uttering the words 'I promise' Jones makes his promise (cf. Austin's account of performatives, Chapter 3, pp. 57–8). But these extra details, Searle urged, just spell out the institutional facts involved; so the need for them does not show that an argument which makes them explicit does not provide a derivation of an 'ought' from mere 'facts'.

The standard criticism of this argument is that although, in making his promise, Jones represents himself to Smith as accepting an obligation to pay Smith five dollars, the question of whether Jones is under such an obligation is not so simply settled. There certainly have been those (e.g. the poet Shelley) who have regarded themselves as under no obligation to keep their promises, and to argue against them it is not sufficient to insist that a promise is a promise; instead one will point to the unfairness of a situation in which Jones is under no obligation to fulfil an undertaking he has given to Smith precisely in order to lead Smith to think that he can rely on Jones' fulfilment of this undertaking. Thus, the critics urge, the step from (3) to (4) requires a duty of fairness as a further premiss. But if this extra moral premiss is needed, then Searle's supposed derivation of an 'ought' from mere 'facts' alone collapses.

Although Searle can respond that the appeal to fairness is just a way of reminding Jones of the obligation inherent in his promise, Searle's case is not as strong as Foot's because promising is an institution which can, on the face of it, be described in value-free terms, whereas the 'fact' constituents of a virtue or vice cannot be readily disentangled from its value. Hence most critics of the fact/value gap tend to base their case on the fundamental status of the virtues and vices in moral practice and thought. This last point was a central theme of Elizabeth Anscombe's remarkable paper 'Modern Moral Philosophy' which is not just a polemic against Hare and like-minded analytical moral philosophers since it is also a critique of moral philosophy from the time of 'modern' (i.e. post-medieval) philosophy. Anscombe's fundamental complaint against this tradition is that it takes morality to comprise a set of rules concerning what we 'ought' to do, without realizing that this way of thinking about morality presupposes a religious conception of life according to which morality is what is 'owed' to God (the etymological origin of 'ought' is that it is the past tense of 'owe', much as 'bought' is the past tense of 'buy'). Hence the attempt, characteristic of the European tradition of moral philosophy that stems from Grotius (1583–1645), to continue to conceive of morality in terms of principles prescribing what we ought to do, while abstaining from a religious conception of life is, Anscombe suggests, bound to fail. This failure,

Anscombe holds, is especially evident in the inability of 'modern' philosophers to give any validity to strict moral prohibitions. All that we are normally offered are what she terms 'consequentialist' calculations in which moral deliberations are reduced to an assessment of the expected consequences of action. Since these assessments neglect the distinction between intended and merely foreseen consequences, the moral theory of modern moral philosophers permits in principle any kind of awful conduct simply by imagining cases in which it is foreseeable that such conduct is the lesser of two evils.

So what is to be done? Anscombe suggests that, in a secular culture, we should abandon the conception of morality as a system of prescriptive 'oughts', and construct a new way of thinking founded on our understanding of particular virtues and vices. Such a way of thinking, however, cannot be easily developed; for it requires, she argues, a new philosophy of mind which will show how the practice of the virtues connects with an Aristotelian understanding of human life as organized around a potentiality for 'human flourishing', and which will also break with the ways of thinking about the role of beliefs and desires in the explanation of action that is characteristic of Hume and his successors (her own work on intention is obviously intended as a contribution to this new philosophy of mind—cf. Chapter 9, pp. 193–4).

Anscombe paints with a broad brush, and her denunciation of post-medieval moral philosophy is overstated. Nonetheless, she anticipated many of the central themes of subsequent debate, and her claim that ethics is dependent upon the philosophy of mind is well illustrated by her reference to Hume. For, returning to the issue of the fact/value gap, most contemporary defenders of this appeal not to Hare's distinction between descriptive and prescriptive language, but to what they call 'Humean moral psychology', by which they mean Hume's distinction between 'reason', i.e. beliefs concerning what 'is' the case, and 'sentiment', typically desires or preferences concerning what 'ought' to be case. For Hume held that our desires and preferences are not answerable to our beliefs; as he famously put it: 'Tis not contrary to reason to prefer the destruction of the whole world to the scratching of my finger' (*A Treatise of Human Nature*, p. 416). Thus those who want to repudiate Hume's 'is/ought' gap have to provide a persuasive alternative to his moral psychology. As we shall now see, this challenge has been a central theme of recent debates in ethics.

Moral Psychology and the Internalism Debates

The framework for these debates was established in 1958 by the American philosopher William Frankena (1908–94) who distinguished the 'internalist' thesis that motivation is 'somehow logically internal' to moral judgement from the 'externalist' thesis which denies that this is so (it needs to be stressed that this 'externalist'/'internalist' distinction has no connection with other 'external'/'internal' distinctions drawn earlier in the book; I am afraid that recent philosophers have found the spatial metaphor inherent in this terminology irresistibly attractive and have used it for a variety of quite different purposes).

Hume is a paradigm internalist in this sense, since he holds that our moral judgements just express certain of our motivations, and some contemporary philosophers such as Simon Blackburn follow Hume in this respect (I discuss Blackburn's position later). But it is worth considering first the externalist view that moral judgements are not inherently motivating. Those who take this view usually agree with Hume in sharply distinguishing beliefs from desires; they just differ from Hume in treating moral judgements as beliefs. This position certainly fits well with much of our ordinary thought concerning morality, for example concerning the possibility of moral ignorance and knowledge. In severing the logical connection with motivation, however, the externalist position implies that moral judgements have no intrinsic connection with practical judgements concerning what one is to do. But Frankena observes that an externalist can readily allow that people are normally motivated to do what they judge to be morally required of them; for it is one of the aims of education to instil a standing desire to behave properly. Frankena recognizes, however, that the concept of a reason for action appears to provide just the logical connection between moral judgement and motivation that internalists assert there to be. For in judging that an action is obligatory, it seems that one accepts that there is a reason to perform it; and from this it seems to follow that one acquires a rational motivation to do it.

In response to this, Frankena distinguishes between 'justifying' and 'motivating' reasons: although obligations and similar moral requirements are justifying reasons for action, it does not follow, he suggests, that in accepting that one has a justifying reason one thereby acquires a motivating reason for action. This distinction is, however, open to criticism: for, his critics argue, it is precisely a mark of reasons for action that they provide motivations via their role in justifying action.

To take this matter further it is worth introducing to Bernard Williams' influential discussion in 1980 of reasons for action. He begins by distinguishing two conceptions of reasons for action, which he calls conceptions of 'internal' and 'external' reasons (that terminology yet again! But Williams' use of it must be distinguished from Frankena's). An agent's 'internal' reasons for action are reasons which depend on his motivations, although, Williams holds, they are not similarly dependent on his beliefs: the fact that I want a glass of gin does not give me an internal reason to drink the contents of a glass which I believe to contain gin if in fact it contains petrol. Thus although the identification of the actions which an agent has an internal reason to do is conceived as determined by the conclusions of the agent's deliberations as to what to do, some idealization is allowed in characterizing these deliberations—the agent is thought of as having relevant information he lacks and as better at seeing the implications of his existing motivations than he often is. Nonetheless, the conception of the actions which an agent has an internal reason to perform remains based upon his actual motivations, and it is this constraint which is lifted when 'external' reasons for action are considered: for these are conceived as reasons for action which arise directly from the agent's duties, responsibilities, obligations and so on, irrespective of his actual motivations.

So far, Williams' distinction between internal and external reasons is largely a refinement of Frankena's distinction between motivating and justifying reasons. What is distinctive about Williams' discussion is his further claim that there can be no external reasons for action. This claim rests on the general thesis that the reasons for action someone has must be capable of figuring in explanations of his actions, combined with the externalist thesis (in Frankena's sense) that acceptance, or belief, that one has a moral obligation to do something is not, of itself, motivating. The general claim implies that external reasons could enter into an explanation of someone's actions only if his acceptance of them was itself such as to motivate him to action. But it is just this which the externalist thesis denies. So there are no external reasons for action. We can criticize those who fail to live up to their responsibilities as selfish, inconsiderate, or worse; but to accuse them of being irrational if there is nothing in their actual motivations which connects rationally with the fulfilment of their responsibilities is, Williams says, just 'bluff'. It is to pretend that they are not the people that they are.

Williams shows, therefore, how an externalist position can be elaborated and defended. One question to which his position gives rise, however, is whether the degree of idealization in his conception of internal reasons permits one to construe at least some moral judgements as registering (internal) reasons for action because they are implications of the agent's being motivated at all, even though they are not explicitly represented among his motivations. A good case to think of here is prudence: for, as the works of moralists from Aesop onwards indicate, there is a strong inclination to regard imprudence as irrational whatever someone's actual motivations may be.

This case was discussed by Thomas Nagel in his book *The Possibility of Altruism* (1970) which provided one of the first detailed developments of a non-Humean moral psychology (Nagel remarks at the start 'I conceive ethics as a branch of psychology', a remark to be compared with Hare's description of ethics twenty years earlier—p. 233). Nagel takes his inspiration from Kant and seeks to develop a position which treats moral judgement as an exercise of 'practical' reason—i.e. a form of reason which is inherently motivating, so that the position is, in Frankena's sense, internalist. Hence he argues that the rationality of prudence does not depend on the existence of a concern for one's future welfare; instead it reflects a structural feature of rational motivation—that one has 'timeless' but potentially motivating reasons to do whatever is required to achieve one's ends. Thus if I need to be able to speak Italian when I visit Italy I have a 'timeless' reason to learn

Italian in advance of my visit. So if the time when I am to visit Italy is six weeks hence, I have a reason to be learning Italian now—whatever my present motivations may be.

This argument is not by itself persuasive. Reasons for action are not timeless since they change; and once temporal qualifications are inserted into Nagel's argument, it fails to deliver the intended conclusion. If I need to be able to speak Italian when I visit Italy I have a reason when visiting Italy to have learnt Italian in advance. Hence if I am to visit Italy in six weeks, I will then have a reason to be learning Italian now. But this is not the conclusion Nagel seeks to establish, which is that if I am to visit in Italy in six weeks' time, I now have a reason to be learning Italian now, whatever my current motivations are. There is, however, a way of reaching this conclusion, namely by taking into account my sense of my own identity through time. For if I can now predict with confidence that in six weeks I will have a reason to be learning Italian now, then I do now have a reason to learn Italian now, since I now recognize that future reason as my own.

Nagel also proposed that an argument similar to that which he had used to argue for the rationality of prudence can be used to establish the rationality of 'altruism', conceived as impartial concern for others. His new argument rested on the thesis that reasons for action are essentially impersonal, that it cannot be the case that there is a reason for me to act in some way on my own behalf without there being a reason for me to act similarly on behalf of any others who are similarly situated. This thesis is as unpersuasive as the thesis that reasons are timeless: the fact that I am going to sit an examination which I want to pass gives me a reason to prepare for it without giving me a similar reason to prepare the other candidates who will sit the exam. But the interesting question here is whether there is an analogue in the case of altruism to the argument for the rationality of prudence which draws on our sense of our own identity through time. Straightforward extrapolation of that argument requires the hypothesis that the differences between different persons are illusory, that 'their' interests are 'mine', and vice-versa, because we are all just aspects of some one inclusive Mind. Although some philosophers have entertained this hypothesis, it is not an easy position to understand, let alone argue for. I myself think that to do better requires a two-stage argument: first, for the rationality of concern for the welfare of an inner circle of those to whom one is intimately related ('family and friends'); and then for the irrationality of restricting this concern when one recognizes that others ('strangers') have similar needs and interests. It is this second stage which is notoriously difficult to establish.

A very different challenge to Williams' position has come from John McDowell. McDowell begins from the thought that there are straight-forward cases in which someone notices what is required of them and acts accordingly (e.g. by helping a child across a road). In such a case, McDowell says 'the requirement imposed by the situation, and detected by the agent's sensitivity to such requirements, must exhaust his reason for acting as he does' ('Virtue and Reason', pp. 142–3). Thus, according to McDowell, in understanding the agent's reason for her action we do not need to find a deliberative route which connects her antecedent motivations with the requirement she has just noticed; her character is such that what she has noticed is reason enough for action. Her reason for action is therefore, in Williams' sense, an external reason; but the resulting position is, in Frankena's sense, internalist, since the judgement that some action is required of her is inherently motivating.

McDowell takes it that 'properly brought up' people are such that in recognizing their obligations, they are thereby motivated to do what is required, and he regards this point as central not only to his disagree-ment with Williams but also to his rejection of the Humean psychology which treats motivations as fundamentally detached from beliefs. Externalists may object that since the role of education is to inculcate a standing desire to live properly, it is this desire in McDowell's 'properly brought up' people which ensures that noticing the requirements of morality motivates action. But McDowell can reply that the reflective endorsement of this desire to live properly is itself best understood as motivated by a recognition of the general demands of morality in a way which is not compatible with externalism. McDowell has also pointed to cases of moral 'conversion' whereby someone (Dostoevsky's Rashkolnikov, for example) comes to recognize and be motivated by responsibilities he had not previously acknowledged. In such cases, McDowell suggests, a new awareness of external reasons for action brings about by itself a radical shift in motivation without drawing on any antecedent disposition to do what is required to live properly.

These considerations are attractive, though not by themselves decisive; but I hope that the discussion at least indicates the main points at issue in this complex series of debates. We have encountered four broadly defensible types of position—Humean internalism, Nagel's Kantian internalism, McDowell's internalism, and Williams' form of externalism. So far the positions have been primarily conceived as alternative accounts of our moral psychology, but the disagreements between them connect with 'metaethical' debates concerning the status of moral values, and I turn now to these—and first to the issue of 'moral realism'.

Moral Realism

Contemporary discussions of moral realism, the thesis that moral values are 'real' properties, start from John Mackie's sceptical treatment of this thesis in his book *Ethics: Inventing Right and Wrong* (1977).

Mackie (1917–81) accepted that our ordinary moral thought embodies a commitment to the reality of moral values: when we agonize over a difficult moral question we seek to reach a conclusion which is decisive because it identifies real, authoritative, moral facts. Mackie argued, however, that no such facts are to be found since values so conceived are impossibly 'queer'. Discovering the real properties of things cannot, of itself, tell us how to act; so they cannot be authoritative in the way that values are supposed to be. And when we reflect on the variety of moral practices described in history and anthropology it is impossible to believe that these practices incorporate more or less accurate judgements concerning some underlying moral reality—they are much more like different ways of preparing food, and thus only 'matters of taste'.

Mackie's argument incorporates an internalist assumption in his thesis that moral values are intrinsically authoritative, and one realist response to it starts by rejecting this assumption. Without this assumption, it is argued, there is no reason to regard values as especially queer;

instead they are best conceived as natural properties to be identified by inquiries in anthropology and sociology.

This type of externalist moral realism, 'Cornell realism' (so-called because it has been especially propounded by philosophers at Cornell University such as Richard Boyd and Nicholas Sturgeon), is not vulnerable to G. E. Moore's famous objection that any proposed definition of values in terms of natural properties (e.g. 'duty is what the sovereign commands') can be called into question in a way which no proper definition ('a bachelor is an unmarried man') can. For quite apart from Quine-inspired doubts as to whether any definitions are beyond question, the Cornell realists take as their model the familiar identity 'Water = H_2O': so they hold that the precise identification of values in terms of natural properties depends upon the results of empirical inquiries and is therefore not like the definition of a bachelor. Thus their position resembles the materialist identity theory of mind discussed in the previous chapter. Indeed there is an Australian version of Cornell realism, 'moral functionalism', which uses the functionalist theory of mind as a model for the identification of the natural properties which are, or realize, moral values.

As the comparisons with the identity theory of mind and functionalism show, the Cornell realists think of moral values as explanatory properties; for example, they say, Hitler's wickedness is part of the explanation of the Holocaust; and the injustice of racial discrimination is part of the explanation of the passing of laws which prohibit it. This is disputed by those who hold that it is only our moral judgements, and not moral values themselves, that have this explanatory role; but the role of virtues and vices (e.g. Hitler's wickedness) is not covered by this response, and, anyway, realists hold that our moral judgements themselves are normally to be explained as the recognition of values, which thereby regain their explanatory role. So the thesis that values have an explanatory role in human affairs is a defensible claim which provides a powerful consideration in favour of some form of moral realism.

For the Cornell realists, however, the explanatory role of values is to guide the identification of the natural properties which supposedly underpin this role. As with the functionalist treatment of rational explanations discussed in the previous chapter, there are grounds for considerable unease here: for it is now implied that explanations which invoke values such as injustice are reducible to explanations which talk only of natural properties. Thus although no conceptual reduction of values is proposed, ethical concepts are not in fact required for the formulation of explanations of human affairs. This is plainly revisionist and undercuts the realist thesis that values have an explanatory role in the first place.

But are there any plausible natural identifications of values anyway? The Cornell realists argue for the utilitarian position that it is our duty to act in a way which maximizes expected welfare and this position, with its single fundamental moral principle, provides the basis for an identification of moral values (e.g. 'Duty = Action which maximizes welfare') in terms of a concept—welfare—which can be given a naturalistic treatment, e.g. as the satisfaction of preferences. It is not clear to me how tight the connections are between utilitarianism and the project of finding a naturalistic identification of values which elucidates their explanatory role in the context of a materialist theory of mind. But the coherence of the resulting position (materialism + moral realism + utilitarianism) undoubtedly gives it strength, while showing how there can be significant connections between positions in metaphysics, philosophy of mind, and moral theory.

The similarities we have just encountered between ethics and the philosophy of mind are also apparent in the applicability within ethics of considerations concerning supervenience (cf. Chapter 9, pp. 209–10). In ethics, supervenience amounts to the thesis that moral values supervene on natural facts in the sense that situations which are alike in respect of all natural facts must also be alike in respect of moral values. This thesis implies that statements ascribing a moral value to a situation admit of at least a disjunctive equivalence to statements about natural properties, namely to the disjunction of all the statements describing the natural properties of possible worlds in which the same moral value applies to a situation of the kind specified. This disjunctive equivalence provides no conceptual reduction, but it does imply an ontological thesis: moral values are given through the distribution of natural properties in all the possible worlds. As in the philosophy of mind, so in ethics, 'attribute dualism'—i.e. the conception of values as real properties distinct from all natural properties or combinations of them—is ruled out.

It will be obvious that this conclusion fits readily with Cornell realism. What alternatives are there? One is to deny the realist thesis that values are real properties at all, and to interpret the supervenience thesis as the principle that moral judgements are inherently precedent-setting, so that a person who makes different moral judgements concerning apparently similar situations is committed to accepting that there is a further difference between the situations. This claim can be readily accommodated by a Kantian rationalist since he holds that moral judgements draw on inherently general considerations. In the case of a Humean who holds that moral judgements just express desires matters are different, since desires can be 'fickle'—changing for no reason. Hence the Humean has to add some further consideration to his account of moral judgements in order to vindicate their supervenience—for example, that moral judgements have a social function in suggesting guidance and criticism which would be undermined if they were permitted to be fickle. This is clearly a very different kind of explanation of supervenience from that offered by the Kantian, pragmatic rather than a priori, thus giving a different status to the supervenience thesis itself, one which reflects the difference between Kant's philosophical rationalism and Hume's philosophical naturalism.

Are there any other alternatives? If one thinks again of the philosophy of mind, there ought to be an ethical analogue of the dual aspect theory of mind. I suggested (Chapter 9, pp. 210–15) that the essence of the dual aspect theory of mind was that mental properties have explanatory significance as such, and not via their physical realizations or identifications. Similarly, then, the essence of a 'moral aspect' theory will be that moral values have explanatory significance as such. Some conception of values as external reasons (in Williams' sense) is therefore required, so that by recognizing such a reason a person acquires a motive for action which helps to explain what the person does. Indeed if values are to have an irreducible explanatory role as reasons for action, then reasons must themselves have such a role in the explanation of human action, as the dual aspect theory holds; so a moral aspect theory of value requires a dual aspect theory of mind (the reverse implication also holds: the irreducibility of the explanatory role of reasons depends on their role as justifications of action).

A moral aspect theory implies, therefore, that moral values are real 'aspects' of the world. McDowell's position, which I introduced earlier in connection with the internalism debates, is such a theory, since he combines moral realism with an insistence upon the irreducible role of values as external reasons for action. McDowell elaborates his position by means of a comparison between values and colours: the fact that the identity of colours is dependent upon the visual experiences of human perceivers ('red things are things which normally look red to a human observer') does not, he suggests, imply that colours lack reality; similarly, he suggests, the fact that the identity of moral values is dependent upon a human point of view does not undermine their reality. For the different virtues enable us to identify the different values to which the virtuous person responds just as the identity of different colours is fixed by our different visual experiences: in this way 'a conception of right conduct is grasped, as it were, from the inside out' ('Virtue and Reason', p. 141).

This comparison between colours and values, though familiar, is, I think, potentially dangerous for a moral aspect theorist. For there is a well established science of colour vision ('colour science') which has achieved a great deal in unravelling the physical and psychological facts concerning colour. There is at present no comparable 'moral science' for value judgement, but if there were, I suspect that it would tend to support the position of a Cornell realist. Furthermore McDowell's 'inside out' account of the role of the virtues in the identification of right conduct is misguided. If we think of our impersonal duties and obligations to others, there is little plausibility in the thesis that our understanding of these values is based upon an antecedent understanding of the virtue of justice. On the contrary, a just person is someone who acts justly in the light of a grasp of these values. Plato correctly observed that the virtue of justice involves more than doing one's duty as specified by some list of principles; but the ways in which just persons justify their willingness to depart from such rules show their antecedent understanding of the values they invoke.

Expressivism

In moral philosophy from the 1930s onwards one often encounters a distinction between 'cognitivist' and 'non-cognitivist' conceptions of moral judgement. This is sometimes taken to be the belief/desire distinction characteristic of Humean moral psychology; alternatively these terms are often used to mark the epistemological distinction between a conception of moral judgement as capable of objective validity, and one according to which this is not possible. It is of course natural to connect these distinctions, since beliefs are capable of objective truth whereas desires are not normally thought of as capable of this or indeed any kind of objective validity. But this last point can be challenged: one can argue that it is possible to start from a Humean conception of moral judgements as expressive of desires, and yet end up with an account whereby some of them are legitimately regarded as objectively valid. This is the 'expressivist' position recently defended by Simon Blackburn (1944–) in *Ruling Passions* (1998).

A side issue here concerns the connection between these distinctions and moral realism. Clearly there is some overlap: moral realism implies that moral judgements are capable of objective truth; the disputed question is whether one can uphold the objective validity of moral judgement without committing oneself to moral realism. Blackburn himself makes no distinction here, but Kantian positions, such as Hare's utilitarian prescriptivism, attempt a defence of objectivity without moral realism; so the answer to this question depends on whether any such position is tenable. I shall return to this issue in the next section.

The starting point of Blackburn's position is that in our moral judgements we 'express' our feelings (which he takes to be a species of desire); thus on his account my judgement that infanticide is wrong is an expression of my abhorrence of infanticide. These expressions of feeling are distinguished from descriptions of feeling; so the expressivist position differs from the untenable subjectivist position that one's moral judgements are merely descriptions of one's feelings. In fact on almost any account of moral judgement, in judging that infanticide is wrong I express my abhorrence of it. But the non-Humean holds that my feeling about infanticide is based on my belief that it is wrong, whereas Blackburn regards the expression of feelings as fundamental and interprets our ordinary talk of the wrongness of infanticide as a 'projection' of our feelings about it onto the world.

This last point can be illustrated by returning to the comparison between colours and values which McDowell employed, but now with a very different presumption about the status of colours. Once the role of visual experience in the identification of colours is acknowledged, it can appear plausible to infer that physical objects are not really coloured at all despite the fact that they look coloured to us (cf. the earlier discussion of Williams' 'Absolute' conception of the world—Chapter 8, pp. 187–9). This position provides a model for the expressivist's conception of values, according to which they are products of the ways in which our feelings 'colour' our experience of the world by projecting values onto it. As Hume himself famously put it, the suggestion is that feeling or sentiment has the power of 'gilding or staining all natural objects with the colours, borrowed from internal sentiment' so that it 'raises, in a manner, a new creation' (*Enquiry*, p. 294)

A central concern for expressivists has been to show that this projective conception of value has the resources to provide an account of moral reasoning, such as that which employs the judgement that if infanticide is wrong then abortion is wrong too. For someone who makes such a judgement expresses no feelings about infanticide or abortion; so it is not clear how the role of this judgement in moral reasoning is to be accommodated in an expressivist account of moral judgement.

Blackburn provides a neat solution to this problem by taking conditional judgements to involve a commitment to a disjunction of feelings: in saying 'if infanticide is wrong, then abortion is wrong too' I express my commitment to either accepting infanticide or rejecting abortion. Hence, if I go on to express my rejection of infanticide by saying that infanticide is wrong I am committed to rejecting abortion. Blackburn thereby validates the reasoning whereby someone who holds both that if infanticide is wrong then abortion is wrong, and that infanticide is wrong, is committed to holding that abortion is wrong.

These ideas enable him to construct an interpretation of much of the apparently 'fact-stating' structure of ordinary moral discourse in terms of the commitments inherent in our attitudes. Equally, he avoids any commitment to obviously unacceptable theses such as that had our feelings been different, things which are wrong would not have been wrong (for in expressing my rejection of infanticide I am certainly not committing myself to accepting the practice of infanticide under the circumstance that my feelings about it had been different). Hence, as Hume's remark about 'raising, in a manner, a new creation' suggests, Blackburn believes that the expressivist thesis that moral judgements are expressions of our feelings can be used as a basis for an account which captures all that matters when we demand objectivity for moral judgement and reality for moral values.

Is this persuasive? One ground for dissatisfaction arises from Blackburn's revisions to our conceptions of our moral feelings. We normally take it that the feeling of guilt is a response to the thought that one has done something wrong. But since Blackburn constructs the judgement that one has acted wrongly on the basis of feelings such as guilt, he has to hold that the fundamental characterization of guilt does not involve any reference to the thought that one has acted wrongly. This point applies generally, and conflicts radically with the way we normally think of feelings such as shame, abhorrence, offence, etc.

A different point concerns public moral justifications of actions. Such justifications are a central feature of the legitimate exercise of political power, so their validity is a matter of considerable practical importance. Consider then the claim that one ingredient in the justification of punishment is that what the convicted offender did was seriously wrong, and that an important element in punishment is that the offender should come to see that his punishment is just because he recognizes that what he did was wrong. The challenge for Blackburn is to provide a construction of these thoughts which shows why they are reasonable. There is clearly no difficulty about a speaker's expressing a commitment to either not seriously disapproving of someone's conduct or approving of their punishment and then seriously disapproving of their action. But this barely captures the proposed justification of punishment, and certainly does not offer a way in which this justification might be internalized by the offender himself.

The difficulty here arises from the fact that the expressivist account of moral rationality is essentially individualist: each person is thought of as having attitudes whose commitments constitute reasons for moral judgements made by them. But their expression of these attitudes cannot provide anyone else with reasons; the reasons others have for moral judgements are constituted by commitments inherent in their own attitudes. Much the same point applies when we consider the possibility of objective moral knowledge. Blackburn holds that his position allows for this; but it turns out that he regards talk of moral knowledge as simply the expression of those of our feelings which we are confident we will not want to modify. Yet knowledge is not confidence: as we saw in Chapter 9, knowledge requires an objective justificatory relationship between someone's beliefs and that which they believe, and the construction of fact-like judgements essayed by Blackburn does not validate a conception of moral facts capable of standing in such a relationship to someone's expression of their feelings. So Blackburn cannot represent himself as securing moral knowledge.

Blackburn's expressivist position turns out, therefore, to be revisionist in its account of our feelings and sceptical in its account of morality. Hence the discussion so far suggests that for a non-sceptical account the alternatives are Cornell realism, a Kantian theory, and a moral aspect theory such as McDowell's. For the reasons given earlier I find Cornell realism excessively reductive, and having already discussed McDowell's position I want to discuss a different position which combines elements of a moral aspect theory with a Kantian approach.

Objectivity

In his book *What We Owe to Each Other* (1998) Tim Scanlon begins from a point discussed in connection with Blackburn, that where strict morality—'what we owe to each other'—is in play we should able to justify our judgements to others. These judgements, Scanlon maintains, are based upon judgments about what would be permitted by principles that could not reasonably be rejected, by people who were moved to find principles for the general regulation of behavior that others, similarly motivated, could not reject. (p. 4)

Scanlon calls this position 'contractualist'. This term reflects the fact that he developed it through reflection on John Rawls' account of justice as grounded on a hypothetical social contract. What is important here is Rawls' idea of procedural rationality: Scanlon's conception of strict morality is that it is what we arrive at through the reflective procedure set out in the passage quoted above. Some values are here presupposed concerning the grounds for the reasonable rejection of principles, but the procedure is supposed to be one through which the scope of these values is determined in such a way as to achieve a coherent moral framework.

Scanlon's reliance on procedural rationality to determine strict morality is indicative of a Kantian approach, and this point is confirmed by his affirmation of an internalist attitude to the resulting judgements. Once we come to understand a course of action we are contemplating as one which we could not justify to others because it relies on a principle which they could reasonably reject, he argues, we have a powerful reason to abandon it.

Rawls took the view that the construction of justice is guided by our recognition of a range of primary, i.e. fundamental, goods. Scanlon replaces this view with the view that it is reasons for action that are fundamental, where these are conceived as considerations which count in favour of action. Scanlon conceives of these as essentially similar to reasons for belief and therefore sensitive to other considerations concerning the situations to which they apply, so that they can on occasion be completely undermined; thus friendship is not a reason for favouring a friend when making an appointment to a public office. Reasons for action so conceived are external reasons, in Williams' sense, and Scanlon argues that so far from being dependent upon desires, finding such reasons normally motivates desires. Values, i.e. goods, are then defined in terms of reasons for action: for example, friendship is valuable because there are reasons to promote the relationship involved.

This is an attractive thesis. The conception of reasons for action as a fundamental aspect of the world constituted by considerations which count in favour of action fits well with the rationale of what I have called a moral aspect theory. These reasons provide a 'material' input into the more formal procedure which Scanlon constructs for determining strict morality. Thus they show why Scanlon's position is not vulnerable to the familiar criticism of Kantian theories that they rely on formal considerations alone to determine the content of morality. Equally, the Kantian aspect of Scanlon's account of strict morality shows why his position is not vulnerable to the objection I made earlier to McDowell's moral aspect theory, namely that it does not do justice to our sense that a virtuous agent is one whose conduct is informed by an understanding of the demands of strict morality.

Prima facie, then, Scanlon's position is an attractive hybrid. But much depends on whether he can vindicate the presumptions of objectivity inherent in his accounts of reasons for action and strict morality. In the case of the former he follows Rawls by arguing that claims to objectivity are best vindicated by the method of 'reflective equilibrium' whereby we start from our ordinary common-sense judgements and then refine them, taking into account our understanding of the world and ourselves, until we reach 'the most coherent and complete account of what reasons there are' (p. 68). In the case of the latter, he distinguishes a hard core of fundamental human rights, whose universality he takes to be demonstrable by his procedure, from judgements which exhibit a degree of cultural relativity in virtue of their dependence upon assumptions about priorities among other values (e.g. privacy, liberty, honour) which vary from one culture to another. This variation, he argues, should not worry us: we should no more expect all cultures to assign the same priorities among values, i.e. reasons for action, than we expect all individuals to have the same ideals. The objectivity of reasons for belief and action does not require uniformity of thought and practice.

In thinking about this position it is worth briefly reviewing the options available for an account of objectivity in ethics. One common suggestion is that in ethics we can take our lead from Wittgenstein's account of rule-following (cf. Chapter 2, pp. 20–3): if there is a collective

practice, sustained by widespread agreement and recognized procedures for handling, if not always resolving, disagreements when
they occur, then that is all we should ask for. As Williams has observed,
this Wittgensteinian approach applies reasonably well to 'thick' concepts, such as rudeness and patience where, because there is no sharp
distinction between 'descriptive' and 'evaluative' components, the
scope for disagreement is slight. By extension, this point applies also to
reasons for action as conceived by Scanlon: for thick concepts are essentially labels for clusters of reasons for and against action. As Williams
also observes, however, once one turns to 'thinner' concepts such as
right and wrong, whose descriptive implications are less determinate, the scope for disagreement is greater and the merits of a pure
Wittgensteinian approach are correspondingly diminished. It is for this
reason, therefore, that Scanlon and others suggest that the way to find
objectivity here is to use the idea of procedural rationality in order to
add some discipline to our informal judgements of right and wrong.

As Scanlon indicates, we should not expect too much here, but his
thesis that there is an element of cultural relativity in this domain of
strict morality requires careful handling. It is often suggested that the
existence of deep and persisting disagreements, e.g. concerning the
permissibility of abortion, shows that all moral requirements are relative
to the culture of those involved. But this is a problematic hypothesis,
since if I ask myself what the right thing to do is, a relativized answer of
the form 'relative to my culture, X is the right thing to do' does not
answer my question, but simply raises a further question as to the
merits of my culture. Moral relativism is often associated with toleration; but the judgement that toleration is the right policy to adopt
towards people whose moral outlook is very different from ours has to
present itself to us as an unqualified judgement, and not simply as the
judgement that toleration is right relative to our own culture. Thus,
insofar as moral relativism is a position we can sensibly entertain, it has
to concern the morality of those (the Homeric Greeks, for example)
whose lives are lived at a distance from us. For it is when a morality is
viewed at a distance that we can appreciate how a culture that is rooted
in very different material and intellectual conditions from our own
gives rise to a morality with which we can imaginatively sympathize

even though in some respects (e.g. concerning the permissibility of retaliation) it is different from our own. As soon as this distance is removed, however, and we confront these others as neighbours, living under much the same material and intellectual conditions as ourselves, the relativist position is no longer helpful. We confront instead the difficult, non-relative, question as to how best we are to live in harmony with people whose value-judgements differ very greatly from our own—e.g. how far we should practise toleration towards those who are themselves intolerant.

This is not a question requiring metaethical analysis, but a grasp of the moral and political issues involved, and I turn now to discuss the ways in which ethical theories which address this type of issue have evolved since 1945.

Virtues, Duties, and Consequences

There are three main types of ethical theory, distinguished by the relative priority they give to different moral values. We have already encountered versions of all three types: (i) Foot and McDowell affirmed the priority of the virtues, and this priority is characteristic of 'virtue ethics'—theories which concern the kind of person we should aim to become; (ii) Scanlon emphasized the strict morality of right and wrong, and strict 'deontologists' take this morality, often thought of as a system of duties, to be fundamental; (iii) the Cornell realists supported utilitarianism, the position which gives priority to the value of states of affairs by maintaining that our fundamental duty is to lead our lives in such a way that the value, or goodness, of the state of the world is thereby maximized.

I have already discussed and rejected McDowell's 'inside out' thesis that the virtues have priority over other values. In dissenting from this, however, I do not imply that virtues are simply reducible to other values. But what of the priorities characteristic of the other types of theory?

In holding that the morality of duty is fundamental, strict deontologists (unlike Scanlon himself) hold that the specification of one's duties is not dependent upon other values; Hare's prescriptivism is a strict deontology in this sense. Thus deontologists hold that things which are good or bad are so primarily because one has a duty either to bring them into existence or to minimize their existence: their goodness or badness is not a reason for this duty—it is an implication of it. The result is a demanding morality which lacks its usual rationale: the duty not to cause unnecessary suffering, for example, would normally be thought to be based on the fact that suffering is, in itself, bad, rather than vice-versa. Another counter intuitive feature of this position is that there is only one fundamental virtue, the sense of duty: other virtues are admissible only as applications of this virtue within some specific domain. This makes some sense in the case of loyalty and other virtues whose practice involves fulfilling difficult duties, but it completely omits important virtues such as humility.

For these reasons, the strict deontologist's position is not seriously tenable either, though this conclusion does not imply that the conception of strict duty or obligation does not make an irreducible contribution to morality. Utilitarianism offers a simple way to conceive how this might be, for it takes us to have a fundamental duty to maximize valuable states of affairs, which utilitarians specify as welfare, usually conceived now as the satisfaction of preferences.

Utilitarianism has been the most influential ethical theory of modern times, especially since it received a definitive formulation from J. S. Mill (1806–73), and Henry Sidgwick (1838–1900) at the end of the nineteenth century. The traditional objection to utilitarianism was that it is repugnant to common sense. If we have a single fundamental duty to maximize welfare, then where fulfilment of familiar obligations conflicts with this duty, it seems that utilitarianism requires us to ditch them. Thus if keeping a promise prevents me from doing something else which would bring greater welfare to the world, it is my duty to do this something else and break my promise. Utilitarians from J. S. Mill onwards have responded to this that the objection fails to take account of the fact that utilitarianism itself implies that we should stick closely to the rules of public institutions such as contract, since these are institutions of great public benefit which depend on confidence that their rules are followed strictly. Indeed, Sidgwick argued, we do the right thing on utilitarian grounds in educating children to regard these rules as strict duties, and thus inculcating moral intuitions which support them, even though it may then appear to people thus educated that utilitarianism itself is counter-intuitive.

Most contemporary utilitarians, therefore, advance an 'indirect' form of utilitarianism which restricts the primary application of the utilitarian principle to the justification of general rules, rather than particular acts, though whether this position altogether deflects the traditional common-sense objection remains disputed. For it is not obvious that this position will justify respect for our familiar rules in preference to rules which permit exceptions whenever the results of such exceptions are better, all things considered; and the critics argue that comon-sense objections to such permissive rules cannot be dismissed as merely the product of early training in following simple rules of conduct. The main focus of recent discussion has, however, been the feature that Anscombe identified (p. 238), that utilitarianism is a 'consequentialist' theory according to which one's duty is determined by the relative value of the consequences of the actions available to one.

Anscombe's objection was that, as a result, utilitarianism neglects the distinction between intended and merely foreseen consequences, and is for this reason unable to sustain any strict prohibitions. It is, however, difficult to justify the assignment of any great ethical significance to the distinction between a consequence which is intended, but only as a means to the achievement of some good end, and one which is merely a foreseen side-effect of the way of achieving that end. In neither case is the consequence wanted for its own sake, and in both cases it is something which the agent chose to bring about. Bernard Williams has argued, however, that there are two other distinctions which utilitarianism neglects because of its exclusive concern with the value of consequences: (i) the distinction between direct consequences of one's action and consequences that are mediated by acts of others; (ii) the distinction between consequences of one's positive actions and consequences of one's omissions, of what one fails to do. Because it neglects these distinctions, utilitarianism implies that in the determination of duty full weight is to be given to those consequences of our own acts which arise through the actions of others which we could have prevented but did not prevent. It is, he argues, because of this feature, rather than its neglect of the foresight/intention distinction, that utilitarianism will not sustain any strict prohibitions; for this feature licenses the moral blackmail whereby one is required to violate a putatively strict prohibition in order to forestall the even worse consequences which some 'Evil Genius' threatens to attach to one's refusal to violate the prohibition.

The intuitive basis of the distinctions which utilitarianism overlooks lies in the priority we give to the fulfilment of negative duties, duties *not* to do something (of the Ten Commandments, nine are primarily negative). For in fulfilling a negative duty such as the duty not to cause unnecessary suffering, we are not required to intervene to prevent the infliction of unnecessary suffering by others; we violate such a duty by what we do rather than by what we fail to prevent others from doing. It may seem at first that a morality which gives priority to negative duties is inferior to one which reformulates them in consequentialist terms— e.g. as the duty to prevent the infliction of unnecessary suffering. For if we think about the matter from the perspective of potential victims, it seems better to live in a community with a morality which enjoins such interventions. There is in fact no reason why an upholder of negative duties should not also acknowledge some positive duties such as a duty to help those in danger; but he will still want to give priority to negative duties and to place limits on the scope of his positive duties. For a utilitarian morality which requires one to intervene to prevent bad consequences radically restricts what one is permitted to do, as compared with our familiar morality which permits one to act as one likes as long as one neither does that which is prohibited, nor fails to do that which is required in appropriate contexts. This intermediate space of permitted acts is largely eliminated within a utilitarian morality, and with it is lost the opportunity for each of us to construct a life of our own in which, without doing anything wrong, we choose what to do from an indefinitely large range of permitted alternatives.

This point connects with a further point stressed by Williams, namely that in a utilitarian assessment of duty the agent's own identity is irrelevant: his own welfare counts simply as someone's welfare, alongside that of everyone else. This is a form of alienation: for it implies that in moral deliberation we are to detach ourselves from our own interests, including those which arise from our relationships, commitments and aspirations, and determine our duty purely by reference to what is best overall, impersonally considered. This form of impartial deliberation is indeed mandatory in certain contexts—e.g. in judicial contexts, as in the famous case of the Roman consul Lucius Brutus who condemned his own sons to death for treason. But such contexts are special and we cannot live our lives as if we were impartial judges without destroying the relationships and concerns which give to our lives most of the value they have. If morality were to require this of us, then we should, and would, be amoralists.

Utilitarians reply that these objections show only the importance of giving due weight to individual liberty and personal relationships when considering how welfare is to be assessed. This reply, however, fails to take account of the fact that these objections derive from the consequentialist structure of utilitarianism, and thus cannot be offset simply by adjusting the account of welfare. So Williams' basic complaint, that utilitarianism is unacceptable because it relies on an impersonal consequentialist determination of duty, looks hard to refute, though contemporary supporters of indirect utilitarianism continue to argue that they can defuse it, by restricting the application of the utilitarian test to the assessment of general rules and institutions within which individuals are supposedly free to think of their own lives and relationships in non-utilitarian ways. As I have indicated, I am sceptical of this claim, but this is not the place to pursue the argument.

The Dimensions of Morality

What structure should one look for in moral values once a utilitarian position is discarded, alongside that of the strict deontologist and the virtue theorist? There is no consensus, and I shall simply take points from recent discussions which indicate the dimensions an answer would need to include.

An initial point connects with the criticism of utilitarianism as too impersonal: if we think about our values, there are indeed some which are impersonal in the sense that in specifying what is good, or what our duty is, we make no essential reference to ourselves, except perhaps as agent. Thus in holding that suffering is bad, we do not restrict our judgement just to our own suffering or to the suffering of those whom we care about: our judgement is impersonal. Similarly, if we judge that we have a duty not to cause unnecessary suffering, we think of the duty as similarly unrestricted. Impersonal values of this kind are called 'agent-neutral', and contrasted with 'agent-centred' values in which we do make essential reference to ourselves in specifying the value. Examples of such values are the responsibilities of parents for their own children, and the obligations we owe to those to whom we have made a promise; for in these cases the value is specified by reference to a relationship 'centred upon' the person to whom the value is attributed.

Ordinary morality includes both agent-centred and agent-neutral values. It is relatively easy to understand the basis of those agent-centred values which represent the significance of the personal relationships that inform the lives of the people concerned. In the case of contractual obligations matters are more complex: although they are agent-centred, they arise within an institution which draws on the agent-neutral duty of fairness. What then is the basis of agent-neutral values? The recognition of neutral goods and evils (or reasons for and against action) is not inherently problematic; what is more contentious is the way in which this recognition is transformed into a normative system of duty. A utilitarian approach, as we have seen, threatens to swamp everything else. A familiar and, I think, preferable alternative is the recognition of some fundamental personal goods (interests) as individual rights which others have a duty to respect and which legitimate political institutions that define and protect them. For this provides the basis for a way of thinking about the duties that we owe to each other and about the ways in which a personal interest in liberty should be balanced against duties which prescribe assistance for others. The resulting dialectical context for the determination of rights and duties is, I think, largely equivalent to Scanlon's procedural treatment of 'what we owe to each other': the reasons for action others have for the 'reasonable rejection' of principles will map out those of their interests which are to be treated as rights requiring respect and protection.

The fact that the resulting position is one in which the precise demarcation of rights and duties is always open for argument is worth stressing. For the same point applies more generally to the relationship between agent-neutral and agent-centred values, and this points to a different dimension within moral theory, that which concerns the relative importance, or stringency, of values. For utilitarians this is, of course, essentially a matter of calculation; for non-utilitarians such calculations, while always important, cannot be decisive. Instead, a more or less tacit theory of human nature, of political community, and of the cosmos, tends to be presupposed in identifying the fundamental interests of persons, the basic structures of political community, and the 'order of being' within the cosmos at large. The traditional position, which goes back to Plato, has been that priority belongs to the claims of justice, and since the seventeenth century these claims have been conceived in terms of respect for human rights. But this has been challenged in much recent debate.

First, the priority of humans over all other species has been challenged, notably by Peter Singer (1946–) in his book *Animal Liberation* (1975). Initially, this position was developed by extrapolating to animals the considerations developed in discussions of the injustice of racial discrimination, leading to the accusation that traditional attitudes to animals are 'speciesist' and to the claim that we should recognize animal rights alongside human rights. But this claim has been resisted by those who take it that the recognition of rights brings with it potential membership of a shared political community, which misrepresents our relationships with animals; indeed, the critics point out, since rights require protection, acceptance of animal rights might legitimate human interference in order to protect the rights of animals from their 'violation' by animal predators, thus inviting people to 'police' the animal world in ways that would be very destructive of it. For these reasons I think it is preferable just to acknowledge that animals have interests (e.g. in not suffering) comparable to those of humans, and then bring them within the scope of duties which prescribe respect for such interests generally.

This approach will not underpin the moral concern for plants or for the preservation of natural environments which many ecologists feel;

for trees, forests, and mountain ranges do not have interests in any straightforward sense. Nonetheless, the fact that we find it straightforward to apply concepts such as 'pollution', 'sickness', and 'health' to ecosystems shows that we recognize that at least the values associated with health are inherent in such systems, and these provide one basis for moral concern. But it remains an urgent and as yet incomplete task for moral philosophy to articulate the values inherent in the natural environment in such a way that their normative implications can be properly understood.

A different challenge to the conventional priority of the claims of justice has come from feminists. In her book *In a Different Voice* (1982) Carol Gilligan (1936–) showed that women tend to assign much more importance to the responsibilities that arise from relationships with people than to the more abstract claims of justice. This has led her and others to elaborate 'an ethics of care' which challenges what they regard as the characteristically masculine assumption that the claims of justice, as represented by the structure of rights and duties which constitute public life, should be given priority over the personal responsibilities which structure private life and which have been traditionally undertaken by women. For, as they rightly urge, the public domain of justice can only flourish where people—especially those who cannot look after themselves—are cared for within relationships that are not simply a matter of one person doing their duty by others.

Gilligan does not argue that the claims of justice should be supplanted by an ethics of care, nor that the introduction of claims of justice into family affairs (e.g. under the concept of the 'rights of the child') is a mistake. Instead her central claim is that in thinking about how we should lead our own lives (and how we should bring up our children), it would be a mistake to think that living in accordance with the claims of justice is the most important element in living well; on the contrary, we need also to recognize our personal responsibilities and find ways of meeting them, however inconvenient they sometimes are. In particular, as women at last begin to take their rightful places within the public domain, men must learn to accept and value properly those personal responsibilities which have been traditionally fulfilled by women.

The feminist stress on responsibilities rather than rights connects with a further dimension of moral theory, that of the extent to which morality is a matter of following explicit rules (laws, principles, etc.) and how far it is a matter of responding to requirements that arise within particular contexts, albeit within broad domains of responsibility. Justice is typically a matter of rules, for the good reason that in our impersonal dealings with those whom we have no occasion to understand well we need an explicit understanding of what is permitted or prohibited. The more personal domains covered by an ethics of care are correspondingly domains in which moral judgements are not best thought of as applications of explicit rules. It is plain that morality needs to make space for values of both types.

This informal side of morality is closely bound up with the virtues. For these are dispositions which essentially involve the exercise of judgement in particular situations: there could be no explicit rules that specify the requirements of courage or patience in all the indefinitely varied situations in which we have to make difficult choices under conditions of uncertainty. As a result, virtues cannot be regarded as just the internalization of some separately specified moral concerns. Instead, they make a separate contribution of their own to the structure of morality. For us, as for the Greeks, from whom we derive our concept, they are 'excellences' of character which point us towards ways of living well which go beyond doing our duty and fulfilling our responsibilities, even though both of these often involve virtues such as courage and patience. Thus it is important for the possibility of the general practice of virtues that the demands of duty and responsibility which prescribe and prohibit courses of action should not exhaust the options available to us: the home for the virtues is that space for conduct which is permitted but not required, a space which, I suggested earlier, is threatened within a utilitarian morality.

As Alastair MacIntyre (1929–) explained in his influential book *After Virtue* (1981), it is easy to understand how there are such excellences within practices that contribute their own goods to life: we can identify the characteristic virtues of a doctor (sensitivity, trust, knowledge, etc.) by reference to the purposes of medicine. What is less clear is how the identity of the general excellences which we think of as 'moral' virtues (courage, self-control, patience, honesty, kindness, etc.) is to be under-stood: for life in general is not a focused activity comparable to medicine. Unless a good deal of theology is assumed, there is no purpose inherent in human life by reference to which a set of all-important virtues could be specified as the distinctive excellences of human life as such (MacIntyre took this to be a reason for finding a way back to religion).

My own view is that there are two ways of specifying a role for excellences which one might identify as 'moral' virtues, albeit of two rather different types. The first just points to the ways in which the demands of everyday life provide occasions in which the exercise of social virtues (e.g. kindness, honesty) contributes something of value to the lives of those involved. We do not need to think of ourselves as engaged in some special co-operative enterprise to recognize that the quality of our relationships with our neighbours often depends on the dispositions of those involved. The second route to an identification of moral virtues points to the fact that, despite the absence of any inherent purpose in life, most people give a meaningful structure to their lives by finding or creating goods within it. Though the ways in which we do this vary indefinitely, it remains a general truth that the achievement of these goods involves personal virtues such as self-control, patience, and courage.

In this brief exploration, drawing selectively on recent moral philosophy, I have suggested that morality involves a range of values which include at least

(1) the traditional claims of justice: rights, duties, and obligations (these are typically negative and agent-neutral);
(2) more informal, but equally important, personal responsibilities (these are typically positive and agent-centred);
(3) moral virtues (and vices), both social and personal.

I have offered no hierarchy among these moral values, and I do not believe that there is one; instead they are interdependent. All of them make reference to further values, the goods and evils inherent in the lives of humans, animals and in the existence of broader ecosystems, all of which arise from reasons for and against action. But morality is not based upon such goods in a means/end (consequentialist) fashion, and although there are goods that are not dependent upon morality, many of the most important ones are.

Indeed as I conceive it, moral practice and reflection have an iterative structure whereby simple systems of rules, responsibilities, and virtues are progressively qualified and enhanced as human cultures become more complicated, self-conscious, and self-critical, finding value in their own moral practices and institutions, most notably the state. If this is right, then it is as vain to hope for a complete account of morality as it is to hope for a complete theory of arithmetic. Nonetheless, the task remains for ethics to articulate and justify a moral consciousness that is adequate to the conditions and possibilities of human life as we find it.

11

The End of Philosophy?

The last half of this book bears witness to the remarkable revival of philosophical inquiry and debate that has flourished in the English language from the early 1960s onwards. The early post-war presumption that the only proper business for philosophy was to explore our ways of thinking about the world by looking to our uses of language, has melted away in the face of a renewed confidence in the possibility of developing arguments which deal directly with questions of metaphysics, epistemology, and ethics. An important symbol of this transformation was the publication in 1998 of the new *Routledge Encyclopedia of Philosophy* which replaced the 1967 Macmillan *Encyclopedia of Philosophy*. Despite much impressive scholarship, the 1967 *Encyclopedia* was still constrained by positivist anxieties about the possibility of metaphysics, and largely guided by analytical concerns with logic and language. The 1998 *Encyclopedia*, by contrast, has no such constraints and takes on the task of providing unapologetic essays on central topics of recent philosophical debate, including the themes of the second half of this book (as well as much more, including due recognition of the importance of non-European traditions of philosophy).

The Renewal of Philosophy

There have been many reasons for this transformation: while Quine's criticisms of the analytic/synthetic distinction implied that there is no firm partition between the analysis of language and the study of things themselves, Kripke showed how a revised understanding of language resurrects old metaphysical questions concerning essence and identity which Quine had sought to bury. Strawson's revival of transcendental arguments suggested that one can argue for ambitious conclusions by considering the presuppositions of knowledge or thought, while the mind/body identity theorists argued that some philosophical positions also involve scientific hypotheses. And the critical reaction against the narrow conception of ethics as primarily the study of the language of morals has led to a tremendous variety of ethical debates, some making connections with new positions in metaphysics and the philosophy of mind, while others address new practical issues in areas such as bioethics and feminism. In all this, however, what has contributed most has been the ability of philosophers to find interesting new arguments for positions which advance our understanding of the world and our place within it, sometimes drawing on considerations of language but often without any overt reference to it. And despite the wide variety of assumptions and methods discussed in this book, what continues to unify philosophy in English is a determination that philosophical discussion and debate are to be conducted through the critical construction and discussion of such arguments.

Arguments in philosophy are never proofs; they always have assumptions that can be called into question. Whatever one thinks in general of Quine's radicalization of Duhem's thesis (cf. Chapter 4, p. 73), it is certainly a mark of philosophy that nothing is immune from revision. This cuts both ways: new arguments are never by themselves decisive; but, equally, old presumptions can always be challenged. Philosophy comes to life where such challenges are created and debated; the deep challenges come from arguments which require us to rethink our understanding of the world and ourselves—either by embracing their conclusion, however uncomfortable, or by rejecting the apparently uncontentious assumptions which they employ. Such arguments cannot be brushed side; they set the context for further debate. In this book I have tried to present the dimensions of contemporary debate precisely by exploring the arguments which constitute the frame of reference of contemporary philosophy in the English language.

For this reason contemporary philosophy is dialectical in its method: new arguments necessarily make reference back to earlier positions which provide the background for understanding the commitments which the arguments seek to challenge. This dialectical conception of philosophy brings with it, however, no commitment to the existence of a Hegelian final vocabulary. On the contrary, there is no avoiding the philosophical version of Laudan's pessimistic meta-induction (cf. Chapter 7, p. 160), that we have excellent inductive grounds to expect that all contemporary philosophical positions will be shown to be unsatisfactory in the course of future debates. But there is no need in philosophy for a teleology of truth. The relation of present arguments to past debate provides by itself good enough reasons for regarding the continuation of such debates as the only way of improving our understanding. Although there is, necessarily, no guarantee that the course of future debates will be such that we would regard them as leading to further advances in understanding, it is reasonable to expect that as long as there are people of sufficient imagination and insight to come forward with new arguments, philosophy of this kind will continue to flourish. And yet, surprisingly, there is currently an influential opinion which holds that this optimism is altogether misguided, and that philosophy is now only a largely futile and anachronistic cultural relic, comparable to scholastic theology. Instead, we are told, we must prepare ourselves for 'post-philosophical' modes of discussion and debate.

Rorty the Sceptic

Contemporary cultural theory makes much use of the 'post-' prefix, especially in its talk of 'post-modernism' and 'post-structuralism'. Both of these are essentially philosophical responses to difficulties inherent in 'modernism' and 'structuralism', and there is much of interest in the debates which surround the use of these terms. In both cases, however, the primary works are French—post-modernism is especially associated with the work of Michel Foucault (1926–84), and post-structuralism with that of Jacques Derrida (1930–), so it has not been appropriate to discuss them here. But it is worth stressing that although both Foucault and Derrida call into question many of the assumptions of traditional philosophical discussion, neither of them suggest that philosophical discussion cannot be continued at all; Derrida, in particular, has emphatically repudiated any such position. It has instead been left to the contemporary American philosopher Richard Rorty (1931–) to put forward a version of this thesis, to the effect that there is no longer any merit in philosophical discussion of questions concerning knowledge, meaning, consciousness, value, and so on. Such discussions belong to 'Philosophy' (capital 'P') which has become a cultural disease of which we should seek to cure ourselves. In its place, Rorty maintains, we should look forward to a 'post-Philosophical culture' in which 'philosophy' (lower-case 'p') amounts only to 'a study of the comparative advantages and disadvantages of the various ways of talking which our race has invented' (*The Consequences of Pragmatism*, p. xl).

Rorty's metaphilosophical scepticism is based on the thesis that philosophical discussion from the time of Descartes has been dominated by questions that arise within the conception of the mind launched by Descartes and refined by Kant, namely as a system of ideas, or representations, which provide each of us with our understanding of the world and ourselves. For this conception of the mind as a putative 'mirror of nature' makes it easy to appreciate epistemological anxieties as to whether things really are as our ideas represent them, and equally easy to understand metaphysical disputes as to whether certain central features of our conception of the world (e.g. necessity) really inhere in things themselves or are only inserted into our understanding through the mind's way of developing its ideas into a systematic representation of a world. Rorty's claim is then that 'Philosophy' is largely constituted by debates involving these epistemological and metaphysical issues; and what motivates his scepticism concerning Philosophy is his conviction that this conception of the mind has been definitively overthrown through the arguments of Dewey, Heidegger, Wittgenstein, Sellars, Quine, and Davidson.

I shall not attempt to discuss this claim in any detail, but it is worth briefly connecting it to the positions of those philosophers on his list whose work I have discussed here—Wittgenstein, Sellars, Quine, and Davidson. Rorty's scepticism about Philosophy has obvious similarities with Wittgenstein's determination not to advance any positive 'theses'; and Wittgenstein's commitment to rejecting a 'mirror of nature' conception of the mind is an implication of the primacy he gives to language-games as the context for meaning and truth, since they are essentially connected into worldly activities and thus are not detached representations of the world. Sellars was not in the same way a critic of the possibility of Philosophy (or, indeed, philosophy); but Rorty uses him as an important critic of the 'mirror of nature' story. For he takes it that Sellars' critical discussion of the 'Myth of the Given' is a way of showing the flaws in empiricist conceptions of mental representation, and he further argues that Sellars' emphasis on the 'space of reasons' characteristic of the 'manifest image' of man should lead us to think of epistemology as a matter of interpersonal 'conversations' that can lead to the justification of beliefs, rather than sensory 'confrontations' with a world that we seek to represent accurately.

In the case of Quine, Rorty's attitude is more equivocal: he endorses Quine's criticisms of the analytic/synthetic distinction, which he takes to show that there is no absolute distinction between the contributions of language and the world to the truth of what we say, and thus that it is a mistake to think of language as a transparent medium for representing facts as they are. But Rorty rejects the scepticism about meaning that Quine attaches to his criticisms of analyticity; hence he rejects the priority which Quine gives to physics as a guide to reality, in preference to disciplines such as history which draw essentially upon the meanings of human acts. This attitude to Quine's work is similar to that of Davidson and it is no surprise, therefore, that Rorty declares himself to be an enthusiastic disciple of Davidson: what particularly attracts him is Davidson's claim that there is no such a thing as 'language' conceived as a shared means of communication and thus in principle available as a common medium of linguistic representation.

Even if Rorty's interpretation of these philosophers is in some respects selective, he is, I think, unquestionably correct in taking them all to be opposed to the conception of the mind as a mirror of nature. But the interpretation of these philosophers (and indeed of Descartes and Kant) is not the point at issue here; what matters is Rorty's thesis that once one has grasped the significance of their work one should see that philosophical discussion and debate cannot continue remotely as before. In effect, in terms of this book, Rorty's claim is that the material presented in the first four-and-a-half chapters implies that the arguments discussed in the rest of the book are largely worthless. Although he does not prescribe an end to philosophy, since it is not a cultural practice that can have an end, philosophy, he holds, cannot any longer be regarded as a 'constructive' discipline, aimed, liked the sciences, at the determination of truth; instead it can be only an 'edifying' discipline, concerned to expose illusion and to sustain conversation by generating new descriptions which do not purport to 'represent reality' but simply to engage the interest of our conversational partners.

The claim that is central to Rorty's position is that the possibility of 'constructive' Philosophy is dependent upon a conception of the mind as a system of representations. Thus Rorty argues that contemporary discussions of 'realism' and 'anti-realism' have this conception as a premiss, and that once one adopts his own 'antirepresentational' position the whole 'realism/anti-realism' debate is undermined. Let us try to apply this to the issue of 'modal realism' discussed in Chapter 6. Modal realists such as Lewis hold that possibilities are best thought of as real worlds, unified by space and time though disjoint from the actual world with which they share no parts. Anti-realists such as Kripke hold that all that is real is actual, and thus that non-actual possibilities are only fictions, the contents of ideally coherent representations whose constituents are all real. So it is perfectly true that in this debate an issue concerning the relationship between 'representation' and 'reality' arises; but it would be quite wrong to suggest that either Kripke or Lewis hold that the debate is to be settled by some general theory of representation. Instead the debate follows the course I tried to set out in Chapter 6, in which the realist Lewis argues that the anti-realist does not have the resources to capture all the modal distinctions we want to draw, whereas the anti-realist argues that the realist's account of modal judgements is inherently sceptical and does not capture the ways in which we think about possibilities which concern particular things. So far as I can see, neither party to this dispute has, even in the background, some neo-Cartesian or neo-Kantian theory of representation; so it is entirely baffling to be told that the dispute is pointless because it assumes such a theory.

Rorty suggests at one point that these realist disputes require 'an *independent* test of accuracy of representation' (*Philosophical Papers* I, p. 6). His thought seems to be that unless there is a way of standing right outside the relevant part of our language and comparing it to a reality that is understood without reference to that language, the issue of realism cannot be sensibly posed because it cannot be definitively resolved. It is immediately obvious that there cannot be 'an *independent* test' of this kind: we cannot detach ourselves from our modal concepts while still retaining the ability to understand possibilities and impossibilities. But why should modal realists and their critics suppose we need any such thing? Their dispute concerns the best way for us to understand the implications of our modal concepts in the light of our general understanding of the world and ourselves. The realist holds that our common-sense talk of the existence of mere possibilities should be taken at face value; the anti-realist holds that we make more trouble for ourselves than it is worth if we take the realist option, and that there is an alternative which enables us to save appearances. Neither party to this dispute envisages the impossible test which Rorty hypothesizes for them; both seek to vindicate their different accounts of the implications of our modal concepts on the basis of an understanding of them that works from within.

This kind of critique of Rorty's metaphilosophical scepticism can be applied to all the debates discussed in the latter part of this book. Even in the area of the philosophy of mind, about which Rorty has written a good deal, there is no straightforward route to a dissolution of the dispute between functionalists and dual-aspect theorists from the rejection of the Cartesian conception of mind. Rorty is understandably keen to promote Davidson's 'non-reductive physicalism', but he does not tangle with the details of Davidson's anomalous monism. Indeed it is not clear to me whether he holds that the dispute between functionalists and dual-aspect theorists is as misguided as other Philosophical disputes, or whether he thinks that in this case the position of dual-aspect theorists is to be preferred because of the conception of mental representation employed by functionalists. In truth in this area, as elsewhere, Rorty's recent writings are neglected because they seem to have little rational connection with the positions discussed in current debates.

The result is a strange impasse: on the one hand, among many writers about philosophy, especially those whose background and sympathies are in the humanities, Rorty's writings are esteemed as an indication of our 'post-Philosophical' situation. On the other hand, among most philosophers, Rorty's writings are largely neglected because his abstract critique of Philosophy simply does not make contact with current philosophical debates.

Philosophy and Method

A regular feature of Rorty's complaints about Philosophy is that we lack a 'method' for resolving Philosophical disputes. Thus he writes that 'the death of meaning' (by which he means Quine's critique of analyticity) brings with it 'the death of philosophy as a discipline with a method of its own' (*The Linguistic Turn*, p. 370). So, he holds, once we recognize that there is no such method for determining whether our conceptual schemes (ways of talking etc.) are accurate, we should reject all truth-oriented questions concerning their merits. This attitude is reminiscent of Carnap's attitude to 'external' questions concerning the merits of conceptual schemes (cf. Chapter 4, p. 89)—that, because there is no disciplined method for answering them, they are not cognitive at all: we can discuss their relative efficiency, fruitfulness, and simplicity, but we should not take ourselves to establish thereby that one scheme is closer to the facts than another. Indeed, because the comparison with Carnap fits other aspects of Rorty's work (for example, Rorty frequently invokes the verificationist thesis that there can be no difference which makes no difference) it is tempting to suggest that Rorty's critique of Philosophy is just a revival of the logical empiricist critique of metaphysics.

This is not quite right. For although both reject traditional philosophy as the illusory attempt to construct a 'super-science', Rorty inveighs also against 'scientism', the belief that the natural sciences provide the only acceptable methods of inquiry, whereas the logical empiricists, because of their empiricism, exemplified all too often precisely this attitude (though Carnap's 'principle of tolerance'—cf. Chapter 7, p. 155—manifests a more complex attitude). Thus a better way to think of Rorty is as a logical empiricist who has shed the dogmas of empiricism, i.e., as he himself often declares, as a pragmatist in the tradition of William James.

Yet this comparison threatens Rorty's sceptical position. For James famously combined his pragmatism with an enduring concern for truth—as in his notorious claim that 'if the hypothesis of God works satisfactorily in the widest sense of the word, it is true' (*Pragmatism*, p. 299). Thus James provides an example of a philosopher who, while certainly rejecting the conception of the mind as a passive mirror of nature, offers his pragmatism as an alternative method of establishing the truth in philosophy as much as elsewhere. Contemporary defenders of Philosophy will not, I think, want to follow James in detail; instead, at least within the English-language tradition explored here, they will invoke the 'dialectical' method of presenting and assessing new arguments which I described at the start of this chapter. As I stressed there, it is a feature of this method that nothing is beyond question; but the absence of a decision-procedure concerning the issues raised by philosophical arguments shows, not that they are not truth-oriented, but that they concern questions which are so fundamental to our understanding of ourselves and the world that no assumptions can be legitimately regarded as beyond question. Anyone who really thinks that, in the absence of a decision-procedure, questions of truth are empty or illegitimate, is simply committed to the self-refuting positivist thesis that the only truths are those which can be conclusively established as true.

Rorty presents his own account of post-Philosophical, edifying, philosophy as one whose participants seek 'to keep the conversation going rather than to find objective truth' (*Philosophy and the Mirror of Nature*, p. 377). Since where there is no concern for truth there can be no arguments, and thus no conclusions whose truth is supposed to follow from stated premises, the 'conversations' of 'edifying' philosophers will be very different from the debates discussed here—so different that indeed it will be difficult to regard them as members of the same cultural tradition. But in fact there is no need to accept the terms of Rorty's contrast. For contemporary philosophers 'keep the conversation going' precisely by creating new arguments with premises that cannot be readily repudiated because they are deeply embedded in the conclusions of past conversations, despite the fact that these premisses are taken to imply the objective truth of conclusions which challenge our current convictions.

Rorty's metaphilosopical scepticism is unwarranted. The arguments discussed in the second half of this book do not have an erroneous 'mirror of nature' assumption as an implicit premiss; and only an indefensible positivist demand for a decision-procedure in philosophy could yield the conclusion that the debates to which these arguments give rise are not directed at the objective truth of their conclusions. Philosophy in the English-language tradition is not a decaying cultural tradition stuck in an unimaginative rut; it is a flourishing tradition of overlapping debates that remain perpetually open to new arguments.

References and Further Reading

References to the main works mentioned in each chapter are given below, using the editions that are currently the most readily available. In the references for Chapters 1–5 there is a section of 'Further Reading' in which I mention some other relevant discussions. In the references for Chapters 6–11 I do not attempt to separate out references to the main works mentioned from references to further discussions.

Chapter 1

Moore, Russell, and Wittgenstein

G. E. Moore *Selected Writings* (London: Routledge, 1993) contains Moore's early paper 'The Nature of Judgment' (1899) in which his method of analysis is proposed, and his paper 'A Defence of Common Sense' (1925) in which his conception of common sense is developed. Bertrand Russell presented his theory of descriptions in 'On Denoting' (1905) which is reprinted in volume 4 of *The Collected Papers of Bertrand Russell* (London: Routledge, 1994). His 1918 lectures on 'The Philosophy of Logical Atomism' provide a classic statement of his 'logical-analytic method of philosophy'; they are reprinted in volume 8 of *The Collected Papers of Bertrand Russell* (London: Routledge, 1986). His later philosophy takes off from the position advanced in *The Analysis of Mind* (London: Routledge and Kegan Paul, 1921). L. Wittgenstein's *Tractatus Logico-Philosophicus* was first published in German in 1921; in 1922 it was republished with an English translation by C. K. Ogden (and F. P. Ramsey), and an introduction by Russell (London: Routledge and Kegan Paul).

Logical empiricism

The English translation of Rudolph Carnap's 1932 paper 'The Elimination of Metaphysics Through Logical Analysis of Language' occurs in *Logical Positivism* (ed. A. J. Ayer; New York: Free Press, 1959), a collection which includes many important papers by members of the Vienna Circle. *Essential Readings in Logical Positivism* (ed. O Hanfling; Oxford: Blackwell, 1981) also contains a useful selection of texts. A. J. Ayer's *Language, Truth and Logic* (London: Gollancz, 1936; repr. Harmondsworth: Penguin, 1971) is the classic English-language statement of the logical empiricist position.

American philosophy

There is a useful selection from Dewey's numerous writings: *The Essential Dewey* (2 vols., ed. C. A. Hickman and T. M. Alexander; Bloomington, Oh.: Indiana University Press, 1998). C. I. Lewis' most influential work was *Mind and World Order* (New York: Charles Scribner, 1929).

Further reading

J. Skorupski *English-Language Philosophy 1750–1945* (Oxford: Oxford University Press, 1993) esp. chs. 4–6 provides a helpful general guide. For the development of the analytical project see parts I and II of P. Hylton *Russell, Idealism and the Emergence of Analytical Philosophy* (Oxford: Clarendon Press, 1990) and T. Baldwin *G. E. Moore* (London: Routledge, 1990). For the development of logical empiricism see part 2 of J. A. Coffa *The Semantic Tradition from Kant to Carnap: To the Vienna Station* (Cambridge: Cambridge University Press, 1991). There is not, to the best of my knowledge, a helpful survey of American philosophy during the first half of the twentieth century; but one can get a reasonable sense of it from a collection of essays by many of the leading philosophers of the time: *Contemporary American Philosophy II* (ed. G. P. Adams and W. Pepperell Montague; London: George Allen and Unwin, 1930).

Chapter 2

The main works by Wittgenstein discussed here are *Tractatus Logico-Philosophicus* (op. cit. Ch. 1), *Philosophical Investigations* (*PI*) tr. G. E. M. Anscombe; Oxford: Blackwell, 1953), and *On Certainty* (*OC*) tr. G. E. M. Anscombe and D. Paul; Oxford: Blackwell, 1969). From among his other writings, the most interesting is the collection *Philosophical Occasions* (ed. J. Klagge and A. Nordmann; Indianapolis: Hackett, 1993). For the topic of rule-following, consult part VI of his *Remarks on the Foundations of Mathematics* (tr. G. E. M. Anscombe; Oxford, Blackwell: 3rd edn. 1978). The English translation of Otto Neurath's 1932 paper 'Protocol Sentences' is in *Essential Readings in Logical Positivism* (op. cit. Ch. 1).

Further reading

The secondary literature concerning Wittgenstein is vast. I am indebted to D. Pears *The False Prison* II (Oxford: Clarendon, 1988), M. Budd *Wittgenstein's Philosophy of Psychology* (London: Routledge, 1989), and M. McGinn *Wittgenstein's* Philosophical Investigations (London: Routledge, 1997). Ray

Monk's biography *Ludwig Wittgenstein* (London: Jonathan Cape, 1990) provides a credible account of his life. The complex history of the publication of Wittgenstein's writings is described in 'The Availability of Wittgenstein's Philosophy' by David Stern, in *The Cambridge Companion to Wittgenstein* (ed. H. Sluga and D. Stern; Cambridge: Cambridge University Press, 1996).

Chapter 3

Ryle, Austin and Strawson

Gilbert Ryle's major work is *The Concept of Mind* (London: Hutchinson, 1949; repr. Harmondsworth: Penguin, 1963). His papers, including 'Systematically Misleading Expressions' (1932), 'Taking Sides in Philosophy' (1937), and 'Ordinary Language' (1953), can be found in his *Collected Papers* I, II (London: Hutchinson, 1971). J. L. Austin *Philosophical Papers* (Oxford: Clarendon, 1961; 3rd edn. 1979) contains all the papers Austin published during his lifetime, including 'Other Minds' (1946), and 'A Plea for Excuses' (1956). *Sense and Sensibilia* (Oxford: Clarendon, 1962) is the text of Austin's famous lectures on perception, reconstructed from his notes by G. J. Warnock. *How to do Things with Words* (Oxford: Clarendon, 1962) is the text of his William James lectures, posthumously edited by J. Urmson. Sir Peter Strawson's early criticisms of Russell are to be found in *Introduction to Logical Theory* (London: Methuen, 1952), and in some of the papers collected in his *Logico-Linguistic Papers* (London: Methuen, 1971), especially his seminal paper 'On Referring' (1950). References to Strawson's later writings are given in the references to Chapter 8.

Cavell and Grice

Stanley Cavell's 1969 essay 'Must we Mean What we Say?' is published in his collection *Must we Mean What we Say?* (Cambridge: Cambridge University Press, 1976) which also includes useful discussions of Wittgenstein and Austin. H. P. Grice's theory of conversational implicature is developed in his 1961 paper 'The Causal Theory of Perception' which is reprinted in his *Studies in the Way of Words* (Cambridge, Mass.: Harvard University Press, 1989).

Further reading

Chapter 2 of L. Hudson *The Cult of the Fact* (London: Jonathan Cape, 1972) contains a vivid description of Oxford philosophy in the 1950s. The style of writing of this time is readily apparent in *The Revolution in Philosophy* (ed. A. J. Ayer et al.; London: Macmillan, 1956) which contains essays by many Oxford philosophers of the period. The contrast between this style and that of the works of phenomenology discussed by Ryle such as M. Heidegger *Being and Time* (tr. J. Macquarrie and E. Robinson; Oxford: Blackwell, 1973) could scarcely be greater. B. Magee (ed.) *Modern British Philosophy* (London: Secker and Warburg, 1971) is a record of a series of lively interviews with several of the philosophers discussed in this book.

Chapter 4

Quine

Willard van Quine's famous paper 'Two Dogmas of Empiricism' (1950) is reprinted in his collection *From a Logical Point of View* (Cambridge, Mass.: Harvard University Press, 1953; revised edn. 1961). He advanced other important criticisms of logical empiricism in 'Truth by Convention' (1935), and 'Carnap and Logical Truth' (1954), both reprinted in his collection *Ways of Paradox* (New York: Random House, 1966). His indeterminacy thesis is propounded in chapter 2 of *Word and Object* (Cambridge, Mass.: MIT Press, 1960). 'Epistemology Naturalized' was published in his collection *Ontological Relativity and Other Essays* (New York: Columbia University Press, 1969). His conception of logic is expounded in *Philosophy of Logic* (Englewood Cliffs, NJ: Prentice-Hall, 1970). Among his later writings *The Pursuit of Truth* (Cambridge, Mass.: Harvard University Press, 1990) provides an exceptionally clear and succinct statement of his position.

Carnap and Sellars

Carnap's crucial acknowledgement that even analytic statements are revisable in the light of experience occurs on pp. 318–19 of *The Logical Syntax of Language* (tr. A. Smeaton; London: Kegan Paul, 1937). His 1950 paper 'Empiricism, Semantics and Ontology' is reprinted in a useful collection of essays *The Linguistic Turn* (ed. R. Rorty; Chicago: University of Chicago Press, 1967). Wilfred Sellars's most important papers are collected in *Science, Perception and Reality* (London: Routledge and Kegan Paul, 1963).

Further reading

Words and Objections (ed. D. Davidson and J. Hintikka; Dordrecht: Reidel, 1969), includes Chomsky's critical discussion of the indeterminacy thesis and Quine's brief reply to it. *The Philosophy of W. V. Quine* (ed. L. E. Hahn and P. A. Schilpp; La Salle, Ill.: Open Court, 1986) starts off with Quine's interesting 'Autobiography of W. V. Quine'. G. Evans criticizes Quine's indeterminacy argument in 'Identity and Predication' which is reprinted in his *Collected Papers* (Oxford: Clarendon, 1985). R. Gibson *The Philosophy of W. V. Quine* (Gainsville, Fla.: University Presses of Florida, 1982) provides an authoritative exposition of Quine's philosophy; C. Hookway *Quine* (Cambridge: Polity Press, 1988) provides a critical assessment of it to which I am indebted.

Chapter 5

Davidson

Most of Davidson's papers in the philosophy of language are collected in his *Inquiries into Truth and Interpretation* (Oxford: Clarendon, 1984). *Truth and Interpretation* (ed. E. LePore; Oxford: Blackwell, 1986) is a useful collection which contains essays on Davidson's position, and further papers by Davidson including 'A Nice Derangement of Epitaphs'. Davidson has also provided a helpful summary of his general position, in his entry 'Davidson, Donald' in *A Companion to the Philosophy of Mind* (ed. S. Guttenplan; Oxford: Blackwell, 1994).

Dummett

In my account of Dummett's position I have relied primarily upon *The Logical Basis of Metaphysics* (London: Duckworth, 1991) and *The Seas of Language* (Oxford: Clarendon, 1993), which is a collection of Dummett's main papers from 1975 onwards. *Truth and Other Enigmas* (London: Duckworth, 1978) is a useful collection of Dummett's earlier papers.

Meaning and convention

H. P. Grice's famous 1957 paper 'Meaning' is reprinted in his *Studies in the Ways of Words* (op. cit. Ch. 3). David Lewis presented his account of convention in *Convention* (Cambridge, Mass.; Harvard University Press, 1969). Jonathan Bennett propounds a detailed theory of language which draws on the ideas of Grice and Lewis in *Linguistic Behaviour* (Cambridge: Cambridge University Press, 1976). Davidson's criticisms of convention-based theories of language are propounded in 'Communication and Convention' (in *Inquiries into Truth and Interpretation* (op. cit.)), and 'A Nice Derangement of

Epitaphs' (in *Truth and Interpretation* (op. cit.)). Chomsky's criticisms are to be found in *Rules and Representations* (Oxford: Blackwell, 1980). He gives a straightforward account of his own position in chapter 2 of *Knowledge of Language* (New York: Praeger, 1986).

Further reading

W. Lycan *Philosophy of Language* (London: Routledge, 2000) is a useful introductory guide to analytical philosophy of language. Apart from the essays in *Truth and Interpretation* (op. cit.), the best study of Davidson's philosophy of language is in French: P. Engel *Davidson et la philosophie du langage* (Paris: Presses Universitaires de France, 1994). For further elucidation and critical discussion of Dummett's position, see C. McGinn 'Truth and Use' in *Reference, Truth and Reality* (ed. M. Platts; London: Routledge, 1980), the essays in *Michael Dummett* (ed. B. Taylor; Dordrecht: Nijhoff, 1987) and C. Wright's 'Introduction' to his book *Realism, Meaning and Truth* (Oxford: Blackwell, 1987). In my remarks about intuitionistic and classical logic I am indebted to Ian Rumfit ' "Yes" and "No" ', *Mind*, 109, (2000), 781–823, which draws on a beautiful paper by T. J. Smiley: 'Rejection', *Analysis*, 56 (1996), pp. 1–9. Gareth Evans presents his revision of Dummett's account of understanding in chapter 4 of *The Varieties of Reference* (Oxford: Clarendon, 1982).

Chapter 6

Quine's sceptical doubts about essentialism were set out clearly in his 1953 paper 'Three Grades of Modal Involvement', which is reprinted in his collection *The Ways of Paradox* (New York: Random House, 1966). Saul Kripke's famous defence of the possibility of essentialism is *Naming and Necessity* (Oxford: Blackwell, 1980). This book is the annotated text of lectures given in 1970 and is remarkably accessible. A standard textbook of modal logic, with a full development of 'possible world semantics' for different systems of modal logic, is G. Hughes and M. Cresswell *A New Introduction to Modal Logic* (London: Routledge, 1996). The Stalnaker/Lewis accounts of counterfactuals (they are not quite the same) are set out in D. Lewis *Counterfactuals* (Oxford: Blackwell, 1973), and R. Stalnaker *Inquiry* (Cambridge, Mass.: MIT Press, 1984).

Hilary Putnam's 'Twin Earth' argument is presented in 'The Meaning of "Meaning" ' in his collection *Language, Mind and Reality* (Cambridge: Cambridge University Press, 1975). For my criticisms of it I am indebted to Hugh Mellor: see his paper 'Natural Kinds' in his *Matters of Metaphysics*

(Cambridge: Cambridge University Press, 1991). David Lewis sets out his modal realism with exemplary clarity in *On the Plurality of Worlds* (Oxford: Blackwell, 1986). From the plurality of responses to Lewis I am especially indebted to P. van Inwagen 'Two Concepts of Possible Worlds' in *Midwest Studies in Philosophy* 11 (1986), 185–213.

Chapter 7

The classic statement of the logical empiricist position is C. G. Hempel *Aspects of Scientific Explanation and Other Essays* (New York: Free Press, 1965); E. Nagel *The Structure of Science* (New York: Harcourt Brace, 1961) provides a clear systematic exposition of the position. Sir Karl Popper's *The Logic of Scientific Discovery* (London: Hutchinson, 1959) is the classic statement of his critical rationalism; he develops the position further in *Conjectures and Refutations* (London: Routledge, 1962). B. Magee *Popper* (London: Fontana: 1973) provides an accessible account of Popper's philosophy; D. Miller *Critical Rationalism: Restatement and Defence* (La Salle, Ill.: Open Court, 1994) is a more advanced discussion.

Thomas Kuhn set out his position in *The Structure of Scientific Revolutions* (Chicago: University of Chicago Press, 1962; 2nd edn., with an important postscript, 1970). His debate with his critics, including Popper and Paul Feyerabend, and his important 'Reflections on my Critics' in response to them, is to be found in *Criticism and the Growth of Knowledge* (ed. I. Lakatos and A. Musgrave; Cambridge: Cambridge University Press, 1970). Feyerabend's criticisms of logical empiricism are developed in the papers collected in his *Philosophical Papers* I, II (Cambridge: Cambridge University Press, 1981); his 'epistemological anarchism' is propounded in *Against Method* (London: New Left Books, London, 1975).

Laudan set out his 'pessimistic meta-induction' in 'A Confutation of Convergent Realism' (1981), which is reprinted in a useful collection *The Philosophy of Science* (ed. D Papineau; Oxford: Oxford University Press, 1996). The passage quoted from Feynman comes from his book *QED: the Strange Theory of Light and Matter* (Princeton, NJ: Princeton University Press, 1985). 'Inference to the Best Explanation' was identified as such by Gilbert Harman in a paper with this title (*Philosophical Review*, 74 (1965) 88–95); the best discussion of it is P. Lipton *Inference to the Best Explanation* (London: Routledge, 1991). Bromberger's example of the shadow cast by a pole comes from his paper 'Why-Questions', in *Mind and Cosmos* (R. Colodny (ed.); Pittsburgh, Pa.: University of Pittsburgh Press, 1966). The importance of causal explanations in the natural sciences is developed in N. Cartwright *How the Laws of Physics Lie* (Oxford: Clarendon Press, 1983) (esp. essays 3 and 4). W. Salmon *Scientific Explanation and the Causal Structure of the World* (Princeton, NJ: Princeton University Press, 1984) is an advanced discussion of this topic.

Chapter 8

The 'brain-in-a-vat' fiction is developed by Hilary Putnam in *Reason, Truth and History* (Cambridge: Cambridge University Press, 1981). Nelson Goodman propounded his 'new riddle of induction' in *Fact, Fiction, and Forecast* (Cambridge, Mass.: Harvard University Press, 1954). Anthony Flew's paper 'Philosophy and Language' occurs in A. Flew (ed.) *Essays in Conceptual Analysis* (London: Macmillan, 1956). Moore's 'Proof of an External World' is reprinted in G. E. Moore *Selected Writings* (London: Routledge, 1993). Norman Malcolm's (mis)interpretation of Moore is developed in his paper 'Moore and Ordinary Language' which occurs in *The Philosophy of G. E. Moore* (ed. P. A. Schilpp; La Salle, Ill.: Open Court, 1942). The best recent discussions of scepticism are those by Barry Stroud: see *The Significance of Philosophical Scepticism* (Oxford: Clarendon, 1984) and *Understanding Human Knowledge* (Oxford: Clarendon, 2000).

Sir Peter Strawson's works include *Individuals* (London: Methuen, 1959), *The Bounds of Sense* (London: Methuen, 1966), *Scepticism and Naturalism: Some Varieties* (London: Methuen, 1985). Gareth Evans' critical discussion of Strawson's discussion of sounds occurs in 'Things Without the Mind', reprinted in his *Collected Papers* (op. cit. Ch. 4). Barry Stroud's criticism of Strawson occurs in 'Transcendental Arguments', reprinted in *Understanding Human Knowledge* (op. cit.). The context for these discussions is provided by I. Kant *Critique of Pure Reason* (tr. P. Guyer and A. Wood; Cambridge: Cambridge University Press, 1997).

Frank Ramsey's discussion of induction occurs in 'Truth and Probability' in *The Foundations of Mathematics* (London: Kegan Paul, 1931). Edmund Gettier's famous argument occurs in 'Is Justified True Belief Knowledge?', reprinted in *Knowledge and Belief* (ed. A. Phillips Griffiths; Oxford: Oxford University Press, 1967). Robert Nozick's account of knowledge is set out in chapter 3 of his *Philosophical Explanations* (Oxford: Clarendon, 1981). Edward Craig gives his account in *Knowledge and the State of Nature* (Oxford: Clarendon, 1990).

Alvin Goldman expounds his naturalized epistemology in *Epistemology and Cognition* (Cambridge, Mass.: Harvard University Press, 1986). Bernard Williams develops his account of the 'absolute conception' in chapter 8 of *Descartes: The Project of Pure Inquiry* (Harmondsworth: Penguin, 1978). Thomas Nagel discusses objectivity in *The View from Nowhere* (Oxford: Clarendon, 1986). Sandra Harding presents her feminist standpoint epistemology in *Whose Science? Whose Knowledge? Thinking from Women's Lives* (Ithaca: Cornell University Press, 1991).

Chapter 9

Elizabeth Anscombe's *Intention* (Oxford: Blackwell, 1957) was closely followed by Peter Winch *The Idea of a Social Science* (London: Routledge, 1958); and A. I. Melden *Free Action* (London: Routledge, 1961). The thesis that reasons are causes was defended by D. Pears in 'Sketch for a Causal Theory of Wanting and Doing' in his *Questions in the Philosophy of Mind* (London: Duckworth, 1975), and by D. Davidson in 'Actions, Reasons and Causes' (1963) which is reprinted in his *Essays on Actions and Events* (Oxford: Clarendon, 1980); this collection also includes 'Mental Events' (1970) in which he propounds his 'anomalous monism'. This position is debated in *Mental Causation* (ed. J. Heil and A. Mele; Oxford: Clarendon, 1995).

The mind/body identity theory was advanced by David Lewis in 'An Argument for the Identity Theory' (1966) reprinted in his *Philosophical Papers* I (Oxford: Oxford University Press, 1985). Lewis's paper 'Reduction of Mind' (1994) is reprinted in his *Papers in Metaphysics and Epistemology* (Cambridge: Cambridge University Press, 1999). David Armstrong's classic work was *A Materialist Theory of Mind* (London: Routledge, 1968). There was an instructive debate between Armstrong and Norman Malcolm in D. M. Armstrong and N. Malcolm *Consciousness and Causality* (Oxford: Blackwell, 1984). Several functionalist positions are developed and discussed in *Mind and Cognition* (ed. W. G. Lycan; Oxford: Blackwell, 1990). An excellent recent critical exposition and defence of functionalism is D. Braddon-Mitchell and F. Jackson *Philosophy of Mind and Cognition* (Oxford: Blackwell, 1996). T. Crane *The Mechanical Mind* (London: Penguin, 1995) provides a lucid critical discussion of materialist theories of thought.

There is no comparable straightforward exposition of a dual aspect theory: B. O'Shaughnessy *The Will* I, II (Cambridge: Cambridge University Press, 1980) propounds a complex dual aspect theory of perception and action; J. McDowell *Mind and World* (Cambridge, Mass.: Harvard University Press, 1994) provides a more recent position of this kind.

Frankfurt's papers on free will are collected in H. Frankfurt *The Importance of What We Care About* (Cambridge: Cambridge University Press, 1988). An important discussion informed by a dual aspect theory was P. F. Strawson 'Freedom and Resentment' (1962) which is reprinted in his collection *'Freedom and Resentment' and Other Essays* (London: Methuen, 1971). The suggestion that our understanding of others involves replicating their reasonings is advanced in J. Heal 'Replication and Functionalism' in *Language, Mind and Logic* (ed. J. Butterfield; Cambridge: Cambridge University Press, 1986).

Fodor's influential computational theory of thought is set out in *Psychosemantics* (Cambridge, Mass.: MIT Press, 1987), and *The Elm and the Expert* (Cambridge, Mass.: MIT Press, 1994). There is a good discussion of Fodor's position and some alternatives to it in D. Braddon-Mitchell and F. Jackson *Philosophy of Mind and Cognition* (op. cit.). Dennett's position is set out in D. Dennett *The Intentional Stance* (Cambridge, Mass.: MIT Press, 1989).

The Externalist issue was raised by Putnam in 'The Meaning of "Meaning"' (op. cit. Ch. 6). Burge developed the position further in T. Burge 'Individualism and the Mental' (1979) reprinted in *The Nature of Mind* (ed. D. Rosenthal; New York: Oxford University Press, 1991). G. McCulloch advocates a strongly externalist philosophy of mind in *The Mind and Its World* (London: Routledge, 1995). Burge discusses the relationship between his position and that of Chomsky in 'Wherein is Language Social?' in *Reflections on Chomsky* (ed. A George; Oxford: Blackwell, 1989). Chomsky returns to the issue in 'Language From an Internalist Perspective' and 'Internalist Explorations' in his collection *New Horizons in the Study of Language and Mind* (Cambridge: Cambridge University Press, 2000).

Nagel's anxiety about what it is like to be a bat is articulated in 'What is it Like to be a Bat?' (1974) reprinted in his *Mortal Questions* (Cambridge: Cambridge University Press, 1979). Richard Dawkins offers an informed answer to Nagel's question in *The Blind Watchmaker* (London: Longman, 1986) Ch. 2. David Lewis advances a materialist response to Nagel's anxieties in 'Mad Pain and Martian Pain' (1980) reprinted in his *Philosophical Papers* I (op. cit.). Frank Jackson sets out Mary's tale in F. Jackson 'What Mary Didn't Know' (1986) reprinted in *The Nature of Mind* (ed. D. Rosenthal; op. cit.). Lewis responds to this in 'What Experience Teaches' in *Mind and Cognition* (ed. W. G. Lycan; op. cit.). The 'explanatory gap' thesis has been developed by Colin McGinn in *The Problem of Consciousness* (Oxford: Blackwell, 1991). An excellent general discussion of recent debates concerning consciousness is M. Tye *Ten Problems of Consciousness* (Cambridge, Mass.: MIT Press, 1995).

Chapter 10

G. E. Moore expounds the 'naturalistic fallacy' in chapter 1 of *Principia Ethica* (Cambridge: Cambridge University Press, 1903). Chapter 6 of *Language, Truth and Logic* (op. cit. Ch. 1) by A. J. Ayer is a classic presentation of the emotivist position of the logical empiricists. Ayer later wrote his 'Preface' for P. Nowell-Smith *Ethics* (Harmondsworth: Penguin, 1954), a book which is a characteristic expression of the analytical moral philosophy of the period. An important contribution to the end of this kind of philosophy was the publication of John Rawls *A Theory of Justice* (Oxford: Clarendon, 1971). For a recent discussion of Rawls' work, see chapter 5 of J. Wolff *An Introduction to Political Philosophy* (Oxford: Oxford University Press, 1996).

R. M. Hare's major works are: *The Language of Morals* (Oxford: Clarendon, 1952), *Freedom and Reason* (Oxford: Clarendon, 1963) and *Moral Thinking* (Oxford: Clarendon, 1981). Philippa Foot's early papers, such as 'Moral Arguments' (1958) in which she discusses Hare, are collected in her volume *Virtues and Vices* (Oxford: Blackwell, 1978). John Searle's 1964 paper 'How to Derive "Ought" from "Is"' is reprinted in *Theories of Ethics* (ed. P. Foot; Oxford: Oxford University Press, 1967) which also includes a useful introduction by Foot and other critical discussions of Hare. Elizabeth Anscombe's 1958 paper 'Modern Moral Philosophy' is reprinted in an excellent recent collection *Virtue Ethics* (ed. R. Crisp and M. Slote; Oxford: Oxford University Press, 1997). Hume sets out his moral psychology in *A Treatise of Human Nature* (ed. L. Selby-Bigge; Oxford: Clarendon, 1888) esp. Book II part III, and again in his 'An Enquiry Concerning the Principles of Morals' in *Enquiries concerning Human Understanding and concerning the Principles of Morals* (ed. L. Selby-Bigge; Oxford: Clarendon, 3rd edn. 1975) esp. Appendix I.

W. Frankena's classic 1958 paper 'Obligation and Motivation in Recent Moral Philosophy' is reprinted in *Perspectives on Morality: Essays by William K. Frankena* (ed. K. E. Goodpaster; Notre Dame, Ind.: University of Notre Dame Press, 1976). Bernard Williams' paper 'Internal and External Reasons' occurs in his collection *Moral Luck* (Cambridge: Cambridge University Press, 1981). Thomas Nagel has qualified the position presented in *The Possibility of Altruism* (Oxford: Clarendon, 1970) in chapters 8 and 9 of his later book *The View From Nowhere* (op. cit. Ch. 8) where he introduces the distinction between agent-neutral and agent-centred values. John McDowell's 1979 essay 'Virtue and Reason' is reprinted in *Virtue Ethics* (ed. R. Crisp and M. Slote; op. cit.).

The title of J. L. Mackie's book *Ethics: Inventing Right and Wrong* (Harmondsworth: Penguin, 1977) indicates his rejection of moral realism. The position of the Cornell Realists is set out by Richard Boyd in 'How to be a Moral Realist' and Nicholas Sturgeon in 'Moral Explanations', which are in *Essays in Moral Realism* (ed. G. Sayre-McCord; Ithaca: Cornell University Press, 1988). Simon Blackburn's expressivist position in *Ruling Passions* (Oxford: Clarendon, 1998) owes a good deal to Allan Gibbard's *Wise Choices, Apt Feelings* (Cambridge, Mass.: Harvard University Press, 1990). Tim Scanlon's book *What We Owe to Each Other* (Cambridge, Mass.; Harvard University Press, 1998) develops his paper 'Contractualism and Utilitarianism' in *Utilitarianism and Beyond* (ed. A. Sen and B. Williams (Cambridge: Cambridge University Press, 1982).

Bernard Williams discusses the issue of objectivity in ethics in chapter 8 of *Ethics and the Limits of Philosophy* (London: Fontana, 1985) in the context of a critical discussion of traditional conceptions of morality (part of which is reprinted in *Virtue Ethics* ed. R. Crisp and M. Slote; op. cit.). His main critical discussion of utilitarianism occurs in J. Smart and B. Williams *Utilitarianism: For and Against* (Cambridge: Cambridge University Press, 1973). Discussion of the foresight/intention distinction was revitalized by Judith Thompson's 'Trolley-cases'; see her collection *Rights, Restitution and Risk* (Cambridge, Mass.: Harvard University Press, 1986).

Peter Singer refined the position presented in *Animal Liberation* (London: Cape, 1975) in chapter 5 of his later book *Practical Ethics* (2nd edn. Cambridge: Cambridge University Press, 1993), which provides a stimulating introduction to several issues of applied ethics. The basis of environmental ethics is discussed in R. Attfield *The Ethics of Environmental Concern* (2nd edn. London: University of Georgia Press, 1991). Carol Gilligan's ideas in *In a Different Voice* (Cambridge, Mass.: Harvard University Press,1982) are taken further in Nell Nodding *Caring: A Feminine Approach to Ethics and Moral Education* (Berkeley, Calif.: University of California Press, 1984). Alastair MacIntyre's *After Virtue* (London: Duckworth, 1981) is a development of the criticisms of 'modern moral philosophy' advanced by Anscombe (op. cit.) and includes an excellent discussion of the concept of virtue (part of which is reprinted in *Virtue Ethics* ed. R. Crisp and M. Slote, op. cit.). Some of MacIntyre's criticisms of 'modernity' are developed and qualified in Charles Taylor's suggestive work *The Sources of the Self* (Cambridge: Cambridge University Press, 1989).

Chapter 11

The two encyclopedias of philosophy mentioned are the *Encyclopedia of Philosophy* (ed. P. Edwards; New York: Macmillan, 1967), and the *Routledge Encyclopedia of Philosophy* (ed. E. J. Craig; London: Routledge, 1998).

Among Richard Rorty's writings those most relevant to his metaphilosophical scepticism are his book *Philosophy and the Mirror of Nature* (Oxford: Blackwell, 1980), his introduction to *The Consequences of Pragmatism* (Brighton: Harvester, 1982), volume I of his *Philosophical Papers* (Cambridge: Cambridge University Press, 1991), and his 'retrospective essays'—'Ten Years After' and 'Twenty-five Years After'—in the 1992 edition of *The Linguistic Turn* (op. Cit. ch. 4). The best discussion of Rorty's work is *Rorty and his Critics* (ed. R. Brandom; Oxford: Blackwell, 2000). William James expounded his pragmatism in *Pragmatism* (London: Longmans, 1907).

Index